Nicaragua in Revolution:
The Poets Speak

Nicaragua en revolución:
Los Poetas hablan

LOS Heroes, nuestros Heroés no dijeron que morian si no que murieron, Fieles al Juramento de patria Libre o morir.   Leonel Rugama Rugama

Nicaragua in Revolution: The Poets Speak

Nicaragua en revolución: Los poetas hablan

Editors:
Bridget Aldaraca
Edward Baker
Ileana Rodríguez
Marc Zimmerman

Studies in Marxism, Vol. 5
Marxist Educational Press
Minneapolis

Library of Congress Cataloging in Publication Data

Main entry under title:

Nicaragua in revolution.

    (Studies in Marxism ; 5)
    Bibliography: p.
    1. Revolutionary poetry, Nicaraguan – Translations
into English. 2. Revolutionary poetry, English –
Translations from Spanish. 3. Revolutionary poetry,
Nicaraguan. I. Aldaraca, Bridget, 1938-
II. Title: Nicaragua en revolución. III. Series:
Studies in Marxism (Minneapolis) ; 5.
PQ7516.Z5N5   861'.008'0353   80-16304
ISBN 0-930656-10-5
ISBN 0-930656-09-1 (pbk.)

●

First Printing - 1980
Second Printing - 1981

Printed in the United States of America

●

MARXIST EDUCATIONAL PRESS
c/o Anthropology Department
University of Minnesota
215 Ford Hall, 224 Church St. S.E.
Minneapolis, Minnesota 55455

Contents

Preface i

Introduction. 1

A Brief History of Modern Nicaragua. 3

Important Dates 11

PART 1 NICARAGUA UNDER IMPERIALISM
AND SANDINO'S UPRISING (1898-1933). 16

Sección 1 Preludio: El imperialismo crea la
Brown Brothers Republic
Section 1 Prelude: Imperialism Creates the
Brown Brothers Republic 21

Sección 2 El levantamiento de Sandino
Section 2 Sandino's Uprising. 33

Sección 3 Las campañas de Sandino
Section 3 The Campaigns of Sandino. 45

Sección 4 La muerte de Sandino
Section 4 The Death of Sandino 57

Sección 5 La lucha continua
Section 5 The Struggle Continues. 69

PART 2 THE TYRANNY (1936-1956) 76

Sección 1 Los primeros años
Section 1 The Early Years 81

Sección 2 El exilio: Ida y vuelta
Section 2 Exile: Departure and Return 89

Sección 3 Los últimos años de Anastasio I
Section 3 The Last Years of Anastasio I. 95

Sección 4 La muerte de Anastasio I
Section 4 The Death of Anastasio I 111

PART 3 THE STRUGGLE CONTINUES (1956-1970) . . . 122

Sección 1   Edwin Castro y
            el régimen de Luis Somoza: 1956-67
Section 1   Edwin Castro and
            the Regime of Luis Somoza: 1956-67 127

Sección 2   Muerte y miseria al comenzar Tacho
Section 2   Murder and misery as Tacho's Reign Begins 141

Sección 3   La llamada a la lucha
Section 3   The Call to Struggle 149

Sección 4   Los que pelean: Los que caen
Section 4   The Fighters: The Fallen 157

Sección 5   Vida y muerte de Leonel Rugama
Section 5   The Life and Death of Leonel Rugama 179

PART 4 THE MARCH TO VICTORY (1970-1979) 202

Sección 1   Prisión y tortura, muerte y esperanza:
            Los sobrevivientes de los años 60
Section 1   Prison and Torture, Death and Hope:
            Those Who Survived the 1960s 207

Sección 2   El terremoto
Section 2   The Earthquake 217

Sección 3   De las cenizas renace la esperanza
Section 3   The Rebirth of Hope out of the Ashes 227

Sección 4   La lucha se prolonga
Section 4   The Struggle is Protracted 237

Sección 5   Matanza y levantamiento
Section 5   Slaughter and Uprising 259

Sección 6   El comienzo
Section 6   The Beginning 273

Epílogo
Epilogue 285

Bio-Bibliographies of the Principal Poets 289

Bio-Bibliographies of the Editors 299

Bibliography 300

Preface

This book was conceived during the Sandinista offensive of 1978. While the social forces which had been repressed by Somoza's tyranny for forty-six years were organizing and responding to the call of the Sandinista vanguard, a group of intellectuals living in Minnesota, a Nicaraguan and three Americans, decided to gather together and publish a collection of Nicaraguan revolutionary poetry. Our purpose was to create a book which would tell the story of the Nicaraguan people's struggle to free themselves from their oppressors and which, at the same time, would be of some use in organizing international solidarity campaigns.

By early June, 1979, we had collected all the poetry we were going to use. At that point, the final offensive began. As we followed the advances of the Sandinista columns, we spurred ourselves to finish our translations. When the book was half finished, the Nicaraguan revolution had triumphed. As telephone calls and letters from friends began coming in, we felt the victory of the Nicaraguan people with ever greater immediacy, but the book was not yet done.

After the victory, we became more ambitious; we wanted a book which would illustrate the process leading to that victory, a well-made book which would pay tribute to the sacrifices of the people of Nicaragua and aid the effort of national reconstruction; a book which, because it is bilingual, would help English-speaking progressives familiarize themselves with Nicaraguan reality so that they too might join the solidarity effort. *Nicaragua in Revolution: The Poets Speak* is, then, a book which we hope will be an expression of solidarity which progressive Americans offer the new Nicaragua.

We wish to thank our collaborators and advisors for their aid and advice:

Carlos Johnson and John Beverley made a detailed critical reading of the first version of the book; Beverley also secured for us the important collaboration of Iván Uriarte in Pittsburgh, and, in Cuba, obtained hard to find material in Margaret Randall's private collection; he translated some poems of Francisco de Asís Fernández; he literally rescued this book.

Steve Kowit and others gave us their excellent translations of the passages from Ernesto Cardenal's *Canto nacional* which appear in the book, in addition to important fragments from Cardenal's *Oráculo sobre Managua* and some lines from "Viaje a Nueva York."

Roberto Márquez translated "La tierra es un satélite de la luna" by Rugama, as well as "La cortina del país natal;" he also placed at our disposal the Nicaraguan pages from *Poesía trunca*, the superb anthology done in Cuba by Mario Benedetti. Márquez also gave us his ongoing support and advice.

Carlos Eduarte, a Mexican student at the University of Minnesota, gave us some decisively important help in typing the manuscript, making critical observations, and first drafts of translations.

Judy Sayad did the layout and typesetting of our "preview" pamphlet, *Nicaragua: Canto y lucha / Song and Struggle*. Her work, in which she was so effectively aided by Hardy Wright, was not fully acknowledged at the time.

Both in Minnesota and Managua, William Rowe gave us innumerable hours of intelligent and effective work. Without his support, neither *Canto y lucha* nor this book would have been possible.

Some final observations on the translations. We would like to thank Donald Gardiner for his translation of Cardenal's *La hora cero*. It helped us to do our own which, nevertheless, is substantially different from his. Except for those which have already been mentioned, all the translations are our own.

We have made some changes in Fonseca Amador's versification of Rigoberto López Pérez's "Carta testamental," leaving Rigoberto's prose intact in the part on "mundane matters." We have followed Fonseca's example, versifying one of his best known statements. We have done likewise with Cardenal's "Carta sobre Solentiname."

We would like to thank Ernesto Cardenal and Nicaragua's Ministry of Culture which he heads for authorizing the inclusion of the works and translations of the Nicaraguan poets which appear in this volume (see Bibliography for sources). Our thanks also to the following parties for the other materials we have included: Rafael Alberti, for the poem, "Aterrizando", found in *50 poemas sobre el General Sandino*, ed. Jorge Eduardo Arrellano and José Jirón Terán (Managua, 1972), as transcribed by Ernesto Mejía Sánchez, in "Sandino comunista" (*La Prensa*, 24 de Junio, 1958). Published originally in Alberti's *13 bandas y 48 estrellas* (Madrid, 1938), p. 23. Nicolas Guillén, for the excerpt from "Coplas americanas", in *Tengo* (Editorial El siglo ilustrado: Montevideo, 1967). *The Massachusetts Review*, where Roberto Márquez's translation of the anonymous Nicaraguan poem, "La cortina del país natal" first appeared. Copyright © 1971 by *The Massachusetts Review*. Carmen Balcells Agencia Literaria, Barcelona, for our selections from poems by Pablo Neruda. Siglo XXI Editores for our excerpt from Pedro Mir's *Contracanto a Walt Whitman* from *Viaje a la muchedumbre*, copyright© 1972 by Siglo XXI Editores, S.A., Mexico. Rogelio Sinán, for the excerpt from his poem, "Acertijo nicaraguense", which appeared in the journal *Encuentro*, published by Nicaragua's Universidad Centro-Americana. Margaret Randall, who, in Cuba and Nicaragua, provided us with poems and photos. Our cover photo is her work.

Aldaraca, Baker and Rodríguez would like to express their thanks to Marc Zimmerman. In the last instance, the global conception of the book was his. But, especially, it was his seemingly limitless intellectual energy which transformed our individual and collective ideas into realities.

The editors would also like to give special thanks to the following people who assisted in the final stages of production: to Doris Marquit for her preliminary copy-editing of the script; to our typesetter and layout person, Jack Nelson, who cheerfully took on the added task of copy-editing the final material and volunteered innumerable hours of labor; and to the following members of the Nicaragua Solidarity Committee of Minnesota who gave crucial aid in correcting the galleys: Deborah Adleman, Colleen Aho, Judy Gold, and once again, Carlos Eduarte. A special thanks to Cecilia Ubilla Arenas for her help beyond words.

Finally, Rodríguez and Zimmerman would like to express their profound debt of gratitude to Manuel Andara Ubeda and Eduardo Contreras (Comandante Marcos), who, in Baja California, Mexico, transmitted to them their profound understanding of the Nicaraguan people's struggle. In addition, Dr. Andara placed at their disposal his personal archives, with its collection of Nicaraguan poetry, *Gacetas Sandinistas,* and articles from the Latin American press. He has lived out his long years of exile with dignity, and now he has returned to Managua to help in the task of national reconstruction, currently serving as Nicaragua's ambassador to Cuba. Comandante Marcos ("Noel") was killed by the Somocistas in Managua in 1976. Nonetheless, he lives on every page of this book.

We dedicate this book to those who died fighting, and to those who survived to carry on the long and difficult task of national reconstruction; our own work is only a minimal part of a vast human undertaking.

In solidarity,
Bridget Aldaraca, Edward Baker, Ileana Rodríguez, Marc Zimmerman. Nicaragua Solidarity Committee of Minnesota, May, 1980.

Introduction

In the preface to *Poesía nueva de Nicaragua,* Ernesto Cardenal states: "... literature should fulfill a purpose. It should ... be at the service of mankind. For that very reason, poetry should also be political."[1] According to Cardenal, the new Nicaraguan poetry "is the finest social poetry that any people of America has ever produced."[2]   Gregorio Selser, one of the most knowledgeable students of Nicaraguan national reality and the historian of Sandino's struggles, echoes Cardenal's words when he notes that "until they were able to do so with arms, the Nicaraguan people fought with poetry."[3]

Nicaragua in Revolution: The Poets Speak is a reaffirmation of this poetic tradition of social commitment. It brings together more than forty Nicaraguan poets whose work was dispersed in small anthologies, mimeographed. sheets, *Gacetas Sandinistas* and Latin American newspapers. Woven in as well are the voices of several well-known foreign – we could say internationalist – poets whose work bears witness to their solidarity with the cause of Nicaraguan liberation. These revolutionary poets or poet-revolutionaries, whose solidarity is such an essential part of their poetic-political activity, blend their voices together to form one continuous narrative line. The result is *not an anthology of poems, but rather a poetic collage* in which one narrative voice breaks off and cedes to another, and in the process a collective poem of Nicaragua's century-long struggle for national liberation is written.

The major voice is the poet whose prolific creation encompasses all of Nicaraguan national life, from animals, birds, trees, flowers and fruits, down to the smallest detail of everyday life. The poetry of Ernesto Cardenal lends order and measure to the story. But in the final analysis, it is the collective poetic testimo-

1

ny of more than forty vanguard poets which has brought this book into existence. Not a few of these poets risked their lives standing fast against torture, the immense loneliness of jail, hunger and the harsh life of the mountains. And some of them lost their lives in the struggle. Yet they express in their poems an unbreachable faith in a better future for their country.

This future, ever present in the poets' verse, speaks to human and material needs which must be satisfied, from fields sown with wheat and corn, to paved roads, full silos, shoeshine boys turned poets and the purification of the language in which public and private documents, constitutions and love letters, will be written.

It is both astounding and exemplary that in the midst of violent repression, of life literally in the lion's den, the poets derived strength from an unbreakable conviction that they were part of a process which would ultimately result in a radically different future. There is a recurring theme of death as new life – as blood, seed, struggle, as the birth pains which precede the creation of a new world and a new people. The negation of love by violence done to the human body – the rape of women, the castration of men – is itself negated through the affirmation of solidarity. As Ricardo Morales says, *somos millones*, we are millions.

The raw material of history is transformed into poetry through a series of common and recurrent images which bear witness to the fact that a poetic tradition is derived from a historical process into which the poet *can* choose to integrate himself. The coincidence of the poets – both Nicaraguan and foreign – in their use of imagery is a further testimony of their feelings of solidarity as they unite in depicting the ferocity of exploitation and the strength of the people's resistance. From this common ground of images extracted from "the mud of history" grows a fraternal vision, the fertile and human vision of *Our America*.

---

1. Ernesto Cardenal, *Poesía nueva de Nicaragua* (Buenos Aires: Carlos Lohle, 1974), p. 9.
2. In the "Prólogo" to *Poesía revolucionaria nicaragüense* (Mexico: Ediciones Patria y Libertad, 6th edition, 1968).
3. *El Día* (Mexico), July 30, 1979.

A Brief History of Modern Nicaragua*

Due to its privileged geographic situation on the Caribbean, to its natural interoceanic waterway which could so easily be made into a canal, and to the natural wealth of its soil, rich in farm, forest and mining products, Nicaragua occupied one of the most desirable strategic locations in the United States empire's defense and security system. This natural geographic position sealed the neocolonial pact between the United States and Nicaragua from the very beginning of her political independence (1821), and determined the future development of the country. This development would be characterized by a fierce struggle between the capitalist interests of the Republic of the north and the democratic interests of the Nicaraguan people.

From this initial situation come the salient features of the nation's history: 1) the prolonged history of American intervention; 2) the brief liberal parenthesis of José Santos Zelaya; 3) the agonizing polemic over the feasibility of building a canal; 4) forty-three years of uninterrupted military dictatorship; 5) the semi-colonial status which this political structure imposed on the country; 6) precarious economic development based on a single-product economy which was subordinated to the United States' strategic interests in times of peace as well as in times of war; 7) the Somoza family's monopolization of the nation's wealth and consequently, the limited development of a national bourgeoisie;

---

* The material presented here comes from the following sources: Gregorio Selser, *Sandino: general de hombres libres* (La Habana: Ciencias Sociales, 1976); Jaime Wheelock, *Imperialismo y dictadura: crisis de una formación social* (Mexico: Siglo XXI, 1975); and a variety of pamphlets published by the FSLN.

8) the Nicaraguan people's constant and heroic resistance to United States invasion and the Somoza tyranny.

The political-economic history of contemporary Nicaragua has its origins in the nineteenth century. In 1850, the Clayton-Bulwer Treaty was signed. It stipulated that England and the United States would share in the profits from any canal built on Nicaraguan soil. In 1855, the American adventurer William Walker arrived in Nicaragua with the first group of invaders, using as a pretext an invitation from the Conservative Party. The U.S., having taken a substantial portion of Mexican territory in 1848, was looking for other outlets for expansion. Walker came to Nicaragua to help the Conservatives defeat the Liberal government, but he himself governed the country until 1857, when the Central American republics formed an army to expel him. The Nicaraguans' resistance spared their country from the annexation which awaited Puerto Rico in 1898.

The changes which took place in the nineteenth -century Nicaraguan economy, especially in coffee production, are a result of the restructuring of the landholding system during the second half of the nineteenth century and Nicaragua's consequent entry into the world market as a producer of a single commodity. Large cattle- raising *haciendas* and pre-capitalist grain-growing collectives were the old forms of land ownership corresponding to a subsistence economy. They were gradually replaced during the decades which preceded the Liberal takeover of José Santos Zelaya by large commercial estates, or latifundium. This transition came about through post-independence wars, nominally between the Conservatives and Liberals. But in reality these wars were an expression of class struggle and were the social cost exacted by the dominant sector's drive for free trade relations. The demands of the peasants also played an important role in the struggle. Their attempts to retain possession of their small holdings and common lands were also attempts to democratize the social process. The forcible separation of the peasants from their means of subsistence –the land– forced them to sell their labor power on the market and thus the mobile agricultural proletariat necessary to work the latifundia was created.

The struggles between the different sectors of the ruling class did not prevent the sealing of the first oligarchic pact, represented by the Liberal Zelaya's seizure of power from 1893 to 1909. In the sixteen years of his presidency, Zelaya attempted to institutionalize the road toward progress begun by the consolidation of the latifundium and Nicaragua's entry into the world market. Zelaya wanted to strengthen the oligarchic pact, to facilitate development of a strong national bourgeoisie and to create a domestic market which would be partially beneficial to the labor force and indispensable to the power of the national bourgeoisie itself. He began to modernize the archaic legal and administrative institutions; fiscal reforms and the writing of a liberal constitution were undertaken. Zelaya also attempted to create a strong infrastructure by investing in roads, railways and shipping.

But the process of liberalization initiated during Zelaya's presidency was halted by a force which was alien to the country's organic development. The nationalist and protectionist policies, which strengthened the national bourgeoisie by facilitating the accumulation of national finance capital, ran counter to United States strategic interests in the area. The policy of Dollar Diplomacy – appropriation of foreign resources through the export of American finance capital backed up by the Marines – required that Zelaya's attempts at liberal reform be truncated. Using the century-old struggles between Liberals and Conservatives as a pretext, and fomenting discord between the still unconsolidated oligarchy, the United States intervened in 1909 and helped the Conservative candidate Estrada to overthrow Zelaya.

During this first period of domination, the United States eliminated all protectionist barriers erected by the Zelaya government. U.S. loans and investments were not long in coming and foreign capital soon gained complete hegemony over national investments. With finance capital, monetary reform, the banks, customs and transportation controlled by the United States, the stage was set for an overtly colonial regime. Nicaragua became "The Brown Brothers Republic."

U.S. colonization was given legitimacy by the signing of the onerous Chamorro-Bryan Treaty in 1914. In it, Nicaragua ceded to the United States in perpetuity the right to build a canal and to establish military bases. Between 1917 and 1925, United States intervention was institutionalized. Army occupation troops controlled key administrative functions. Natural resources were exploited without restrictions in the capitalist enclaves and the wealth generated by exports ended up in U.S. controlled banks. Executive power, still in Nicaraguan hands, was only symbolic, since it was limited to transmitting the State Department's plans through the current American ambassador.

What sovereignty Nicaragua maintained during the period between 1912 and 1933 was due to Benjamín Zeledón's resistance in 1912 and that of Augusto César Sandino in 1927. Sandino was of peasant extraction and a Liberal. Born in 1895 in Niquinohomo in the province of Masaya, he emigrated in his youth first to Honduras and then to Guatemala and Mexico where he worked, respectively, for the Montecristo sugar plantation, the United Fruit Company and the Huasteca Petroleum Company. His early ideological apprenticeship came when he witnessed Americans dragging Zeledón's body through the streets. In Mexico, he watched Alvaro Obregón's struggles with the United States, and no doubt he had heard of the United States invasions of Cuba, Santo Domingo, Haiti and Puerto Rico. As a result of these lessons he resolved in 1925 that "if there were in Nicaragua one hundred men who loved her as I do, the nation would regain its absolute sovereignty."

In search of that symbolic hundred, he returned to his country and gradually familiarized himself with the people's economic conditions. He saw the precarious labor situations of workers paid in coupons which were worthless outside the company store. Entire families were forced to work fifteen hours a day or more, living in shacks, sleeping on bare boards, eating badly and bereft of social services. Sandino and his men began their stuggle in 1927 alongside the Constitutionalist Army led by José María Moncada, fighting against the Conservatives and their allies, the American troops. But when Moncada decided to make a deal with the enemy and hand over his weapons, the "General of Free Men" and his "Crazy Little Army" went up to the mountains, to the Segovias, and kept on fighting. Sandino understood the enemy very well. When he broke with the Liberal Army he stated that "the sons of the people are without leaders and new men are needed."

Sandino fought until 1933; in that year, he defeated the invading army. But before U.S. troops left the country, the United States had maneuvered to protect its interests by creating a structure through which they could exert control. That structure was the National Guard headed by Anastasio Somoza, Sr. Somoza, following the plan laid down by his American advisors, offered Sandino a peace settlement. Sandino accepted, but the peace offer was a trap, and upon leaving the banquet in celebration of the pact, Sandino was murdered. Somoza's payment for services rendered was state power, which he took in 1936. The semi-colonial nature of Nicaragua became more evident in the following years, since Somoza acted as the American governor of the country, while the National Guard functioned as an army of occupation.

The first Somoza consolidated his power during the years of World War II. The main features of this period were, politically, the oligarchic pact sustained by brute force, and economically, the intensification of coffee growing, followed by the introduction of cotton, rubber and, marginally, of precious woods and metals to accomodate the Nicaraguan economy to United States strategic needs.

Scientific analysis of coffee production has succeeded in uncovering the social cost of Nicaragua's subordinate development during those years. The seasonal employment of the labor force, its underemployment and unemployment were the social consequences. A seasonal economy mobilized the work force and took it from one production center to another, from one harvest to the next, turning it into an insecure nomadic population barely able to keep itself alive. Living conditions in the barracks, the food, the low and uncertain pay, and the superexploitation of women and children took on forms similar to those of Black slavery in the nineteenth century. The variety of occupations and work situations – peonage, sharecropping, tenant farming, etc. – masked the capitalist nature of exploitation.

The Somoza family fortune and the extent of its property holdings have always been difficult to document. Research on this aspect of the nation's economy was blocked during the reign of the dynasty; any attempt to conduct research could result in jail or execution. Nevertheless, it is believed that from the beginning of Somoza's rule, the family began to control a substantial part of the nation's wealth, and that with the aid and support of their allies, the Somozas gradually took possession of most of the major agricultural and commercial enterprises. When the economy began to modernize, the family cast its net more widely over the banking establishment and even raked off profits from public services, the customs houses, hospitals and the communications media. It therefore became proverbial in Nicaragua to speak of the country as though it were Somoza's private estate.

The second period of *somocismo* began in 1956 when Luis, Somoza's eldest son, inherited both the economic structure and the political power of his father. But it also fell to Luis to deal with the *sandinista* heritage represented by the Sandinista National Liberation Front (FSLN). Revolutionary movements

7

began to appear all over Latin America, culminating in the Cuban Revolution. This wave of revolutionary activity was the result of a process of consolidation of popular resistance to the bourgeoisie's offensive, whose most visible manifestation was the McCarthyism of the late '40s and '50s and the Cold War. During the '50s and '60s Nicaragua's strategic position was utilized by the United States as a launching platform for attacks against other Latin American countries: the invasion of Guatemala in 1954 during Eisenhower's presidency; the invasion of Cuba at the Bay of Pigs during Kennedy's term; and the invasion of the Dominican Republic in 1965 during Johnson's presidency.

Following the Cuban Revolution, the United States changed its global strategy in Latin America to include some attempt at conciliating the disfranchised masses by a reformist campaign, the Alliance for Progress. In Nicaragua, the Alliance favored a better distribution of income, changes in the tax structure, land distribution and above all a change of government from Somoza militarism to a charade of civil rule under René Schick.

In fact, the Alliance for Progress was part of a strategy of counterinsurgency intended to operate on two distinct but mutually supportive levels: superficial social reform to pacify the "natives" and intensified military control to halt the revolutionary upsurge. This two-pronged counterrevolutionary strategy resulted in two permanent structures: one, the Central American Defense Council (CONDECA), and two, the Central American Common Market. Both organizations were adjuncts of AID (Agency for International Development). The cosmetic quality of the reforms undertaken by the Alliance was particularly visible in the pattern of land distribution, which tended to take place only in those areas where insurgency existed.

Under the influence of the Central American Common Market the process of import substitution began in Nicaragua. The door was opened to the massive entry of U.S.-dominated multinationals which profited from the "free zone" tax exemption. The multinationals seized control of the most important sectors of industry. They installed prefabricated factories which were easily transferable to other countries in case of labor trouble or political emergencies. The majority of these corporations were involved in light industry, but they also succeeded in dismantling traditional industry and took a share of wealth from the already precarious national bourgeoisie. Corona Oil was acquired by United Brands; the biscuit factory was taken over by Nabisco; the ceramics industry was controlled by American Standard.

Designed to operate in countries that had reached a high level of division of labor, the industries installed by the Common Market continued to depend on semi-manufactured products and raw materials produced outside of Nicaragua, bringing on a state of acute circular decapitalization and acute dependency. The factories set up in Nicaragua enjoyed, from the very beginning, the privilege of loans, free exchange, and complete freedom in the quantities of their exports, resulting in a situation of absolute dependence on foreign finance in the form of loans to cover the government's growing deficits.

Thus, imperialism's plan to eliminate growing popular agitation through grandiose reform programs served only to intensify the Central American economies' structural dependence on the imperial metropolis. Without minimum changes, which the foreign consortium and Somoza's oligarchy did not wish to implement, it was foreseeable that the Alliance's developmental perspective would be impracticable. Furthermore, social and economic conditions were maturing which would give rise to revolutionary violence. In Nicaragua, this violence intensified from 1958 on, especially after Pancasán in 1967, when the revolutionary movement, having survived an early period of difficulties, began a phase of consolidation.

In the '60s, the United States began to confront a situation in which Nicaragua, its most loyal Central American client, paradoxically became the weakest link in the imperialist chain. Its vital interests endangered by increasing revolutionary activity, the United States abandoned its reformist policies. The democratic façade gave way to stepped-up military programs and counterrevolutionary violence.

In 1967, Luis Somoza died and the last phase of the dynasty began. Anastasio Somoza, Jr., educated militarily and politically in the United States, took over the presidency. On January 22, he left his calling card when the National Guard massacred more than three hundred citizens participating in a popular demonstration. "Tacho" reinforced militarism in the region by strengthening programs which complemented the "Civic Action" projects, by equipping the National Guard with modern arms, by importing specialized personnel to train the Guard, by turning the police and security agencies into modern organizations to combat subversion, and by coordinating National Guard activities with CONDECA.

9

The imposition of the new Somoza coincided, however, with the crisis of the Central American Common Market. At this point, the nontraditional capital interests of the U.S. Sunbelt — Vesco, Hughes, Nixon — entered Nicaragua and began to develop a new area of social exploitation; on the one hand, tourism, gambling casinos, the hotel industry, drug traffic, and in short, an entire constellation of businesses linked to the Mafia, to Cuban counterrevolutionaries and to Nixon; on the other hand, an industrial project centered around research for oil in the San Juan River area. The main investor was Hughes; his main partner, Somoza. Their projects were supported by AID and by Nixon himself, who sent Ambassador Turner Shelton to Nicaragua to facilitate the arrangements. But this program of exploitation never came about.

In 1972, the earthquake which partially destroyed Managua set in motion the final stage of the process which would culminate in the overthrow of the Somoza dictatorship. The influx of economic aid from international agencies was utilized by Somoza to consolidate and increase his own economic holdings and those of the National Guard. This in turn had the effect of further alienating large sections of the bourgeoisie who saw their own economic power threatened. They became more vocal about their support for a liberal alternative to Somoza, the editor of *La Prensa*, Pedro Joaquín Chamorro. In January, 1978, the *somocistas* decided to eliminate this possible threat to their political hegemony and Chamorro was assassinated. The murder of Chamorro meant the end to a liberal alternative and resulted in an alliance between the bourgeoisie and the popular revolutionary forces, led by their vanguard, the Sandinistas.

Between January of 1978 and the summer of 1979, the Nicaraguan populace fought Somoza with a series of strikes and with intensified military actions. Somoza's indiscriminate and genocidal bombing only served to strengthen the people's resistance and to horrify the international community. Finally, on July 17-18, in the face of the Sandinista's final onslaught, Somoza fled the country after pillaging the national treasury. On July 19, 1979, victory was proclaimed and the long and arduous task of rebuilding Nicaragua began.

Important Dates

1821   Independence.

1824-28 Civil Wars between Liberals and Conservatives.

1855   First U.S. invasion of Nicaragua. William Walker governs the country for three years.

1893   José Santos Zelaya becomes president and undertakes the Liberal Reform.

1909   The U.S. intervenes in Nicaragua's internal affairs and expells Zelaya from the presidency.

1912   U.S. troops land at Corinto. They attack the Liberals and remain in Nicaragua until 1925.

1914   The Chamorro-Bryan Pact is signed. For three million dollars, the U.S. obtains perpetual rights to build a canal and military bases.

1927   U.S. troops return to Managua to oppose the Constitutionalist Army of José Santos Moncada. General Augusto César Sandino begins his guerrilla war against the U.S. intervention.

1933   U.S. troops, beaten back by Sandino, withdraw from the country, leaving the National Guard in their place.

1934   On Somoza's orders, Sandino is assassinated February 22. Somoza begins the transition to achieving absolute power, which he will hold until 1956.

1954   Somoza intervenes in Guatemala on the side of reaction. Anti-Somoza opposition grows. In April, the uprising of Adolfo Báez Bone and Pablo Leal is unsuccessful. Báez Bone and Leal are killed.

1956   The rebel poet Rigoberto López Pérez, in collaboration with Edwin Castro, Ausberto Narváez and Cornelio Silva Argüello, assassinates Somoza. López Pérez is killed. The dictator's eldest son, Luis, takes power. He captures and kills the conspirators, unleashing a reign of terror.

1958-60 A few old Sandinistas (Ramón Raudales, Heriberto Reyes, Lázaro Salinas, Zacarías López, etc.) re-emerge, and a new generation begins to be active, starting guerrilla actions in Los Encinos, Jicaro, El Dorado, and especially in El Chaparral. Foundation of a forerunner of the Sandinista National Liberation Front, the Patriotic Youth.

1961   Somoza puts a base at the disposal of the U.S. for its invasion of Playa Girón, Cuba. Foundation of the Sandinista National Liberation Front under the leadership of Carlos Fonseca Amador. The organization, however, does not use the name or the initials FSLN in a systematic way until 1964.

1962-63 Intensification of guerrilla actions in Coco, Bocaycito, Pancasán, etc. in an attempt to broaden the rural base of the Front.

1964   In response, Somoza actively collaborates in the creation of the Central American Defense Council (CONDECA).

1965   The National Guard aids the U.S. in the invasion of the Dominican Republic.

1967   The FSLN sets up a rural base in Pancasán. In major cities (Managua, León, etc.), the organizational work of the Front intensifies. Luis Somoza dies suddenly, and in circumstances which are still unclear. His brother, Anastasio, head of the National Guard, takes power.

1967-71 Somoza's power and wealth increase. The Front advances and retreats.

1972   An earthquake destroys Managua. Somoza increases

12

his wealth by expropriating a substantial share of the emergency aid sent from abroad. U.S. "Rangers" invade. Under the pretext of the emergency situation created by the earthquake, they attempt to destroy the Front. Miguel Obando y Bravo, Archbishop of Managua, breaks with Somoza and calls for a new order.

1974   A commando unit led by Sandinista Eduardo Contreras (Comandante Marcos) occupies the house of an important Somocista politician and demands the liberty of fourteen political prisoners, five million dollars, broadcasts of the incident and free passage to Cuba. The regime accedes to their demands, making manifest its increasing weakness.

1975   The sale of arms to the regime jumps 100%.

1976   The Front broadens its popular support, but several leaders die fighting, among them Comandante Marcos and Carlos Fonseca Amador.

1977   The Front attacks National Guard military installations on the borders of Honduras and Costa Rica. International pressure on the regime increases. The contemplative community of Solentiname founded by Ernesto Cardenal opts for armed struggle and is destroyed by the Guard. The Group of Twelve is formed.

1978   *January.* The Somocistas suspect that the U.S. is searching for a substitute who is more acceptable to the international community, and they assassinate the most likely candidate: Pedro Joaquín Chamorro, leader of the Conservative Party, editor of *La Prensa,* and a long-time opposition figure. His burial turns into a mass demonstration against the regime as opposition extends throughout the country.

June. Students from elementary and secondary schools join a strike of anti-Somoza university students. The widow of Chamorro calls for the international isolation of the Somoza regime.

August. The Catholic Church demands Somoza's resignation. The first general strike is called. A commando of twenty Sandinistas occupies the National Palace during a session of Congress, which is captured.

The commando demands the liberty of numerous political prisoners. The dictator has no choice but to agree to the demands. As the commandos and the ex-prisoners go to the airport, the people cheer them along the route.

September. The Front begins an offensive, taking several northern provinces on the Pacific coast. Somoza compares the mobilization to the Tet offensive of 1968. The Organization of American States wants to intervene, and the U.S. wants a Somoza regime without Somoza. Somoza achieves a military victory, but the opposition to the regime is broadened. Conservative sectors organize around the Broad Opposition Front (FAO), the Democratic Liberal Union (Udel) and the Group of Twelve. The more militant sectors group around the FSLN.

1979   *March 11.* Representatives of the Sandinista National Liberation Front sign a unity pact, agreeing on a strategy to overthrow the dictator, and on a general reconstruction program.

April. Estelí is occupied by the Front. Military coordination of the different fronts is achieved in preparation for the final offensive.

June. The Front calls a general strike and gets a massive popular response. The final offensive begins. The United Popular Movement (MPU) unites all opposition political forces. The Sandinistas begin to take control of the provinces and name a provisional government.

July 17-18. Somoza leaves the country, defeated. During the brief reign of his replacement, Urcuyo, the National Guard surrenders to the Sandinista Front.

July 19. The "Day of Victory." The Provisional Government takes power, and the long, hard road of national reconstruction begins.

Nicaragua in Revolution: The Poets Speak

Nicaragua en revolución: Los poetas hablan

Ernesto Cardenal / LA HORA CERO

> *¡Centinela! ¿Qué hora es de la noche?*
> *¡Centinela! ¿Qué hora es de la noche?*
>
> ISAÍAS, 21, 11

Noches Tropicales de Centroamérica,
con lagunas y volcanes bajo la luna
y luces de palacios presidenciales,
cuarteles y tristes toques de queda.
"Muchas veces fumando un cigarillo
he decidido la muerte de un hombre,"
dice Ubico fumando un cigarillo. . .
en su palacio como un queque rosado
Ubico está resfriado. Afuera el pueblo
fue dispersado con bombas de fósforo.
San Salvador bajo la noche y el espionaje
con cuchicheos en los hogares y pensiones
y gritos en las estaciones de policía.
El palacio de Carías apedreado por el pueblo.
Una ventana de su despacho ha sido quebrada,
y la policía ha disparado contra el pueblo.
Y Managua apuntada por las ametralladoras
desde el palacio de bizcocho de chocolate
y los cascos de acero patrullando las calles.

¡Centinela! ¿Qué hora es de la noche?
¡Centinela! ¿Qué hora es de la noche?

Part 1

Ernesto Cardenal / ZERO HOUR

Tropical Nights of Central America,
with lagoons and volcanoes under the moon
and lights in presidential palaces,
barracks and sad curfew calls.
"I've often decided to send a man to his death
while smoking a cigarette,"
Ubico says, smoking a cigarette. . .
in his palace like a pink cake,
Ubico's caught a cold. Outside
they dispersed the people with phosphorus bombs.
San Salvador shrouded by night with spies
and whispers in homes and boarding houses
and cries from police stations.
Carías's palace stoned by the people:
One of his office windows broken,
his guards have fired on the people.
And Managua a target for machine guns
from the chocolate-cake colored palace
and steel helmets patrolling the streets.

Watchman, what of the night?
Watchman, what of the night?

Nicaragua Under Imperialism
and Sandino's Uprising (1898-1933)

Part One covers the period from 1898, the beginning of imperialism's domination of the Caribbean area, to 1933, the year imperialism suffers its first defeat by the army of General Augusto César Sandino, who is then assassinated by Anastasio Somoza-García working in concert with the U.S. ambassador.

In the poetry, two forces confront each other: the force of destruction and the force of conviction. The dominant images are of darkness, on the one hand, and of light and hope on the other. Repeated allusions are made to the invader, a wild beast whose fangs tear at the people's throat, and to the weak and dispossessed. Animal images intermingle with those of businessmen in their Wall Street uniforms, frock-coated, seated in easy chairs, cigarette and whiskey in hand. Both images portray the U.S. capitalists who negotiate the price of Nicaragua's future with the traitors.

The poetry of the second section tells of the formation of a guerrilla army under Sandino. It speaks, as well, of the old and new consciousness, and describes weapons which in the 1930s bear human names: rifles made by Remington (just like typewriters and electric shavers), Lewis and Thompson machine guns and submachine guns. Later these human names will hide behind technical code words like M-1 and M-3. Rifles and machine guns are the tools of the "civilizers." Sandino must respond with whatever weapons he can find.

The third section tells us exactly what Sandino's weapons are: ancient rifles and machine guns, improvised hand grenades. We descend on the weapon scale all the way down to machetes and ropes. But the jungle comes to the aid of Sandino's army: trees, tortoises, rivers, all "cooperate," as Neruda puts it. These are the Nicaraguans' defense against the beasts of the land and air. And the guerrillas are everywhere, taking advantage of their mobility, hiding behind the fog, the rain, the storm, the dark.

They surface in El Coco, Boaco, Telnaneca, El Chipote, more a community than an army. Finally, the Yankees grow weary of soiling their uniforms and risking their lives in the jungle. They sign the peace treaty at last. The fourth section explains what this treaty really means. Peace is a "civilizing" measure. Since the invaders cannot defeat the Sandinistas or discredit their leader, whom they call an outlaw (in the technical sense of the word, of course), they decide to have him killed. They find a collaborator, a ruthless, made-in-USA sellout. They buy him, they train him, they use him. It is Somoza who organizes the victory banquet, and while Sandino demonstrates his good will by attending, a handful of men, following Somoza's orders, dig his grave. When the time comes, Sandino leaves the banquet and is never seen again. This was the agreement sealed between Somoza and the United States. A cloud of mourning and pain would cover Nicaragua for nearly half a century.

International solidarity with Nicaragua can be seen in the poetry of Alberti, who bids farewell to Sandino; of Neruda, who sings a dramatic response; of Guillén, with his call for the struggle to continue. The Nicaraguan poets search everywhere for Sandino. The fifth section bears witness to this search, of this sense of perspective. Managua seen from the sky, from the clouds, from Managua. Faribundo Martí has fallen in Salvador, Sandino has fallen in Nicaragua. But the struggle continues. There are so many tyrants to overthrow, so many guards to defeat, so many people to educate — to teach to read, write, think, dream. This is why the fifth section concludes with the Cuban poet Guillén's call to struggle, to go up into the mountains with Sandino, to answer the people's cry which the Chilean Neruda invokes: Sandino, Sandino, Sandino.

19

Sección 1
Preludio: El imperialismo crea la *Brown Brothers Republic*

1 / Pablo Neruda / **Centro América**

Delgada tierra como un látigo,
calentada como un tormento,
tu paso en Honduras, tu sangre
en Santo Domingo, de noche,
tus ojos desde Nicaragua
me tocan, me llaman, me exigen,
y por la tierra americana
toco las puertas para hablar,
toco las lenguas amarradas,
levanto las cortinas, hundo
la mano en la sangre:
        Oh, dolores
de tierra mía, oh, estertores
del gran silencio establecido,
oh, pueblos de larga agonía,
oh, cintura de sollozos.

2 / Rubén Darío / **A Roosevelt**

. . . Cazador
primitivo y moderno, sencillo y complicado,
con un algo de Washington y cuatro de Nemrod,
Eres los Estados Unidos,
eres el futuro invasor
de la América ingenua. . .

20

Section 1
Prelude: Imperialism Creates the *Brown Brothers Republic*

1 / Pablo Neruda / Central America

Land as slim as a whip,
hot as torture,
your step in Honduras, your blood
in Santo Domingo, at night,
your eyes in Nicaragua
touch, call, grip me,
and throughout American lands
I knock on doors to speak,
I tap on tongues that are tied,
I raise curtains, plunge
my hands into blood:
                    Sorrows
of my land, death rattle of
the great established silence,
long-suffering people,
slender waist of tears.

2 / Rubén Darío / To Roosevelt

... Hunter
primitive and modern, simple and complex,
one part Washington, four parts Nimrod.
You are the United States,
future invader
of our naive America. . .

3 / Neruda / **Sandino**

Fue cuando en tierra nuestra
se enterraron
las cruces, se gastaron
inválidas, profesionales.

Llegó el dólar de dientes agresivos
a morder territorio,
en la garganta pastoril de América.
Agarró Panamá con fauces duras,
hundió en la tierra fresca sus colmillos,
chapoteó en barro, whisky, sangre,
y juró un Presidente con levita:
"Sea con nosotros el soborno
de cada día"

Luego, llegó el acero,
y el canal dividió las residencias,
aquí los amos, allí la servidumbre.

Corrieron hacia Nicaragua.

4 / Darío / **A Roosevelt**

Crees que la vida es incendio,
que el progreso es erupción,
que en donde pones la bala
el porvenir pones.

No.

Los Estados Unidos son potentes y grandes.
Cuando ellos se estremecen hay un hondo temblor
que pasa por las vértebras enormes de los Andes.
Si clamáis, se oye como el rugir del león.
. . .

. . . Sois Ricos.
Juntáis al culto de Hércules el culto de Mammón;
y alumbrando el camino de la fácil conquista,
la Libertad levanta su antorcha en Nueva York.

3 / Neruda / **Sandino**

That was when they buried the crosses
in our land,
the professional crosses
crippled, used up.
The dollar came to sink agressive teeth
in America's pastoral throat,
to chew up territory.
It seized Panama in its iron jaw,
sank its fangs into the fresh earth,
splashed about in whiskey and mud and blood
and a frock-coated President swore:
"Give us this day
our daily bribe"
            Later the steel came
and the canal divided the dwellings,
here the bosses, there the lackeys.

They ran on toward Nicaragua.

4 / Darío / **To Roosevelt**

You think life is a fire,
progress an eruption,
the future wherever
your bullet strikes.

            No.

The United States is great and strong.
When it trembles, a deep tremor
buckles the Andes' vast backbone.
If you raise a cry, it resounds like the lion's roar.
    . . .
                    . . . You are rich.
You merge Mammon's cult with the cult of Hercules;
and Liberty lights the way to easy conquest,
lofting her torch in New York.

5 / Pedro Mir / Contracanto a Walt Whitman

Ahora,
       escuchadme bien:
si alguien quiere encontrar de nuevo
la antigua palabra
                    yo
vaya a la calle del oro, vaya a Wall Street.
No preguntéis por Mr. Babbitt. El os lo dirá.
— Yo, Babbitt, un cosmos,
un hijo de Manhattan.
            El os lo dirá
— Traedme las Antillas
sobre varios calibres presurosos, sobre cintas
de ametralladoras, sobre los caterpillares de los
       tanques
traedme las Antillas.
            Y en medio de un aroma silencioso
allá viene la isla de Santo Domingo.
— Traedme la América Central.
            Y en medio de un aroma pavoroso
allá viene callada Nicaragua.

6 / Cardenal / Canto nacional

Por los préstamos de 1911 Nicaragua cedió sus aduanas
a los prestamistas y la dirección del Banco Nacional
reservándose también los banqueros el derecho
de adquirir el Banco Nacional. Por los de 1912
comprometió además los Ferrocarriles. El 2 de Feb. de 1911
el grupo de banqueros Brown Brothers & Co.
se interesó en nosotros. Para pagar un empréstito
       se recurriría a otro, y así
sucesivamente. (Una vez que se entra no se puede salir)
       Los banqueros vinieron como barracudas.
       Los marinos desembarcaron a restablecer el orden
y se quedaron en Nicaragua por 13 años. No basta
el control de las aduanas, los bancos, los ferrocarriles.
       Nicaragua también vendió su territorio.
Adolfo Díaz empleado de la mina Ángeles Mining Co.,
con 35 dólares a la semana, fue el "capitalista"   ►

5 / Pedro Mir / **Countersong to Walt Whitman**

So,
  heed me well:
if you want to recover
the old word
  I
go to the gold street, go to Wall Street.
Don't ask for Mr. Babbitt. He'd tell you:
– I, Babbitt, a cosmos,
a son of Manhattan.
  He'd tell you:
– Bring me the Antilles
over many quick calibers, over
machine gun belts, over tank
  treads
bring me the Antilles.
  And in the midst of a silent aroma
  here comes the island of Santo Domingo.
– Bring me Central America.
  And in the midst of a fearful aroma,
  here comes silent Nicaragua.

6 / Cardenal / **National Song**

By the loan agreements of 1911 Nicaragua ceded her customs houses
and the management of the National Bank to the moneylenders.
The bankers reserved for themselves the right
to acquire the National Bank. By the agreements of 1912
the railroad was also compromised. On February 2, 1911,
the banking group Brown Brothers & Co.
took an interest in us. In order to pay a loan
  we would have recourse to another, and so on
forever. (Once begun, there is no way out.)
  The bankers came like barracudas.
  The marines landed to reestablish order
and remained in Nicaragua for 13 years. Not enough
to control the customs houses, the banks, the railroads.
  Nicaragua sold its land as well.
Adolfo Díaz, a $35-a-week employee of the Angeles Mining Co.,
was the "capitalist" ▶

de la "revolución," prestando al movimiento 600 000 dls.
El pago del empréstito a Brown Brothers
quedaba garantizado con las rentas de aduanas.
Corrupción, corrupción nacional fue el banquete de los banqueros
     un banquete de zopilotes
caballeros de negro frac en rueda como zopilotes.
Y los politicos: como murciélagos ciegos que nos cagan
     colgados en lo oscuro cagándonos y orinándonos
cagadas y meadas de los murciélagos de color de tinieblas
     negras alas revoloteando en el aire negro.
Otros 500 000 dls. prestados para la estabilización del cambio
pero — el banquete de los banqueros —
el dinero tampoco sale de manos de los banqeros de Nueva York.
     La garantía era entregar el país a los prestamistas.
El dinero del préstamo de 1911 era para crear el Banco Nacional
pero se dejaba el Banco Nacional en manos de los banqueros.
Los banqueros Brown Brothers compraron todo el papel que
                                    quisieron
o sea todo el papel moneda que quisieron, a 20 por un dólar
y lo vendieron a 12.50 por el dólar, todo el papel que quisieron
o sea 20 pesos comprados costaban 1 dólar (y podían comprar
los que quisieran) y vendidos (cuando ellos quisieran) valían
un dólar sesenta. Es decir
     compraban dinero barato para venderlo caro
se lo compraban al país para venderlo al país
con lo cual encarecieron el maíz, las casas, la educación,
las danzas, el tiquete de tren.
     Ese fue el saqueo de la mafia de banqueros.
     Asaltaron como pistoleros la moneda nacional.
Después los banqueros prestaron al país el dinero del país
al 6% de interés.
Las rentas nacionales recaudadas por banqueros extranjeros
depositadas en un Banco Nacional en poder de tales banqueros
extranjeros, y distribuidas por los banqueros extranjeros
asociados con el Secretario de Estado de los Estados Unidos
(que tenía acciones en la Ángeles Mining Co.)
Como los impuestos de Honduras eran recaudados por Morgan
Morgan el feroz
     como cuando viene el chancho de monte chas-chas-chas
       o hay en el aire un olor a puma
Después fue vendido el territorio nacional en 3 millones   ▶

of the "revolution," loaning the movement $600,000.
The payment of the loan to Brown Brothers
        was to be guaranteed by the revenues of the customs houses.
Corruption, corruption of the nation, the banquet of the bankers
        was a banquet of vultures
gentlemen in black tails hovering like vultures.
And the politicos: like blind bats that shit upon us
        hanging there in the dark crapping and pissing on us
shit and piss of abyss-colored bats
        black wings fluttering in the black air.
Another $500,000 loaned for the stabilization of the currency
but − the banquet of the bankers −
the money doesn't come out of the pockets of the bankers in
                                            New York either.
    The collateral was that the country would be turned over to
                                            the moneylenders.
The money from the loan of 1911 was to found the National Bank
but it left the National Bank in the hands of the bankers.
The bankers Brown Brothers bought all the paper that they wanted
or rather, all the paper money that they wanted, at 20 to the
                                            dollar
and they sold it at 12.50 to the dollar, all the paper they wanted
or rather to buy 20 pesos cost a dollar (and they were able to buy
as much as they wanted) and when sold (whenever they wanted),
they were worth a dollar sixty. That is to say
        they bought money cheap in order to sell dear
they bought it from the country to sell it back to the country and
by doing so increased the price of corn, houses, education,
dances, train tickets.
    That was the plunder of the mafia of the bankers.
    Like stickup men they held up the national currency.
Afterwards the moneylenders loaned back the country the
                                            country's money
at 6% interest.
The revenue of the nation collected by the foreign bankers
deposited in a National Bank controlled by those foreign bankers
and distributed by the foreign bankers
linked to the United States Secretary of State
(who owned shares in the Angeles Mining Co.)
Just as the Honduran taxes were collected by Morgan   ►
Morgan the ferocious

de dólares (Tratado Chamorro-Bryan)
que también fueron directamente a manos de los banqueros
(Los EE.UU. adquieren sin limitaciones una zona de Canal
2 islas en el Caribe
y una base naval
la patria por 3 millones – y el dinero para los banqueros –
y las aduanas siguen regentadas por los prestamistas por
tiempo indeterminado – hasta la cancelación total de los créditos –
y los prestamistas han adquirido el Banco Nacional, y también
los Ferrocarriles, comprando en 1 millón de dls. el 51% de
las acciones, y de lo que era la nación sólo ha quedado la bandera
Oscura la noche y sin kerosín en el rancho.
Un tecolote canta sobre la patria.
Han callado el canto del pequeño pijul.
No había necesidad de anexarse el territorio
le bastaba a EE.UU. dominar al país (con Díaz
y todos los demás presidentes hasta el presente) con
todas las ventajas de la anexión sin sus riesgos ni sus gastos
"a no ser que quiera jugarse con las palabras
– un profesor, por 1928, al Daily News en París –
nadie duda que la independencia de Nicaragua
no existe"
Para colocar capitales en Nicaragua y protegerlos una vez
colocados, para eso estaba el Departamento de Estado.
Expansión política con miras a la expansión económica:
y expansión económica porque el capital no era suficientemente
reproductivo en los Estados Unidos o lo era menos
que en Nicaragua
that is: imperialismo
intervenciones para inversiones o viceversa
La diplomacia mediante los baqueros sojuzgaba el país
los banqueros mediante la diplomacia extraían el dinero
Reunidos, de rigurosa etiqueta, los zopilotes fúnebres.
Alrededor del Producto Nacional Bruto.
– También igual que el tiburón cuando ha olido sangre.
La intervención extranjera era favorecida por la desorganización
y corrupción de adentro, de ahí que la intervención fomentara
la desorganización y la corrupción y las desarrollara
(claro como el ojo del piche)
De ahí pues:
el imperialismo como elemento perturbador desorganizador etc.
▶

like when the wild boar comes shrieking down
        or the smell of puma is in the air
Afterwards the nation's land was sold for 3 million
dollars (Chamorro-Bryan Agreement)
which also went directly into the hands of the bankers
(The U.S. acquires a canal zone without limitations
        2 Caribbrean islands
        and a naval base
the country for 3 million – and the money to the bankers –
and the customs houses continue to be controlled by the money-
                                                            lenders for
an indeterminate period – until the total cancellation of the debts –
and the moneylenders have acquired the National Bank, and
the railroad, buying 51% of the shares for a
million dollars, and all that remains of the nation is its flag)
        The night dark and no kerosene in the farmhouse.
        An owl sings over the nation.
They have silenced the song of the little *pijul*.
No need to annex the land
but enough for the U.S. to control the country (through Díaz
and every president since) with
all the advantages of annexation but neither its risks nor expenses
"unless one wishes to play with words"
– a professor, circa 1928, to the *Paris Daily News* –
"it is perfectly clear that Nicaraguan independence doesn't exist"
To invest capital in Nicaragua, and to protect it once
invested, was the job of the State Department.
Political expansion with an eye to economic expansion:
and economic expansion because capital didn't have sufficient
yield in the U.S. or yielded less
than it did in Nicaragua
that is: imperialism
        interventions for investment or vice versa
Diplomacy operating through the bankers to subjugate the nation
the bankers operating through diplomacy to extract the money
        Together, in impeccable formality, the funereal vultures.
Hovering about the Gross National Product.
        – Or like sharks about the smell of blood.
Internal chaos and corruption set the stage for foreign intervention
which in turn encouraged further chaos and corruption
        (clear as the *piche's* eye – clear as daylight)   ▶

factor de atraso, de corrupción en Nicaragua: ha violado
tratados, constituciones, decisiones judiciales
    provocado guerra civil manipulado elecciones sobornado
ha amparado robos prostituido la política empobrecido al pueblo
impedido la unión sostenido en el poder a sus agentes contra
    la voluntad del pueblo encarecido la vida defendido
    la opresión traído la muerte
Nicaragua se encontraba (cuando apareció Sandino) con
una parte de su territorio enajenado, la deuda exterior
acrecentada, la vida financiera sometida al
Sindicato de Banqueros de Nueva York, y sin ningún progreso.
    El país entero
como lo que es ahora Cabo Gracias a Dios: ya sólo una hilera
de chozas, con una única calle, y en ella, a dos metros del mar
un zopilote y un perro disputándose una tripa de pescado.

7 / Fernando Gordillo / **El precio de una Patria**

3.000.000 es el precio de una Patria,
si alguien quiere venderla.
Y hubo quien quiso y la vendió.
Más tarde dijeron que sus hijos
nacieron para cantarla.
Como si la lucha no es el más alto
de los cantos.
Y la muerte el más grande.

From here then:
imperialism like an obstructing destabilizing element, etc.
factor of backwardness, of corruption in Nicaragua: has violated
treaties, constitutions, judicial decisions
        provoked civil war stolen elections bribed
covered up corruption prostituted politics impoverished the people
impeded unity kept their agents in power against
        the will of the people jacked up prices defended
                oppression unleashed death
Nicaragua found itself (when Sandino appeared) with
part of its territory already in foreign hands, the foreign debt
increased, its financial life subjected to
the New York Banking Syndicate, and completely stultified.
        The whole country
what Cabo Gracias a Dios looks like today: a row
of huts, with a single street on which, a few steps from the sea,
a vulture and a dog wrangle over the guts of a fish.

7 / Fernando Gordillo / The Price of a Country

3,000,000 is the price of a country
if someone wants to sell her.
And there was someone who so wanted and so sold her.
Later they said that her children
were born to sing her praise.
As if struggle isn't the most sacred
of songs.
And death the greatest.

Sección 2
El levantamiento de Sandino

1 / HuGós / 1927

En las tardes de Granada,
los americanos se sentaban
en las butacas coloniales
del Club Social.

("Y era tan bonito oírles hablar Inglés,"
aún comentan algunas viejas de sociedad.)

En la casa nos enseñaron a rezar
la Viasacra todos los Viernes,
a ir a misa todos los Domingos,
y a sentir un gran temor por Dios.

¿Quién no se acuerda de 1927?

Y mi padre les lustraba
sus terribles botas de invasor,
y de ellas aprendió a entender
palabras como "shoe shine boy."

Y en la escuela Padre Missieri
nos daban cuadernos
con el retrato de un dictador,
y lápices número tres hechos en U.S.A.

¿Quién no se acuerda de 1927?

Los machos asesinos
cortaban orejas campesinas
para venderlas en los Estados Unidos
como "souvenirs of war."

Y un obispo granadino,
que había sido inquisidor,
bendijo los rifles "Remington"

▶

Section 2
Sandino's Uprising

1 / HuGós / 1927

In the Granada evenings,
the Americans sat
in the colonial armchairs
of the Social Club.

("It was so nice to hear them speak English,"
some old society ladies still say.)

At home they taught us to pray
the Way of the Cross every Friday,
to go to mass every Sunday,
and fear God in every way.

Who could forget 1927?

And my father shined
their terrible invader boots,
and learned from them to understand
words like "shoeshine boy."

And in the Padre Missieri School
they gave us notebooks
with a dictator's picture
and number three pencils made in U.S.A.

Who could forget 1927?

The hot shot assassins
cut off peasants' ears
to sell in the States
as "war souvenirs."

And a Granada bishop,
ex-inquisitor,
blessed the Remington rifles   ►

y las ametralladoras "Thompson"
con que los marinos masacraron
a la indígena población.

¿Quién no se acuerda de 1927
en esta hora de descubrimiento,
renuncia y rebelión?

Yo sólo me acuerdo de Semana Santa
y la vez que me dieron diez córdobas
por votar en una elección.

2 / Cardenal / La hora cero

Había un nicaragüense en el extranjero,
un "nica" de Niquinohomo,
trabajando en la Huasteca Petroleum Co., de Tampico.
Y tenía economizados cinco mil dólares.
Y no era ni militar ni político.
Y cogió tres mil dólares de los cinco mil
y se fue a Nicaragua a la revolución de Moncada.
Pero cuando llegó, Moncada estaba entregando las armas.
Pasó tres días, triste, en el Cerro del Común.
Triste, sin saber qué hacer.
Y no era ni político ni militar.
Pensó, y pensó, y se dijo por fin:
Alguien tiene que ser.
Y entonces escribió su primer manifiesto.

El Gral. Moncada telegrafía a los americanos:
TODOS MIS HOMBRES ACEPTAN LA RENDICIÓN MENOS UNO
Mr. Stimpson le pone un ultimátum.
"El pueblo no agradece nada. . ."
le manda a decir Moncada.
El reúne a sus hombres en el Chipote:
29 hombres (y con él 30) contra EE.UU.
    MENOS UNO.
      ("Uno de Niquinohomo. . ."
− ¡Y con él 30!

and the Thompson machine guns
the Marines manned
to massacre the "natives."

Who could forget 1927
in this hour of discovery,
sacrifice and rebellion?

All I remember is Holy Week
and the time they gave me ten cordobas
to vote in some election.

2 / Cardenal / **Zero Hour**

There was a Nicaraguan living abroad,
a "Nica" from Niquinohomo,
working with the Huasteca Petroleum Co., in Tampico.
And he'd saved up five thousand dollars.
And he wasn't a soldier or politician.
And he took three thousand of the five thousand dollars
and went to Nicaragua to join Moncada's revolution.
But when he got there, Moncada was laying down his arms.
He spent three sad days on Común Hill.
Sad, not knowing what to do.
And he wasn't a soldier or politician.
He thought and thought and finally said:
Someone has to do something.
And then he wrote his first manifesto.

General Moncada cables the Americans:
ALL MY MEN SURRENDER EXCEPT ONE
Mr. Stimpson sends him an ultimatum.
"The people won't thank you. . ."
Moncada tells him.
He assembles his men in El Chipote:
29 men (30 counting him) against the U.S.A.
        EXCEPT ONE
     ("One from Niquinohomo. . .")
— 30 counting him.

35

3 / Manolo Cuadra / **Elegía simplista**

Flotaban en la luz de una nueva conciencia.
Todavía la leche les blanqueaba en los labios,
así que alegres, jubilosos y fuertes
dijeron adiós a sus primas y a sus amigas.

4 / Neruda / **Sandino**

Bajaron, vestidos de blanco,
tirando dólares y tiros.
Pero allí surgió un capitán
que dijo: "No, aquí no pones
tus concesiones, tu botella."
Le prometieron un retrato
de Presidente, con guantes,
banda terciada y zapatitos
de charol recién adquiridos.

5 / Cardenal / **La hora cero**

"El que se mete a redentor muere crucificado,"
le manda otra vez a decir Moncada.
Porque Moncada y Sandino eran vecinos;
Moncada de Masatepe y Sandino de Niquinohomo.
Y Sandino le contesta a Moncada:
"La muerte no tiene la menor importancia."
Y a Stimpson: "Confío en el valor de mis hombres. . ."
Y a Stimpson, después de la primera derrota:
"El que cree que estamos vencidos
    no conoce a mis hombres."

3 / Manolo Cuadra / **Simplistic Elegy**

They floated in the light of the new consciousness.
Milk still white on their lips,
so happy, radiant and strong
they kissed their cousins and girlfriends goodbye.

4 / Neruda / **Sandino**

Down came the Yankees, dressed in white,
scattering dollars and bullets.
But up rose a captain
who said: "No, you won't set up
your business, not here."
They promised him a presidential
portrait, with gloves, a sash
and shiny new patent leather shoes.

5 / Cardenal / **Zero Hour**

Moncada wrote him again
"If you set yourself up as a savior, you'll die crucified."
For Moncada and Sandino were neighbors:
Moncada from Masatepe, Sandino from Niquinohomo.
And Sandino answered Moncada:
"My death hasn't the least importance."
And to Stimpson: "I trust the courage of my men. . ."
And to Stimpson after the first defeat:
"If you think we're whipped,
    you don't know my men."

6 / Neruda / **Sandino**

Sandino se quitó las botas,
se hundió en los trémulos pantanos,
se terció la banda mojada
de la libertad en la selva,
y, tiro a tiro, respondió
a los "civilizadores."

7 / Cardenal / **La hora cero**

Y no era ni militar ni político.
Y sus hombres:
    muchos eran muchachos,
con sombreros de palma y con caites
o descalzos, con machetes, ancianos
de barba blanca, niños de doce años con sus rifles,
blancos, indios impenetrables, y rubios, y negros murrucos,
con los pantalones despedazados y sin provisiones,
los pantalones hechos jirones,
desfilando en fila india con la bandera adelante
— un harapo levantado en un palo de la montaña —
callados debajo de la lluvia, y cansados,
chapoteando los caites en los charcos del pueblo
    ¡Viva Sandino!

8 / Neruda / **Sandino**

La furia norteamericana
fue indecible: documentados
embajadores convencieron
al mundo que su amor era
Nicaragua, que alguna vez
el orden debía llegar
a sus entrañas soñolientas.

6 / Neruda / **Sandino**

Sandino took off his boots,
plunged into the tremulous marshes,
unfurled the dampened sash
of freedom in the jungle,
and shot for shot, he answered
the "civilizer's" fire.

7 / Cardenal / **Zero Hour**

And he wasn't a soldier or politician.
And his men:
       many were kids,
with sombreros of palm fronds, with sandals
or barefoot, with machetes, old men
with white beards, twelve-year-old boys with rifles,
whites, impenetrable Indians, and blondes, and curly-headed Blacks.
their trousers in tatters, without supplies,
their pants made into pennants,
marching Indian file with their flag in front
– a rag raised on a mountain reed,
silent under the rains, and tired,
their sandals splashing through village puddles
       Viva Sandino!

8 / Neruda / **Sandino**

The Americans were
rabid beyond words:
Ambassadors armed with documents
convinced all the world that
Nicaragua was their love,
that order some day soon
must come to its sleeping womb.

9 / Cardenal / La hora cero

"El abrazo es el saludo de todos nosotros,"
decía Sandino – y nadie ha abrazado como él.
Y siempre que hablaban de ellos decían todos:
"'Todos nosotros. . ." "'Todos somos iguales."
"Aquí todos somos hermanos," decía Umanzor.
Y todos estuvieron unidos hasta que los mataron a todos.
Peleando contra aeroplanos con tropas de zacate,
sin más paga que la comida y el vestido y las armas,
y economizando cada bala como si fuera de oro;
con morteros hechos con tubos
y con bombas hechas con piedras y pedazos de vidrios,
rellenas con dinamita de las minas y envueltas en cueros;
con granadas fabricadas con latas de sardinas.

10 / Neruda / Canción de gesta

. . . Sandino atravesó la selva
y despeñó su pólvora sagrada
contra marinerías bandoleras
en Nueva York crecidas y pagadas:
ardió la tierra, resonó el follaje:
el yanki no esperó lo que pasaba:
se vestía muy bien para la guerra,
brillaban sus zapatos y sus armas
pero por experiencia supo pronto
quiénes eran Sandino y Nicaragua:
todo era tumba de ladrones rubios:
el aire, el árbol, el camino, el agua,
surgían guerrilleros de Sandino
hasta del whiskey que se destapaban
y enfermaban de muerte repentina
los gloriosos guerreros de Luisiana
acostumbrados a colgar los negros
mostrando valentía sobrehumana:
dos mil encapuchados ocupados
en un negro, una soga y una rama.
Aquí eran diferentes los negocios:
Sandino acometía y esperaba, ▶

9 / Cardenal / Zero Hour

"An embrace is the salute for all of us,"
Sandino said, and no one embraced like him.
And whenever they talked of themselves they said *all:*
"All of us. . ." "We're all equals."
"We're all brothers here," Umanzor said.
And they were all united till they killed all of them.
Fighting against airplanes with strawmen troops,
with no other pay but food, clothes and arms,
and hoarding each bullet as if it were gold;
with mortars made from pipes,
and bombs made from stones and broken glass
loaded with dynamite from the mines and wrapped in hides;
with grenades made from sardine cans.

10 / Neruda / Epic

. . .Sandino crossed the jungle
and hurled his sacred powder
against the bandit Marines
New York bred and hired:
the earth burned, the leaves shook:
the Yankees were caught by surprise:
well-dressed for war,
their shoes and weapons shined
but soon they knew first hand
Sandino's Nicaraguans:
the whole land a tomb for blonde thieves:
Sandino's guerrillas sprang
from the air, the tree, the road, the water,
even from untapped whiskey bottles
and they sickened to sudden death —
glory boys from Louisiana
used to hanging Blacks
to show their hot-shot courage
two thousand hoods busy with
a Black, a rope and a bough.
But here the business was different:
Sandino waited and attacked,   ►

Sandino era la noche que venía
y era la luz del mar que los mataba,
Sandino era una torre con banderas,
Sandino era un fusil con esperanzas.

11 / Cardenal / La hora cero

Y de la montaña venían, y a la montaña volvían,
marchando, chapoteando, con la bandera adelante.
Un ejército descalzo o con caites y casi sin armas
que no tenía ni disciplina ni desorden
y donde ni los jefes ni la tropa ganaban paga
pero no se obligaba a pelear a nadie:
y tenían jerarquía militar pero todos eran iguales
sin distinción en la repartición de la comida
y el vestido, con la misma ración para todos.
Y los jefes no tenían ayudantes:
más bien como una comunidad que como un ejército
y más unidos por amor que por disciplina militar
aunque nunca ha habido mayor unidad en un ejército.
Un ejército alegre, con guitarras y con abrazos.
Una canción de amor era su himno de guerra:

Si Adelita se fuera con otro
La seguiría por tierra y por mar
Si por mar en un buque de guerra
Y si por tierra en un tren militar.

Sandino was the night that fell
and the light from the sea that killed,
Sandino was a tower with flags,
Sandino was a rifle with hopes.

11 / Cardenal / **Zero Hour**

And they came from the mountains and returned to the mountains,
marching, splashing through puddles with the banner in front.
An army barefoot or in sandals and almost without arms,
with neither discipline nor disorder
and with neither leaders nor troops earning pay
but no one had to fight
and they had military hierarchy but they were all equal
without distinctions in sharing out their food
and their clothes, with the same ration for all.
And the leaders had no adjutants:
more like a community than an army
and more united by love than by military discipline
though never did an army have such unity.
A happy army, with guitars and embraces.
A love song was their battle hymn:

If Adelita runs off with another
I will follow her by land and over sea,
If by sea in a tanker of war
If by land in a military train.

Sección 3
Las campañas de Sandino

1 / Pablo Antonio Cuadra /
Poema del momento extranjero en la selva   *[A varias voces]*

En el corazón de nuestras montañas donde la vieja selva
devora los caminos como el guás las serpientes
donde Nicaragua levanta su bandera de ríos flameando entre
tambores torrenciales.
Allí anterior a mi canto
anterior a mí mismo invento el pedernal
y alumbro el verde sórdido de las heliconias,
el hirviente silencio de los manglares
y enciendo la orquídea en la noche de la toboba.
Llamo. Grito. ¡Estrella! ¿Quién ha abierto las puertas de la noche?
Tengo que hacer algo con el lodo de la historia,
cavar en el pantano y desenterrar la luna
de mis padres. ¡Oh! ¡Desata
tu oscura cólera víbora magnética,
afila tus obsidianas tigre negro, clava
tu fosforescente ojo ¡allí!
En la médula del bosque
500 norteamericanos!

2 / Neruda / **Sandino**

Los héroes de Wall Street
fueron comidos por la ciénaga,
un relámpago los mataba,
más de un machete los seguía,
una soga los despertaba
como una serpiente en la noche,
y colgando de un árbol eran
acarreados lentamente
por coleópteros azules
y enredaderas devorantes.

44

Section 3
The Campaigns of Sandino

1 / Pablo Antonio Cuadra /
Poem of an Alien Moment in the Jungle   *[For several voices]*

    In the heart of our mountains where the old jungle
devours the roads like the *guás* eats snakes
where Nicaragua raises its flag of rivers twisting and turning
                                amid torrential drums.
There, before my song
before myself, I invent flint and
light the sordid green of the *heliconias,*
the hissing silence of the mangrove,
and I ignite the orchid in the night of the snake.
I call. I cry. Star! Who has opened the doors of the night?
I must do something with the mud of history,
dig in the swamp and pull out the moon
of my ancestors. Oh! Thrust forth
your dark magnetic viper wrath,
sharpen your black obsidian, drive
your phosphorescent eyes – there!
        In the marrow of the woods
        500 Yankees!

2 / Neruda / **Sandino**

Wall Street's heroes
were devoured by the swamp,
a lightning bolt killed them,
machetes followed them,
a rope awakened them
like a serpent in the night,
and hanging from a tree
they were slowly carried off
by blue coleoptera
and man-eating vines.

45

3 / Cardenal / **Canto nacional**

     – La noche es oscura y con neblina y 140 sandinistas
sorprenden a los centinelas del cuartel –
– Al atardecer los sandinistas se apuestan en un camino
por donde van a pasar los marinos –
     – Miguel Angel Ortez surge en la noche
con su larga cabellera rubia y sus pantalones negros –
– Rifles y machetes y 2 viejas ametralladoras Lewis
y gritos VIVA SANDINO! entre los tiros y PATRIA LIBRE O MORIR!
  – Se disipa la neblina, y los sandinistas han desaparecido –

4 / Cardenal / **La hora cero**

"He is a bandido," decía Somoza, "a bandolero."
Y Sandino nunca tuvo propiedades.
Que traducido al español quiere decir:
Somoza le llamaba a Sandino bandolero.
Y Sandino nunca tuvo propiedades.
Y Moncada le llamaba bandido en los banquetes
y Sandino en las montañas no tenía sal
y sus hombres tiritando de frío en las montañas,
y la casa de su suegro la tenía hipotecada
para libertar a Nicaragua, mientras en la Casa Presidencial
Moncada tenía hipotecada a Nicaragua.
"Claro que no es" – dice el Ministro Americano
riendo – "pero le llamamos bandolero en sentido técnico."

3 / Cardenal / **National Song**

    − The night dark and foggy and 140 *Sandinistas*
take the sentries by storm at the barracks −
− At dusk the *Sandinistas* take up positions along a road the
Marines will be traveling −
    − Miguel Angel Ortez springs up in the night
with his long blond hair and his black trousers −
    − Rifles and machetes and 2 old Lewis machine guns
and cries of VIVA SANDINO! amidst the shooting and FREE HOME-
                                       LAND OR DEATH!
− The mist clears, the *Sandinistas* have vanished −

4 / Cardenal / **Zero Hour**

"He's a *bandido*," said Somoza, "a *bandolero*."
And Sandino never owned any property.
Which translated means
that Somoza called Sandino a gangster.
And Sandino never owned any property.
And Moncada called Sandino a bandit at public banquets
and in the mountains Sandino had no salt
and his men shivering from cold in the mountains,
and he mortgaged his father-in-law's house
to liberate Nicaragua, while in the Presidential Palace
Moncada had mortgaged all of Nicaragua.
"It's clear he isn't" − the American Minister says
laughing − "but in a technical sense we dub him *bandolero*."

5 / Neruda / **Sandino**

. . .en todas
partes estaba Sandino,
matando norteamericanos,
ajusticiando invasores.
Y cuando vino la aviación,
la ofensiva de los ejércitos
acorazados, la incisión
de aplastadores poderíos,
Sandino con sus guerrilleros,
como un espectro de la selva,
era un árbol que se enroscaba
o una tortuga que dormía
o un río que se deslizaba.

Pero, árbol, tortuga, corriente
fueron la muerte vengadora.
fueron sistema de la selva,
mortales síntomas de araña.

6 / M. Cuadra / **Elegía simplista**

Pelearon contra un regimiento entero y mejor armado,
contra ametralladoras y fusiles de tiro rápido,
contra prodigiosas bestias de la tierra y del aire
manejados por hombres perfectamente fríos.
. . .
. . .sabemos que por acerbos étnicos,
rotos sus espinazos y sus tibias,
ensarrados los huesos de sus pies ligeros
– ensarrados por el paludismo –
y tembloroso el cuerpo por la quinina,
siempre hicieron gala de una moral muy alta.

5 / Neruda / **Sandino**

. . .Sandino was everywhere
killing Yankees,
slaying invaders.
And when the air force came,
the offensive of the armored
legions, the incision of
overwhelming power,
Sandino with his guerrillas,
like a specter in the jungle,
was a twisting tree
or a sleeping tortoise
or a river gliding by.

But tree, tortoise, current
were vengeful death,
were the jungle's system,
deadly symptoms of the spider.

6 / M. Cuadra / **Simplistic Elegy**

They fought against a whole regiment, better armed,
against machine guns and rapid-fire rifles,
against prodigious beasts of earth and air
driven by perfectly cold-blooded men.
          . . .
. . .tradition has it
that even with broken backbones and shinbones,
rot eating away at their fleet feet
− bodies stricken with malaria −
and trembling from quinine,
they flaunted their morale.

7 / Cardenal / La hora cero

¿Qué es aquella luz allá lejos? ¿Es una estrella?
Es la luz de Sandino en la montaña negra.
Allá están él y sus hombres junto a la fogata roja
con sus rifles al hombro y envueltos en sus colchas,
fumando o cantando canciones tristes del Norte,
los hombres sin moverse y moviéndose sus sombras.

Su cara era vaga como la de un espíritu,
lejana por las meditaciones y los pensamientos
y seria por las campañas y la intemperie.
Y Sandino no tenía cara de soldado,
sino de poeta convertido en soldado por necesidad,
y de un hombre nervioso dominado por la serenidad.
Había dos rostros superpuestos en su rostro:
una fisonomía sombría y a la vez iluminada;
triste como un atardecer en la montaña
y alegre como la mañana en la montaña.

8 / Cardenal / Canto nacional

A la luz de una fogata Sandino leyendo *El Quijote*
     – el cuartel inaccesible como nido de quetzal –
Sandino está otra vez en el Chipote muchachos.
     Ataca otra vez de noche Telpaneca.
Otra vez Pedrón anda por el Coco
          o tal vez por Boaco.
Los campesinos dejan otra vez sin tapiscar el maíz
          sin aporrear los frijoles
y van con Sandino a cercar a las minas, a verguear a los marinos
pegarle fuego a la Standard Fruit.

7 / Cardenal / **Zero Hour**

What's that far off light? Is it a star?
It's Sandino's light in the dark of the mountain.
There he is with his men near their red campfire
rifles on their shoulders, wrapped in their blankets
smoking or singing sad songs from the north,
men without movement, only their shadows stirring.

His face was vague like a ghost,
distanced by thoughts and meditations
grave from the battles and the storms.
And Sandino didn't look like a soldier
but like a poet turned soldier by necessity
like a manic man ruled by serenity.
He had two faces superimposed on his face:
a look at once somber and lit;
sad like a sunset in the mountains
and happy like the morning in the mountains.

8 / Cardenal / **National Song**

By the light of a fire, Sandino is reading *Don Quixote.*
    — the headquarters inaccessible as the nest of the quetzal —
Boys, Sandino is in El Chipote again.
    Again he attacks Telpaneca by night.
Once again Pedrón is in the vicinity of El Coco
      or perhaps near Boaco.
Once again the peasants leave the corn unthreshed
      the frijoles unshucked
and go with Sandino to lay siege to the mines, beat the shit
out of the Marines, put Standard Fruit to the torch.

9 / Cardenal / **La hora cero**

En la luz su rostro se le rejuvenecía,
y en la sombra se le llenaba de cansancio.
Y Sandino no era inteligente ni era culto,
pero salió inteligente de la montaña.
"En la montaña todo enseña" decía Sandino
(soñando con las Segovias llenas de escuelas)
y recibía mensajes de todas las montañas
y parecía que cada cabaña espiaba para él
(donde los extranjeros fueran como hermanos
todos los extranjeros hasta los "americanos")
    —"hasta los yanquis. . ."
Y: "Dios hablará por los segovianos. . ." decía.
"Nunca creí que saldría vivo de esta guerra
pero siempre he creído que era necesaria. . ."
Y: "Creen que yo voy a ser latifundista?"

10 / Neruda / **Canción de gesta**

Eran muy diferentes las lecciones,
en West Point era limpia la enseñanza:
nunca les enseñaron en la escuela
que podía morir él que mataba:
los norteamericanos no aprendieron
que amamos nuestra pobre tierra amada
y que defenderemos las banderas
que con dolor y amor fueron creadas.
Si no aprendieron esto en Filadelfia
lo supieron con sangre en Nicaragua:
allí esperaba el capitán del pueblo:
Augusto C. Sandino se llamaba.
Y en este canto quedará su nombre
estupendo como una llamarada
para que nos dé luz y nos dé fuego
en la continuación de las batallas.

9 / Cardenal / Zero Hour

In the light his face grew young,
and in the shade it pined with fatigue.
And Sandino wasn't bright or well read
but he grew bright in the mountains.
"In the mountains everything teaches," said Sandino
(dreaming of the Segovias filled with schools)
and messages came from all the mountains
and every cabin seemed to spy for him
(where foreigners would be like brothers
all foreigners, even the "Americans")
    –"even the Yankees. . ."
And: "God will speak through the Segovians..." he said.
"I have never believed I'd come out of this war alive
but I have always believed it was necessary. . ."
And: "Do they really think I'll become a landowner?"

10 / Neruda / Epic

The lessons were very different,
in West Point instruction was pure:
school never taught them
that those who kill could be killed:
the Yankees never learned
how we love our poor and dear land
how we'd defend the flags
we'd sewn with so much pain and love.
What they couldn't learn in Philadelphia,
was taught in blood in Nicaragua:
the people's captain waited,
Augusto C. Sandino his name.
And in this song that name
resounds stupendous like a flare
that gives us light and gives us fire
to inflame us in our wars.

11 / Cardenal / **Canto nacional**

— Al oscurecer los marinos van a entrar a un bosque de pinos
   (alcanzan a oír un bordoneo de guitarra tras los pinos)
y de repente te detiene el retén en San Rafael del Norte:
"¿Quién vive?"
"¡Viva Nicaragua!"
"Santo y seña"
"No venda nunca a la patria"
Y otra vez Pedrón y Ortez se juntan para atacar Jinotega
Pedrón va otra vez de pueblo en pueblo diciéndoles que no voten
tras un ataque los marinos oyen los adioses y el
trote del tropel de mulas y traquidos de carretas en la noche.

12 / Cardenal / **La hora cero**

Es medianoche en las montañas de las Segovias.
¡Y aquella luz es Sandino! Una luz con un canto. . .

> *Si Adelita se fuera con otro*

Pero las naciones tienen su sino.
Y Sandino no fue nunca presidente
sino que el asesino de Sandino fue el presidente
¡y 20 años presidente!

> *Si Adelita se fuera con otro*
> *La seguiría por tierra y por mar*

Se firmó el desarme. Cargaron las armas en carretas.
Guatuceros amarrados con cabuyas, rifles sarrosos
y unas cuantas ametralladoras viejas.
Y las carretas van bajando por la sierra.

> *Si por mar en un buque de guerra*
> *Y si por tierra en un tren militar.*

11 / Cardenal / **National Song**

— At dusk the Marines are about to enter a pine forest
    (faintly among the pines they hear a guitar's bass string)
and suddenly there at the police station in San Rafael del Norte
                                        you're stopped:
"Who goes there?"
"Viva Nicaragua!"
"The password"
"Never betray your country"
And once again Pedrón and Ortez reconnoiter to attack Jinotega
again Pedrón travels from village to village telling them not to vote
after an attack the Marines hear the goodbyes and the
hoofbeats of the mules and the rattle of oxcarts in the night.

12 / Cardenal / **Zero Hour**

It's midnight in the Segovia mountains.
And that light is Sandino! A light with a song. . .

    If Adelita runs off with another

But nations follow their fate.
And Sandino was never the president
but his assassin was president
and president for twenty years!

    If Adelita runs off with another
    I will follow her by land and over sea

They signed the ceasefire. They loaded the weapons in carts.
Guns lashed together with cords, rusty rifles
and a few old machine guns
And the carts wind slowly down the mountains.

    If by sea in a tanker of war
    If by land in a military train.

Sección 4
La muerte de Sandino

1 / Neruda / **Sandino**

. . .cuando fuego, sangre
y dólar no destruyeron
la torre altiva de Sandino,
los guerreros de Wall Street
hicieron la paz, invitaron
a celebrarla al guerrillero,
y un traidor recién alquilado
le disparó su carabina. . .

Se llama Somoza. Hasta hoy
está reinando en Nicaragua:
los treinta dólares crecieron
y aumentaron en su barriga.

2 / Cardenal / **La hora cero**

Telegrama del Ministro Americano (Mr. Lane)
al Secretario de Estado – depositado en Managua
el 14 de febrero de 1934 a las 6:05 p.m.
y recibido en Washington a las 8:50 P.M.:
  "Informado por fuente oficial
  que el avión no pudo aterrizar en Wiwilí
  y por tanto la venida de Sandino se retrasa. . ."

El telegrama del Ministro Americano (Mr. Lane)
al Secretario de Estado el 16 de febrero
anunciando la llegada de Sandino a Managua
Not Printed
no fue publicado en la memoria del Depto. de Estado.
Como la guardatinaja que salió del matorral
a la carretera y es acorralada por los perros
y se queda parada delante de los tiradores
porque sabe que no tiene para donde correr. . .   ▶

Section 4
The Death of Sandino

1 / Neruda / **Sandino**

. . .when fire, blood
and dollars failed
to destroy Sandino's proud bastion,
the Wall Street warriors
made peace, invited the guerrilla
to celebrate,
and a newly hired traitor
fired the fatal shot.

His name is Somoza. And still
he reigns in Nicaragua:
the thirty dollars grew
and multiplied in his belly.

2 / Cardenal / **Zero Hour**

Cable from the American Minister (Mr. Lane)
to the Secretary of State – sent from Managua
February 14, 1934, at 6:05 P.M.
and received in Washington at 8:50 P.M.:
    "Informed by official sources
    that the airplane could not land at Wiwilí
    and Sandino's arrival is delayed. . ."

Cable from the American Minister (Mr. Lane)
to the Secretary of State on February 16
announcing Sandino's arrival in Managua
Not Printed
was not published in State Department record.
Like the *guardatinaja* that runs out of the brush
onto the road and surrounded by dogs,
remains still before the hunters
because he knows there's nowhere he can run. . .

I talked with Sandino for half an hour
– dijo Somoza al Ministro Americano –
But I can't tell you what he talked about
because I don't know what he talked about
because I don't know what he talked about.

"Y ya verán que yo nunca tendré propiedades. . ."
Y: "Es in-cons-ti-tu-cio-nal," decía Sandino.
"La Guardia Nacional es inconstitucional."
"An insult!" dijo Somoza al Ministro Americano
el VEINTIUNO DE FEBRERO a las 6 de la tarde,
"An insult! I want to stop Sandino."

3 / Neruda / **Canción de gesta**

¡Oh banquete del vino ensangrentado!
¡Oh noche! ¡Oh luna falsa de los caminos!
¡Oh estrellas amarillas que no hablaron!
¡Oh tierra muda y ciega de la noche!
Tierra que no detuvo su caballo.
¡Oh noche de traición que abandonaste
la torre del honor en malas manos!
¡Oh banquete de plata y de agonía!
¡Oh sombra de traición que prepararon!
¡Oh pabellón de luz que florecía,
desde entonces vencido y enlutado!

4 / Cardenal / **La hora cero**

Cuatro presos están cavando un hoyo.

"¿Quién se ha muerto?" dijo un preso.
"Nadie," dijo el guardia.
"¿Entonces para que es el hoyo?"
"Qué perdés," dijo el guardia, "seguí cavando."

El Ministro Americano está almorzando con Moncada.
"Will you have coffee, sir?
It's very good coffee, sir."
"What?" Moncada aparta la mirada de la ventana
y mira al criado: "Oh, yes, I'll have coffee."
Y se rió. "Certainly."

I talked to Sandino for half an hour
— Somoza told the American Minister —
but I can't tell you what he talked about
because I don't know what he talked about
because I don't know what he talked about.

"And you'll see that I won't own any property. . ."
And: "It is un-con-sti-tu-tion-al," Sandino said.
"The *Guardia Nacional* is unconstitutional."
"An insult!" Somoza told the American Minister
on the TWENTY-FIRST OF FEBRUARY at six in the evening.
"An insult! I want to stop Sandino."

3 / Neruda / Epic

Banquet of bloodied wine
Night of false moon on the roads,
Yellow stars that did not speak,
mute and blind land of the night.
Land that did not slow his horse.
Night of treason that abandoned
honor's tower to sullied hands.
Banquet of agony and silver,
shadow of treason they prepared.
Pavilion of the light that flourished,
draped in mourning ever since.

4 / Cardenal / Zero Hour

Four convicts were digging a pit.

"Who's been done in?" a convict asked.
"No one," said the guard.
"Then who's the pit for?"
"Quit squawking and dig," said the guard.

The American Minister is having lunch with Moncada.
"Will you have coffee, sir?
It's very good coffee, sir."
"What?" Moncada looks away from the window
and looks at the servant: "Oh, yes, I'll have coffee."
And he laughs. "Certainly."

▶

En un cuartel cinco hombres están en un cuarto cerrado
con centinelas en las puertas y en las ventanas.
A uno de los hombres le falta un brazo.
Entra el jefe gordo con condecoraciones y les dice: "Yes."

Otro hombre va a cenar esta noche con el Presidente
(el hombre para el que estuvieron cavando el hoyo)
y les dice a sus amigos: "Vámonos. Ya es hora."
Y suben a cenar con el Presidente de Nicaragua.

5 / Neruda / Canción de gesta

Para la paz en una noche triste
el General Sandino fue invitado
festejando su bravura
con el "Embajador Americano"
(porque el nombre total del continente
estos filibusteros usurparon).
Alegre estaba el General Sandino:
vino y brindis subieron y bajaron:
los yanquis regresaron a su patria
desoladoramente derrotados
y el banquete sellaba con honores
la lucha de Sandino y sus hermanos.
En la mesa esperaba el asesino.
Era un oscuro ser prostibuliario
y levantó la copa muchas veces
mientras en los bolsillos resonaron
los treinta horrendos dólares del crimen.

Five men are in a locked room in the barracks
with guards at the doors and windows.
One of the men has only one arm.
The fat bemedalled officer comes in and says: "Yes."

Another man is going to have dinner with the President tonight
(the man for whom they were digging the pit)
and he says to his friends: "Let's go. It's time now."
And they go to have dinner with the President of Nicaragua.

5 / Neruda / Epic

For the sake of peace one sad night
General Sandino took up the invitation
to celebrate his brave resistance
with the Ambassador from "America"
(Because like pirates, they confiscated
the name of the whole continent.)
Sandino's spirits soared
as toasts of wine were raised and downed:
the Yankees had returned home
desolate in defeat
the banquet paid full honors
to Sandino and his brothers.
Waiting at the table the assassin
an unknown small-time pimp
raised his glass and drank a toast
while thirty horrendous criminal dollars
jingled in his pockets.

"I was in a concierto," dijo Somoza.
Y era cierto, había estado en un concierto
o en un banquete viendo bailar a una bailarina o
quién sabe qué mierda sería.
Y a las 10 de la noche, Somoza tuvo miedo.
De pronto afuera repicó el teléfono.
"¡Sandino lo llama por teléfono!"
Y tuvo miedo. Uno de sus amigos le dijo:
"¡No seas pendejo, jodido!"
Somoza mandó no contestar el teléfono.
La bailarina seguía bailando para el asesino.
Y afuera en la oscuridad siguió repicando y repicando el teléfono.

7 / Neruda / **Canción de gesta**

Se levantó Sandino y no sabía
que su victoria había terminado
y que el embajador lo señalaba
cumpliendo así su parte en el contrato:
todo estaba dispuesto para el crimen
entre asesinos y norteamericanos:
y allí en la puerta mientras lo abrazaban
lo despidieron y lo condenaron.
Enhorabuena! Y se alejó Sandino
con el verdugo y con la muerte andando. . .

8 / Cardenal / **La hora cero**

A las 10 de la noche bajan en automóvil a Managua.
En la mitad de la bajada los detienen los guardias.
A los dos más viejos se los llevan en un auto
y a los otros tres en otro auto para otro lado.
A donde cuatro presos estuvieron cavando un hoyo
"¿A dónde vamos?"
preguntó el hombre para él que hicieron el hoyo.
Y nadie le contestó.
Después el auto se paró y un guardia les dijo:
"Salgan." Los tres salieron,
y un hombre al que le faltaba un brazo gritó "¡Fuego!"

6 / Cardenal / **Zero Hour**

"I was in a Concierto," Somoza said.
And it was true, he'd been at a concert
or a banquet or watching a ballerina dance or
whatever the shit it was he was doing.
And at ten o'clock Somoza grew afraid.
Suddenly the telephone rang outside.
"Sandino is calling him on the phone!"
And he grew afraid. One of his friends told him:
"Don't be chicken-shit, man!"
Somoza ordered them not to answer the phone.
The ballerina went on dancing for the assassin.
And in the dark outside the telephone went on ringing and ringing.

7 / Neruda / **Epic**

Sandino arose unaware
that his victory was at an end
that the Ambassador had fingered him,
according to his share in the deal:
the murderers and North Americans
made ready for the crime:
and there at the door as they embraced him
they saw him off and passed his sentence.
A job well done. And Sandino took his leave
with the executioner and began his walk with death. . .

8 / Cardenal / **Zero Hour**

At ten o'clock they go down by car to Managua.
In the middle of the trip the guards stop them.
They take the two older men off in one car
and the other three in another car in another direction.
To the place where four convicts were digging a pit.
"Where are we going?"
the man for whom they were digging the pit asked them.
       And no one answered.
Then the car stopped and a guard said to them:
"Get out." The three of them got out,
and a man with only one arm shouted "Fire!"

9 / Gordillo / **La circunstancia y la palabra**

En otros países
podríamos crecer al margen de la muerte.
En Nicaragua, no, no en
Nicaragua.
Un asesino de cinco hombres
en la cárcel encendía cinco velas.
¿Será por eso La Loma tan
iluminada?

Como semillas,
a la orilla de ríos desconocidos
que corren por montañas
ignoradas,
con el odio como testigo y el
dolor por compañero
fueron enterrados.
Pero desde ahora lo digo
para que no olvidemos,
por ellos florecerá el Amor.
Y no digo sus nombres ni cuando
fueron muertos,
cada uno sabrá a quienes me refiero
y quienes fueron los asesinos.
Porque ellos podridos, ignorados,
calumniados,
murieron para que pudiéramos
vivir.
Por amor,
se lanzaron a la muerte.
Si despertaron antes de tiempo
y la sombra que nos cubre
les impidió ver la aurora,
sabedlo, el camino hacia el Este
fue trazado por ellos,
que con los ojos abiertos
descubrieron la verdadera Patria.

In other countries
we could grow
on the margin of death.
In Nicaragua, no, not in
Nicaragua.
An assassin of five men
lit five candles in jail.
Is this why
Somoza's Loma is so
lit up?

Like seeds,
on the edge of unknown rivers
that run through unknown
mountains
with hatred as witness
and pain for companion
they were buried.
But from now on I say it,
so we won't forget it,
because of them Love will flower.
And I don't say their names, nor when
they were killed,
every one will know of whom
I speak
and who were their murderers.
Because rotting, ignored,
slandered,
they died so we could
live.
For love
they hurled themselves at death.
If they woke up too early
and the shadow that covers us
kept them from seeing the dawn,
let it be known that the road to the East
was traced by them,
who with open eyes
found our true country.

10 / Cardenal / **La hora cero**

A la luz de una lámpara tubular
cuatro guardias están cerrando un hoyo.
Y a la luz de una luna de febrero.

Es hora en que el lucero nistoyolero de Chontales
levanta a las inditas a hacer nistoyol
   . . .
La Llorona va llorando a la orilla de los ríos:
"¿Lo hallaste?" "¡No!" "¿Lo hallaste?" "¡No!"
   . . .
Y mientras en los salones del Palacio Presidencial
y en los patios de las prisiones y en los cuarteles
y la Legación Americana y la Estación de Policía
los que velaron esa noche se ven en el alba lívida
con las manos y las caras como manchadas de sangre.

"I did it," dijo después Somoza.
"I did it, for the good of Nicaragua."

11 / Rafael Alberti / **Aterrizando**

Nicaragua desde el cielo.

Los yankis por los caminos.
Martí se fue a las Segovias
con el general Sandino.

Managua desde las nubes.

Sangre por los levantados
pueblos de San Salvador.
Martí cayó fusilado.

Managua desde Managua.

Se fueron ya los marinos.
Los yankis firman la paz. . .
pero matando a Sandino.

10 / Cardenal / **Zero Hour**

By the light of a tubular lamp
four guards are closing a hole.
And by the light of a February moon.

It is the hour when the cornmeal light of Chontales
wakes up the Indian girls to grind corn
. . .
The Weeping Woman wanders weeping by the banks of the rivers:
"Did you find him?" "No!" "Did you find him?" "No!"
. . .
While in the Presidential Palace parlors
in the prison courtyards and in the barracks
and in the American Embassy and the Police Station
those who stayed awake that night look at their hands and faces
and in the livid light of dawn they see them stained with blood.

"I did it," Somoza said later,
"I did it, for the good of Nicaragua."

11 / Rafael Alberti / **Landing**

Nicaragua seen from the sky.

The Yankees along the road.
Martí went up to the Segovias
with General Sandino.

Managua seen from the clouds.

Blood spilled in rebel
towns of San Salvador.
Martí has fallen.

Managua seen from Managua.

The Marines have gone at last.
The Yankees sign the treaty. . .
but they kill Sandino first.

Sección 5
La lucha continua

1 / Salomón de la Selva / **La hoja del tallo que se hizo espada**

No fuera Nicaragua traicionada
por enconados odios fratricidas,
no tiranuelo ruin, en maridaje
con extrañas legiones asesinas,
sembrara espanto, y corrompiera al pueblo,
y burlara el honor y la justicia.

Ni fuera soledad la de Sandino,
de la abyección de sus hermanos víctima:
Hombre sencillo que brotó del campo
como la caña que nos da la espiga –
hombre como tus hombres, sin alardes
de vana floración y sin espinas –
y ante el peligro que a la raza arrolla,
y ante el dolor que al continente hostiga,
cada hoja de su tallo se hizo espada
contra la iniquidad de la conquista.
    . . .
No de admirarlo dejes porque brilla
apagada su estrella: Si se apaga,
es quizás porque nace el nuevo día.

2 / Azarías H. Pallais / **Granada y León**

Norte, Sur, Este y Oeste
nuestro país antes lleno
ha caído en el horror
del vacío

Section 5
The Struggle Continues

---

1 / Salomón de la Selva / **The Leaf of his Stalk Became a Sword**

How different it would have been
had Nicaragua not been betrayed
by bitter fratricidal hatreds,
had a petty tyrant, in concert
with murderous foreign legions
not sown terror and corrupted the people,
mocking honor and justice.

Had Sandino not been alone,
victim of his brothers' cowardice:
a simple man who grew from the fields
like plant from seed –
a man like other men, free
of vain florescence, free of thorns –
who, when faced with danger that could rout a people,
and faced with pain that could scourge a continent,
made every leaf of his stalk a sword
against the iniquity of conquest.
            . . .
Cease not to admire him if the light
of his star fades. Should it dim,
then perhaps it is because a new day begins.

2 / Azarías H. Pallais / **Granada and León**

North, south, east and west
our country once full
has fallen into the horror
of emptiness

3 / Cardenal / **La hora cero**

Después EE. UU. le mandó más armas a Somoza;
como media mañana estuvieron pasando las armas;
camiones y camiones cargados con cajones de armas;
todos marcados U.S.A., MADE IN U.S.A.,
armas para echar más presos, para perseguir libros,
para robarle a Juan Potosme cinco pesos.
Yo vi pasar esas armas por la Avenida Roosevelt.
Y la gente callada en las calles las veía pasar:
el flaco, el descalzo, el de la bicicleta,
el negro, el trompudo, aquélla la de amarillo,
el alto, el chele, el pelón, el bigotudo,
el ñato, el chirizo, el murruco, el requeneto:
y la cara de toda esa gente
      era la de un ex teniente muerto.

4 / Cardenal / **Canto nacional**

. . .Y Sandino decía a los campesinos:
"Algún día triunfaremos. Y si yo no lo veo
las hormiguitas llegarán a contármelo bajo la tierra."

5 / Cardenal / **La hora cero**

Esclavo de los extranjeros
            y tirano de su pueblo
impuesto por la intervención
         y mantenido por la no intervención:
SOMOZA FOREVER.

6 / Cardenal / **Canto nacional**

    Todavía tenemos la lucha: . . .
y ay, tantos Rubén Daríos hay en el monte
macheteando. Habitantes de ranchos en perpetua noche.
    El filósofo que se quedó lustrador.
El pintor genial entre los chivos. No sólo
    no saber leer y escribir:
              tampoco pensar, querer, soñar.

3 / Cardenal / **Zero Hour**

Later the U.S. sent more arms to Somoza;
for a full half day the arms rolled past;
truck after truck loaded with cases of arms;
all of them labelled U.S.A., MADE IN U.S.A.,
arms to take more prisoners, to hunt down books,
to rob Juan Potosme of his five pesos.
I saw these arms going down Avenida Roosevelt.
And the people silent in the streets saw them go by:
the skinny man, the shoeless man, the one with a bicycle,
the Black man, the big-nosed man, the one dressed in yellow,
the tall, the blond, the bald, the man with a moustache,
the flat-faced, the scrawny, curly-headed, straight-haired men,
and every one of them with the face
    of a dead ex-lieutenant.

4 / Cardenal / **National Song**

. . .And Sandino used to say to the *campesinos:*
"Someday we will triumph and if I don't get to see it
the little ants will come and bring me the news under the ground."

5 / Cardenal / **Zero Hour**

Slave to the foreigners
                and tyrant to his own people
imposed by intervention
                and kept there by nonintervention:
SOMOZA FOREVER.

6 / Cardenal / **National Song**

    The struggle continues. . .
there are so many Rubén Daríos in the mountains
swinging machetes, living in shacks in perpetual night.
    The philosopher who remained a shoeshine boy...
the marvelous painter among the goats. Not only
    doesn't he know how to read and write:
                he doesn't know how to think, wish, dream.

7 / Cardenal / La hora cero

El espía que sale de día
el agente que sale de noche
y el arresto de noche:
Los que están presos por hablar en un bus
o por gritar una Viva
o por un chiste.
"Acusado de hablar mal del Sr. Presidente. . ."
Y los juzgados por un juez con cara de sapo
o en Consejos de Guerra por guardias con cara de perro;
a los que han hecho beber orines y comer mierda
(cuando tengáis Constitución recordadlos)
los de la bayoneta en la boca y la aguja en el ojo,
las pilas electrizadas y el foco en los ojos,
  — "Es un hijueputa, Mr. Welles, pero es de nosotros."
Y en Guatemala, en Costa Rica, en México,
los exiliados de noche se despiertan gritando,
soñando que les están aplicando otra vez la maquinita.

8 / Cardenal / Canto nacional

          Vengan
vamos a arrancar los cercos de alambre compañeros.
Ruptura con el pasado. ¡Es que no era nuestro este pasado!
      . . .
Como me dijo la muchacha cubana: "La revolución es sobre todo
una cuestión de amor."
      Quisiera ya ver cartelones en la carretera como
                Uno no vale por lo que quita
                sino por lo que da a los demás.
      . . .

                          . . ."¡Que se levanten todos!"
Hay tanto maíz que sembrar tanto niño que instruir tanto
      enfermo que curar tanto amor
que realizar tanto canto.   Yo canto
un país que va a nacer. . .
      . . .
Los tanques convertidos en tractores
las zarandas de la policía en buses escolares
      y la máquina será el mejor amigo del hombre
General de Los-hombres-libres
      te lo contarán las hormiguitas de la tierra!

7 / Cardenal / **Zero Hour**

The spy who goes out by day
the agent who goes by night
and the arrests at night:
those jailed for talking on a bus
or for shouting a *Viva*
or for a joke.
"Accused of speaking ill of Mr. President. . ."
And those sentenced by a judge with a face like a toad
or in the War Councils by cops with faces like dogs
those made to drink piss or eat shit
(when you have a Constitution remember them)
those with bayonets in their mouths and needles in their eyes,
electrocuted in water-troughs with spotlights in their eyes.
—"He's a sonofabitch, Mr. Welles, but he's ours."
And in Guatemala, in Costa Rica, in Mexico,
the exiles wake up in the night and cry out,
dreaming they're in the torture machine once again.

8 / Cardenal / **National Song**

       Come,
let's tear down the wire fences, comrades,
break with the past, a past that was never ours!
   . . .
As the Cuban girl put it: "The Revolution is, above all,
a matter of love."
    How I long to see huge highway placards that say
          One's worth depends not on what one takes
          but on what one gives. . .
   . . .
                . . ."Everyone arise!"
There is so much corn to be sown so many children to teach so many
    sick to be cured so much love
to be had so much singing.   I am singing
a country yet to be born.
   . . .
The tanks turned into tractors
the paddy wagons into school buses
    and the machine will be man's best friend.
General-of-free-men
    the little ants of the earth will bring you the news!

9 / Cardenal / **La hora cero**

Las sombras de las zopiloteras de Wiwilí;
la sombra de Estrada; la sombra de Umanzor;
la sombra de Sócrates Sandino;
y la gran sombra, la del gran crimen,
la sombra de Augusto César Sandino;
Todas las noches en Managua la Casa Presidencial
se llena de sombras.

Pero el héroe nace cuando muere
y la hierba verde renace de los carbones.

10 / Neruda / **Salud, capitán del continente**

Tambores que redoblan
voces que se inflaman,
puños que se yerguen:
Sandino, Sandino, Sandino.

11 / Nicolás Guillén / **Coplas americanas**

Ah, pueblo de todas partes,
ah, pueblo, contigo iré;
pie con pie, que pie con mano,
iremos que pie con pie.

¡Que muera el generalote
sable, mandón!
¡Que viva la primavera
y viva mi corazón!

Ay, mi general Sandino,
vuelve a partir
camino de las Segovias,
que yo te voy a seguir.

9 / Cardenal / **Zero Hour**

The ghost with bones picked by Wiwilí vultures;
Estrada's ghost; Umanzor's ghost;
the ghost of Sócrates Sandino;
and the great ghost, the ghost of the great crime,
the ghost of Augusto César Sandino;
Every night in Managua the Presidential Palace
fills with ghosts.

But the hero is born when he dies
and green grass springs from the ashes.

10 / Neruda / **Hail, Captain of the Continent**

The drums roll
cries of rage,
fists raised on high:
Sandino, Sandino, Sandino.

11 / Nicolás Guillén / **American Rhymes**

Oh, people from every land,
my people, I'll march with you;
step by step, and hand in hand,
we'll go forward side by side.

Death to General Fat-belly
rapacious, sword-toting boss!
Hurrah for spring and long life
to the springtime in my heart!

Oh, my General Sandino,
come back to start again
on the road to the Segovias,
for I want to follow you.

Neruda / LA UNITED FRUIT CO.

Cuando sonó la trompeta, estuvo
todo preparado en la tierra,
y Jehová repartió el mundo
a Coca-Cola Inc., Anaconda,
Ford Motors, y otras entidades:
la Compañía Frutera Inc.
se reservó lo más jugoso,
la costa central de mi tierra,
la dulce cintura de América.
Bautizó de nuevo sus tierras
como "Repúblicas Bananas,"
y sobre los muertos dormidos,
sobre los héroes inquietos
que conquistaron la grandeza,
la libertad y las banderas,
estableció la ópera bufa:
enajenó los albedríos,
regaló coronas de César,
desenvainó la envidia, atrajo
la dictadura de las moscas,
moscas Trujillos, moscas Tachos,
moscas Carías, moscas Martínez,
moscas Ubico, moscas húmedas
de sangre humilde y mermelada,
moscas borrachas que zumban
sobre las tumbas populares,
moscas de circo, sabias moscas
entendidas en tiranía.

Part 2

Neruda / THE UNITED FRUIT CO.

When the trumpets had sounded and all
was in readiness on the face of the earth,
Jehovah divided his universe:
Coca-Cola Inc., Anaconda,
Ford Motors and similar concerns:
the United Fruit Company Incorporated
reserved for itself the most succulent
morsel of all, the midsection
and coasts of my country,
the sweet waist of America.
They rechristened their lands
the "Banana Republics,"
and over the sleeping dead,
the uneasy repose of the heroes
who'd won greatness,
liberty and flags,
the comic opera began:
they mortgaged off freedom,
passed out tin Caesar crowns,
unleashed envy and lured in
the Dictatorship of the Flies:
Trujillo flies, and Tacho flies,
flies called Carías, Martínez,
Ubico, glutted flies sticky and dank
from their banquet of humble blood,
drunken flies buzzing
around people's graves,
circus flies, wise flies,
well-versed in tyranny.

The Tyranny (1936-1956)

The second part surveys the years of the rule of Anastasio Somoza, Sr. from the time he takes power in 1936, until his death in 1956. It depicts the division of the country's wealth among U.S. corporations, the entrenchment of the monopolies and imperialist domination which keeps the dictator in power and impedes all opposition. The people pay the price of exploitation. The most representative struggle of the final decade of Anastasio I is Báez Bone's conspiracy. Two years later, in 1956, and twenty-three years after Sandino's assassination, Anastasio Somoza, Sr. is brought to justice by Rigoberto López Pérez. At this time, the beginnings of organized opposition become visible.

The first section describes the atmosphere of the dictatorship's early years. Even private life is in the government's hands. Street fights, love poems, birthday celebrations, public monuments, everything is subject to the impact of the State. The political situation penetrates the innermost recesses of daily existence and asphyxiates the people's lives. This is the meaning of the *pax americana*. The Nicaraguans cry out for the Yankees to go home, but it is the Nicaraguans themselves who are forced to flee the country.

The second section presents Nicaraguan exile. The first period of resistance has begun. Its protagonist is anonymous; we know neither his name nor his face. Those who do not leave the country are buried dead or alive by the National Guard. This force of repression, an army of occupation, incarnates the implacable forces of destruction. From their exile, the Nicaraguans remember their homeland: "a shitty country" over which a "shit curtain" has fallen. But they also recall happier things: food, popular celebrations, the countryside, "the scent and the heat of Nicaragua."

The third section narrates the return. Ten or more years of exile mean that the returnees virtually do not know their own country and must become reacquainted with it. They must get in touch with the country once again, with its geography, with the way its wealth is systematically wasted, with the possibility of a more just distribution of the national product. They must learn as well to confront the corruption which has taken hold of every aspect of national life; they must learn to overcome the pessimism and cynicism which are reflected in the belief that *somocismo* is eternal; and they must learn to recognize those calm and austere faces that have not been deformed by the regime. And this is not easy. But the human face confronting the tyrant's is real and presents a challenge to the regime. In the face of this challenge, repression becomes even more severe. It is no longer a question of purely psychological warfare, of inspiring fear and circulating false rumors, but rather of barbed wire, jailings, mutilation and death. Báez Bone and his comrades are killed.

The fourth section tells of a metamorphosis: from death comes life. The fallen heroes are the seed which fecundates the land and which eventually will germinate. The people begin to organize. Five men meet to plan the tyrant's execution. The eldest of the five is Edwin Castro, Sr., followed by Rigoberto López Pérez, Edwin Castro, Jr., Ausberto Narváez and Cornelio Silva Argüello. The ruthless dictator meets his end at the hands of Rigoberto and his comrades. The tyrant falls, but so does the hero, and immediately after him, his comrades are taken. In this transaction of death for death, Sandino's assassination has been vindicated, and Sandino's people begin to acquire active consciousness. Rigoberto's act of justice is one of the first successful moments of resistance. The U.S. State Department deplores the death of a friend and collaborator: such a great loss for the Western world! Now the imperialists must rethink their relations with Nicaragua. A new period has begun, and the Yankees decide to back the dynasty in the person of Luis, Somoza's eldest son.

Los primeros años

1 / Ernesto Gutiérrez / **Mi país es tan pequeño**

Mi país es tan pequeño

que 2.000 guardias sostienen el Gobierno.

Mi país es tan pequeño
que la vida privada
tiene que ser a favor
o en contra del Gobierno.

Mi país es tan pequeño
que el Sr. Presidente
arregla personalmente
hasta los pleitos callejeros.

Mi país es tan pequeño
que con los rifles de la guardia
cualquier imbécil lo gobierna.

2 / Cardenal / **Uno se despierta con cañonazos**

Uno se despierta con cañonazos
en la mañana llena de aviones.
Pareciera que fuera revolución:
pero es el cumpleaños del tirano.

Section 1
The Early Years

1 / Ernesto Gutiérrez / **My Country is so Tiny**

My country is so tiny

that just 2,000 guardsmen keep the Government in power.

My country is so tiny
that private life
has to be for
or against the government.

My country is so tiny
that the President
himself even settles
street fights personally.

My country is so tiny
that with the rifles of the guard
any imbecile can govern it.

2 / Cardenal / **You Wake Up to Cannon Fire**

You wake up to cannon fire
on a morning filled with airplanes.
You'd think it was the revolution:
but it's only the tyrant's birthday.

3 / Cardenal /
Somoza desveliza la estatua de Somoza en el Estadio Somoza

No es que yo crea que el pueblo me erigió esta estatua
porque yo sé mejor que vosotros que la ordené yo mismo.
Ni tampoco que pretenda pasar con ella a la posteridad
porque yo sé que el pueblo la derribará un día.
Ni que haya querido erigirme a mí mismo en vida
el monumento que muerto no me erigiréis vosotros:
sino que erigí esta estatua porque sé que la odiáis.

4 / Cardenal / **Epigrama XXXII**

De pronto suena en la noche una sirena
de alarma, larga, larga,
el aullido lúgubre de la sirena
de incendio o de la ambulancia blanca de la muerte,
como el grito de la cegua en la noche,
que se acerca y se acerca sobre las calles
y las casas y sube, sube, y baja
y crece, crece, baja y se aleja
creciendo y bajando. No es incendio ni muerte:
                                    Es Somoza que pasa.

5 / E. Gutiérrez / **La mosquitia**

La paz tipo "made in USA"
los barcos de Eisenhower
(dueños del Caribe
            de Panamá
            de las Islas Vírgenes
            de Puerto Rico. . .)
guardando nuestra Patria
impidiendo las revoluciones
dejando en mueca la soberanía
        libresca la autodeterminación.

**3 / Cardenal /
Somoza Unveils the Statue of Somoza in Somoza Stadium**

Don't think I believe that the people raised this statue to me,
because I know better than you that I commissioned it myself.
Or that I hope thereby to achieve immortality:
I know the people will tear it down someday.
Or that I wished to give myself in life
the monument you won't raise to me when I'm dead:
No, I erected this statue because I know you hate it.

4 / Cardenal / Epigram XXXII

Suddenly a siren signals alarm
long drawn out in the night
the lugubrious howl of the fire alarm
or the death white ambulance shriek
like the *cegua's* scream in the night
closing in, closing in on the streets
and the houses and louder, louder, and softer
and builds, builds, fades and retreats
rising and falling. It's not fire or death:
                    It's Somoza passing by.

5 / E. Gutiérrez / The Mosquitia

"Made in USA" peace,
Eisenhower's ships
(owners of the Carribean
            of Panama
            the Virgin Islands
            Puerto Rico. . .)
keeping watch over our country,
blocking revolutions,
turning our sovereignty into
            words on a printed page.

6 / Cardenal / Epigrama

¿No has leído, amor mío, en *Novedades:*
CENTINELA DE LA PAZ, GENIO DEL TRABAJO
PALADÍN DE LA DEMOCRACIA EN AMÉRICA
DEFENSOR DEL CATOLICISMO EN AMÉRICA
EL PROTECTOR DEL PUEBLO
                    EL BENEFACTOR. . .?
Le saquean al pueblo su lenguaje.
Y falsifican las palabras del pueblo.
(Exáctamente como el dinero del pueblo.)
Por eso los poetas pulimos tanto un poema.
Y por eso son importantes mis poemas de amor.

7 / Cardenal / Epigrama

Tal vez nos casemos este año,
amor mío, y tengamos una casita.
Y tal vez se publique mi libro,
o nos vayamos los dos al extranjero.
Tal vez caiga Somoza, amor mío.

8 / Fernando Silva / Epigrama

Un Capitán G.N. que tiene su cuartel en una de estas
ciudades
me mandó un Telegrama a mí
diciéndome que ni les entendía, ni le gustaban a él
los versos que yo escribo en *La Prensa.*
Yo creo que hasta el momento
ningún Poeta ha recibido mejor elogio.

6 / Cardenal / **Epigram**

Haven't you read in *Novedades,* my love:
WATCHMAN OF PEACE, GENIUS OF LABOR
PALADIN OF DEMOCRACY IN AMERICA
DEFENDER OF CATHOLICISM IN AMERICA
THE PROTECTOR OF THE PEOPLE
                                  THE BENEFACTOR. . .?
They plunder the people's language
and falsify the people's words.
(Just like the people's money.)
That's why we poets polish our poems so much.
That's why my love poems are important.

7 / Cardenal / **Epigram**

Perhaps we'll marry this year,
my love, and live in a little cottage.
And perhaps they'll publish my book,
and we'll go, the two of us, abroad.
Perhaps Somoza will fall, my love.

8 / Fernando Silva / **Epigram**

A National Guard captain stationed in one of our
cities
sent me a telegram
saying that he didn't get and didn't like
the poems I write in *La Prensa.*
I think that up till now
no poet's received greater praise.

9 / Pasos / Desocupación pronta, y si es necesario violenta

Yankees, váyanse,
váyanse, váyanse, yankees.
Váyanse, váyanse, váyanse,
váyanse, váyanse, yankees.
Ésta es tierra con perfume sólo para nosotros.
Crecen mangos, jocotes, guayabas y chocomicos
y un montón más de frutas de monte que se cultivan solas en el
Mombacho.
· · ·
Esta tierra es nuestra con toda su hermosa floración de costumbres
Y su lenguaje, español que dice: "Gringo, macho, andá vete,"
· · ·
Váyanse, váyanse, váyanse
¡VAYANSE!
En este ambiente está el alma de un pueblo
cuyo fondo de belleza no se os puede tirar con un ticket como
objeto de turismo.

10 / Cardenal / Epitafio para Joaquín Pasos

Aquí pasaba a pie por estas calles, sin empleo ni puesto,
y sin un peso.
Sólo poetas, putas y picados conocieron sus versos.
Nunca estuvo en el extranjero.
Estuvo preso.
Ahora está muerto.
No tiene ningún monumento.
                          Pero
recordadle cuando tengáis puentes de concreto,
grandes turbinas, tractores, plateados graneros,
buenos gobiernos.
Porque él purificó en sus poemas el lenguaje de su pueblo
en el que un día se escribirán los tratados de comercio,
la Constitución, las cartas de amor, y los decretos.

86

9 / Pasos / **Kick Them Out With Violence, If Need Be**

Yankees, get out,
out, out, Yankees.
Get out, get out, get out,
out, out, Yankees.
This perfumed land is ours.
Mangos, *chocomicos,* guavas and plums,
and many more mountain fruits that grow wild in Mombacho.
        . . .
This land is ours with all its lovely flowering of customs
and its language, a Spanish which says: "Gringo, man, take a walk."
        . . .
Out, out, out,
GET OUT!
The air stirs with a people's spirit
whose beauty you can't toss out
        like some tawdry tourist souvenir.

10 / Cardenal / **Epitaph for Joaquín Pasos**

He walked these streets, out of a job,
didn't have a dime.
Only poets, whores and bums knew his verse.
He never went abroad.
He did time.
Now he's dead.
There's no monument to him,
                but
remember him when you have concrete bridges,
great turbines, tractors, gleaming silos,
good governments.
Because he purified, in his poems, the language of the people
in which trade agreements, the Constitution, love letters
and decrees will one day be written.

Sección 2
El exilio: Ida y vuelta

1 / Anónimo / La cortina del país natal

Mis amigos demócratas,
comunistas,socialcristianos,
elogian o denigran

La Cortina de Hierro
La Cortina de Bambú
La Cortina de Dólares
La Cortina de Sangre
La Cortina de Caña

Son unos excelentes cortineros.
Pero nadie se refiere
a la Cortina de Mierda
de Mi Nicaragua Natal.

2 / Neruda / Las satrapías

Trujillo, Somoza, Carías,
hasta hoy, hasta este amargo
mes de septiembre
del año 1948,
con Moríñigo (o Natalicio)
en Paraguay, hienas voraces
de nuestra historia, roedores
de las banderas conquistadas
con tanta sangre y tanto fuego,
encharcados en sus haciendas,
depredadores infernales,
sátrapas mil veces vendidos
y vendedores, azuzados
por los lobos de Nueva York.

Section 2
Exile: Departure and Return

1 / Anonymous / The Curtain of the Native Land

My democratic, communist,
christian-socialist friends
eulogize or denigrate

The Iron Curtain
The Bamboo Curtain
The Dollar Curtain
The Curtain of Blood
The Curtain of Cane

They are excellent curtain makers.
But no one ever mentions
the Curtain of Shit
of My Native Nicaragua.

2 / Neruda / The Satraps

Trujillo, Somoza, Carías,
until today, until this bitter
month of September
of the year of 1948
with Moríñigo (or Natalicio)
in Paraguay, hyenas
devouring our history,
gnawing at flags
conquered with so much blood
and so much fire,
wallowing in their haciendas,
infernal predators,
satraps sold out a thousand times over
and salesmen, driven on
by the wolves of New York.

3 / Cardenal / **Epigrama**

La Guardia Nacional anda buscando a un hombre.
Un hombre espera esta noche llegar a la frontera.
El nombre de ese hombre no se sabe.
Hay muchos hombres más enterrados en una zanja.
El número y el nombre de esos hombres no se sabe.
Ni se sabe el lugar ni el número de las zanjas.
La Guardia Nacional anda buscando a un hombre.
Un hombre espera esta noche salir de Nicaragua.

4 / P. A. Cuadra / **Escrita en una piedra del camino cuando la primera erupción**

Abandonaremos nuestra patria y nuestra parentela
porque ha dominado nuestra tierra un dios estéril.

Nuestro pueblo miró al gigante sin mente,
oyó el bramido de la fuerza sin rostro.

¡No viviremos bajo el dominio de la ciega potencia!
¡Quebraremos nuestras piedras de moler
                nuestras tinajas
                nuestros comales
para aligerar el paso de los exiliados!

5 / E. Gutiérrez / **El exiliado**

Un día gané el umbral de la Embajada
¡jodido! mejor me hubieran agarrado
                (y si me torturan
                y si me matan?)

Al otro día en el vuelo 501 salía de mi patria

                (talvez otra suerte alumbre
                talvez otros pulsos latan)

3 / Cardenal / **Epigram**

The National Guard is searching for a man.
A man hopes to reach the border by nightfall.
The name of this man is unknown.
Many more men are buried in a ditch.
The number and name of these men are not known.
Nor are the places and number of the ditches.
The National Guard is searching for a man.
A man hopes to leave Nicaragua tonight.

4 / P. A. Cuadra / **Written on a Stone in the Road at the Time of the First Eruption**

We'll abandon our country, our kin,
for a sterile god rules the land.

Our people looked at the mindless giant,
heard the bellow of a faceless force.

We'll not live under the thumb of a blind power,
We'll break our grinding stones
        our jars
        our pans
to lighten the step of the exiles.

5 / E. Gutiérrez / **The Exile**

One day I made it to the Embassy
shit! I wish they'd caught me
        (and what if they torture
        and what if they kill me?)

The next day on flight 501 I left my country

        (maybe it will go better for them
        maybe others will join the fight)

6 / Cardenal / **Canto nacional**

Cuántas veces hemos dicho los nicaragüenses en el extranjero
'somos un país-de-mierda,' en mesas de tragos, en pensiones
donde se juntan los exilados, pero
hemos recordado los nacatamales, la sopa de mondongo con
  su culantro y su chile congo, los cantos
de la "Purísima" y el perfume de los madroños en diciembre
    el lago azul/azul y sobre él el
      vuelo de una garza como una vela blanca
    o la lanchita de vela como una garza
y uno ha pensado en
el olor de mayo, a patio llovido a tejas mojadas
    el calor y olor de Nicaragua.

7 / E. Gutiérrez / **El exiliado**

Y me pasé 10 años soñando con mi casa

y se pidieron garantías
y me dieron el visado
y me prometí no meterme en nada.

Luego me encontré solo en medio de las calles

y me pregunté desconcertado:
Pero, ¿es ésta la Patria?
       ¿es esto lo soñado?
Y tanta miseria y tanta ignominia
¿podré quedarme sin meterme en nada?

6 / Cardenal / **National Song**

How many times have we Nicaraguans said abroad
"we're a shitty country" around a drinking table, in boarding houses
where the exiled gather, but
we remembered the Nicaraguan tamales, tripe soup with
　its coriander and its *chile congo,* the singing
on Immaculate Conception and the perfumed scent
　of the arbutus in December
　　the blue blue lake and above
　　　a heron's flight like a white sail
　　or the little sailboat like a heron
and one thinks of
the smell of May, a rain-soaked yard and wet clay tiles
　　the heat and smell of Nicaragua.

7 / E. Gutiérrez / **The Exile**

And I spent 10 years dreaming of home

and they demanded guarantees
and they gave me the visa
and I promised to stay out of trouble.

Then I was alone in the streets

and I wondered confused:
Can this be my home?
　　　Is this what I dreamed?
And such misery and such shame
How can I stay out of trouble?

Sección 3
Los últimos años de Anastasio I

1 / E. Gutiérrez / **Oh Patria, mi Patria**

. . .regresé a tí, lleno de ilusiones
— amor, madre mía —
a sumergirme entre tus aguas dulces
a embriagarme en el perfume de tus campos
a germinar bajo tu cielo azul

Y encontré una relación melódica
entre la forma y el color de tu geografía:
No hay altas montañas que hiendan
y recorten el elevado cielo
sino que azul cobija
el tierno verde de tus suaves colinas
No hay anchurosos ríos surcados de vapores
sino pequeñas cintas de plata
donde tus hijas lavan la ropa de sus hijos
No hay extensos valles poblados de trigo
donde la vista se pierda en rubias lejanías
sino la reducida alegría de la milpa
el café que enrojece bajo el sol de noviembre
la mejor caña cortada para U.S.A.
y la nieve del algodón que va desapareciendo
sólo tus lagos desbordan la imaginación
Y allí donde flota una sonrisa
de fértil campo y encendido cielo
el campesino repta y reptan así sus hijos
bajo la casa construida con desechos
Es lástima, ¡ay!
— amor, madre mía —
que sólo dos jóvenes seudopríncipes
se beneficien de todo.

Section 3
The Last Years of Anastasio I

1 / E. Gutiérrez / **Oh Country, My Country**

. . .I returned to you, full of illusions
– my beloved mother –
to dive into your sweet waters
to drink in the perfume of your fields
to flower beneath your blue sky

And I found a melodic relation
between the form and color of your geography:
without high mountains that trace
and tear the elevated sky,
but a blue that covers
the tender green of your soft hills
without broad rivers plowed by steamships
but tiny silver strips
where your daughters wash their children's clothes
without vast valleys of wheat
farther than eyes can see into the blonde distance
but the reduced joy of the cornfield
coffee that reddens under the November sun
the best sugar cane cut for the U.S.A.
and the cotton snow that disappears
your lakes alone overflow imagination
and there where a smile floats
from fertile fields and blazing skies
peasants and their children crawl
It's a great shame
– my beloved mother –
that only two young pseudoprinces
should profit from it all.

Duérmete, futuro ciudadano de Nicaragua.
Arrurrú, mi niño, arrurrú.

Una luna de cobre arroja sobre LA LOMA sus mancillados rayos.
Duérmete ahora, cuando todavía no tienes que esperar
de esa colina la firma todo poderosa: el salvoconducto,
la exención del impuesto, el indulto para el sobrino rebelde,
el rincón en la Nómina, el galardón al mérito... ¡Todo!

Arrurrú, mi niño, arrurrú.

Una nueva agita el hogar. Despierta el alborozo
entre la parentela, tu padre obtuvo el nombramiento:
Portero, Abogado del Banco, Guardaespaldas, Embajador...
Él supo cómo. Probó no ser ningún novicio el viejo.
Pero tú, a dormir. Mientras aún yace en el limbo
tu conciencia y no puedes sentir vergüenza de tu padre.

Arrurrú, mi niño, arrurrú.

Ya crecerás. Y atraparás al vuelo el sentido de la vida
en esta linda Tierra de Darío. Aprenderás a cerrar
el puño, dejando el pulgar entre el dedo-del-corazón
y el índice: la insignia heráldica de tu Patria.
No es visible en el triángulo del escudo
pero está allí, bajo el gorro frigio;
como tú habrás de llevarla, oculta en el bolsillo. Mientras
con la otra mano estrecharás la mano que se te tienda
confiada, rubricarás los decretos y la carta de recomendación
para la viuda, la moverás persuasiva en los discursos.

Pero duérmete, apresúrate a hacerlo ahora
que aún no has empezado a ser deshonesto.

Antes de que hayas empañado la Mitra, alzándola
entre tus temblorosos dedos pastorales en defensa de la Opresión;
antes de que hayas extendido la orden de captura contra el esposo
de tu hermana, y culateado en el calabozo al camarada
de los días de colegio; antes de que escribas
tu pobre nombre en la lista de las adhesiones;

Duerme, porque aún estás incontaminado
duerme, mientras aún eres inofensivo

▶

Sleep, future citizen of Nicaragua.
Hushabye, my child, hushabye.

A copper moon sheds its blemished beam over *LA LOMA*.
Sleep now, while you still don't have to wait
for the all-powerful signature from the palace: the safeconduct,
the tax exemption, the pardon for your rebel nephew,
the choice spot in the payroll, the merit award. . . Everything!

Hushabye, my child, hushabye.

Fresh news stirs the household. Joy awakens
in the family, your father got the post:
Doorman, Bank Attorney, Bodyguard, Ambassador. . .
Your old man knew how to do it. He showed he was no novice.
But you, sleep now. While your conscience remains
in limbo and you can't feel ashamed of your father.

Hushabye, my child, hushabye.

Soon enough you'll grow up. And you'll catch
on the wing the way things go
in this lovely land of Darío. You'll learn to close
your fist, leaving the thumb between middle
and index fingers: the heraldic salute of your country.
It's not visible in the triangle of the shield
but it's there, under the Phrygian cap;
since you'll have to wear it, hidden in your pocket. Meanwhile
with your other hand you'll press the trusting hand
offered you, you'll sign and seal the decrees and the letter
of recommendation for the widow, you'll wax persuasive in
                                        your speeches.
But sleep, hurry to sleep now,
while you've still not begun to be dishonest.

Before you have sullied the Mitre, raising it
between your tremulous pastoral fingers in defense of Oppression;
before you have signed the order of capture against the husband
of your sister, before you've thrown your boyhood friend
into prison; before you add
your miserable name to the loyalty list;

Sleep, because you're still unpolluted   ►

duerme, ahora que aún no te has vendido,
futuro Arzobispo, Teniente, empleadillo
. . . .
Perdóname, esta noche no te he contado ningún cuento.
Vine a fastidiarte con la verdad.
¡Qué sueño tienes! Se te cierran los párpados. . .
Duerme, futuro ciudadano de Nicaragua.
Arrurrú, mi niño, arrurrú.

3 / P. A. Cuadra / **Patria de tercera**

Viajando en tercera he visto
un rostro.
No todos los hombres de mi pueblo
ávidos, claudican.
He visto un rostro.
Ni todos doblan su papel en barquichuelos
para charco. Viajando he visto
el rostro de un huertero.
Ni todos ofrecen su faz al látigo del "no"
ni piden.
La dignidad he visto.
Porque no sólo fabricamos huérfanos,
o bien, inadvertidos,
criamos cuervos.
He visto un rostro austero. Serenidad
o sol sobre su frente
como un título (ardiente y singular).
Nosotros ¡ah! rebeldes
al hormiguero
si algún día damos
la cara al mundo:
con los rasgos usuales de la Patria
¡un rostro enseñaremos!

sleep, while you're still inoffensive
sleep, now, since you've still not sold out,
future Archbishop, Lieutenant, underling employee

.   .   .   .

Forgive me, tonight I haven't told you any tale.
I came to disturb you with the truth.
How tired you are! Your eyelids are closing. . .

Sleep, future citizen of Nicaragua.
Hushabye, my child, hushabye.

3 / P. A. Cuadra / Third Class Country

Traveling third class I have seen
a face.
Not everyone in my country
surrenders to greed.
I have seen a face.
Not everyone makes paper boats
for the pond. Traveling I have seen
the face of a farmer.
Not everyone offers himself to the whip's "no"
or begs.
I have seen dignity.
Because we do not only make orphans
or, inadvertently,
spawn ravens.
I have seen an austere face. Integrity
or sun on its brow
like a title of nobility (ardent and unique).
We, imprisoned
rebels,
if some day we show
our face to the world:
with the true features of our country
we shall truly show a face!

4 / P. A. Cuadra / **Urna con perfíl político**

El Caudillo es silencioso.
   — (dibujo su rostro silencioso) —

El Caudillo es poderoso
   — (dibujo su mano fuerte) —

El Caudillo es el jefe de los hombres armados
   — (dibujo las calaveras de los hombres muertos) —

5 / Ernesto Mejía Sánchez / **El César y la carne**

El César puso un impuesto más
para felicidad de su pueblo.
Los carniceros suben la carne
para pagarlo; los ganaderos
suben el ganado para pagarlo;
sólo el pueblo tiene que arrodillarse
para pagarlo, porque toda la carne
y el ganado, los ganaderos y los carniceros
son del César, menos el pueblo.

6 / M. Cuadra / **Poema a hachazos**

Los déspotas nos atan los pies y las manos
y traban nuestros dientes con alambre
porque los impotentes sienten miedo de la palabra.
Con nosotros barren el suelo de las ciudades,
entaponan las letrinas y nos sumergen en las cloacas.
Pero éste será el año de los grandes milagros.

Porque la libertad no está en la letra de imprenta,
ni nace de diez bandidos que discuten en una mesa,
ni viene de los carneros que mugen en el Parlamento.
Libertad, esa palabra se aferra muy dura a nuestras conciencias
He aquí que un pobre roe su pan seco,
he aquí que una niña no sacia su escondido deseo,
he aquí que muere de cólera un obrero,
un sacerdote, un reportero.

▶

4 / P. A. Cuadra / Urn with a Political Profile

The Chief is silent
— (I draw his silent face) —

The Chief is powerful
— (I draw his strong hand) —

The Chief is the head of armed men
— (I draw the skulls of dead men) —

5 / Ernesto Mejía Sánchez / Caesar and the Flesh

Caesar levied one more tax
for the happiness of his people.
The butchers raise the price of meat
to pay him; the cattlemen raise
the price of cattle to pay him;
only the people have to kneel down
to pay him, because all of the meat
and the cattle, the cattlemen and
the butchers belong to Caesar, everything
but the people.

6 / M. Cuadra / Poem in Pieces

The despots bind our hands and feet
and brace our teeth with wire
because impotent men fear the word.
They sweep the city streets with us,
They stuff the toilets and sink us in cesspools.
But this will be the year of great miracles.

Because freedom is not in the printed word,
nor is it born of thieves' table-talk,
Nor from the bleating of parliamentary sheep.
Freedom — that word grips our conscience like a vise.
Look at them: a poor man who gnaws his dry bread,
a young girl who cannot satisfy her hidden desire,
a worker who dies of rage,
a priest, a reporter.   ►

101

Pero arriba danza ebrio el dinero
¡y he ahí la otra cara de la moneda!
"Nosotros llegamos siempre tarde. Estamos tarde. Morimos tarde."
Decid si no será esto cochino,
pero una gran alba se abre en nuestro camino.
porque Dios se prepara a bajar a media calle.

El pan que no comemos se pudre en lejanos armarios
y el vino hierve en las cráteras lejanas.
Un beso, un sólo beso de la mujer amada
buscadlo ahí donde la tierra se ha hecho pedazos.

Para alcanzar la dicha siempre nos hace falta una pulgada
y está la culpa en nuestra medrosa mirada,
en el barniz que engaña a nuestro tacto,
en los vergeles donde se embriaga el olfato.

La culpa es de nuestros puercos sentidos,
desde que nos hizo saber el señor Ministro
que dos más dos son igual a cinco;
por fin sabemos que dos más dos son cuatro.

Cuando bajen al pueblo estas simples verdades
el mundo ha de tornarse súbitamente claro
como un cuchillo volado por el aire
en pleno día, sobre los duros escenarios.

7 / Anónimo / **Mientras. . .**

Mientras gobierne a Nicaragua una terrible dinastía.
Mientras existan sicarios esperando
patriotas en las cárceles.
Mientras la justicia social sea
indefinidamente postergada.
Mientras la indiferencia y el
conformismo arraigue en las conciencias,
y la libertad sólo sea de palabra.
Mientras la inercia del pueblo
oscureza el porvenir.
Mientras la juventud no se levante. . .

But up there money does a drunken dance
and that's the other side of the coin!
"We always arrive late. We're late. We die late."
Tell me if this isn't filthy,
but a great dawn breaks on our road
because God makes ready to walk in our midst.

The bread we don't eat rots in far-off bins
and the wine sours in far-off vessels.
One kiss, just one kiss of a beloved woman —
seek there where the earth has been torn to pieces.

We are always an inch away from fulfillment
and the fault lies in our faint-hearted look,
in the glaze that fools our touch,
in the flower-garden which deranges our sense of smell.

Our swinish senses are to blame,
ever since Mr. Minister let us know
that two plus two make five;
we know at last that two plus two make four.

When these simple truths and the people are one,
the world will suddenly become clear
like a knife thrown through the air
in broad daylight standing out against the harsh backdrops.

7 / Anonymous / **As Long As. . .**

As long as a terrible dynasty rules Nicaragua.
As long as there are hired assassins awaiting
patriots in the prisons.
As long as social justice is
indefinitely put off.
As long as indifference and conformity
take   root in consciousness,
and freedom is only freedom of speech.
As long as the inertia of the people
darkens the future.
As long as the young do not rise up. . .

8 / Cardenal / **Epigrama XIX**

Se oyeron unos tiros anoche.
Se oyeron del lado del Cementerio.
Nadie sabe a quién mataron, o los mataron.
Nadie sabe nada.
Se oyeron unos tiros anoche.
Eso es todo.

9 / M. Cuadra / **La admonición: gritad en las esquinas**

Fraterno lustrador, deja tu pasta.
¡Poeta, oculta tu cepillo!
Es hora de pedrada y de chilillo,
de decir: ¡alto ahí! y de decir: ¡basta!

Que no haya división, que no haya casta
de rico y pobre entre la pobre gente.
Es la hora roja del iconoclasta:
Hora del llanto y del crujir de diente

Hora de huevos podridos y gengibres
y de mujeres con los brazos en jarras;
hora de pueblos libres
que al fin han soltado sus amarras.

10 / P. A. Cuadra / **Tomasito, el Cuque**

— ¿En qué lancha las llevaron?
　　　　¡Contesta, Tomás, contesta!
— ¿Desde cuál isla zarparon?
　　　　¡Jodido, Tomás, contesta!
— ¿A quiénes las entregaron?
　　　　¡Hijo de puta, Tomás!
— ¿Quiénes llevaron las armas?
　　　　¡Cabrón, contesta, Tomás!

Pero no habla Tomás.
¡Qué huevos de hombre. No habla!
　　　　Ya nunca hablará más
　　　　　　Tomás!

8 / Cardenal / Epigram XIX

Shots rang out last night.
Over by the Cemetery.
Nobody knows who they killed, or how many.
Nobody knows anything.
Shots rang out last night.
That's all.

9 / M. Cuadra / The Warning: Shout on the Corners

Brother shoe-shine boy, put aside your polish.
Poet, hide your pen!
It's the time for stone and whip,
to say: stop there! and to say: enough!

An end to divisions, to castes
of richer and poorer among the poor.
It's the red time of the iconoclast:
a time of weeping and gnashing of teeth.

A time of rotten eggs and ginger,
of women with arms akimbo;
the time of a free people
who have finally thrown off their bonds.

10 / P. A. Cuadra / Tomasito

— What boat did they take them in?
      Tell me, Tomás, tell me!
— What island did they sail from?
      Damn it, Tomás, tell me!
— Who'd they turn them over to?
      Son of a bitch, Tomás!
— Who took the weapons?
      Tomás, tell me, you bastard!

But Tomás doesn't talk.
What balls he has, he doesn't talk!
      Now Tomás will never talk.
            Never!

11 / P. A. Cuadra / **Interioridad de dos estrellas que arden**

Al que combatió por la Libertad
se le dió una estrella, vecina
a la luminosa madre muerta al alumbrar.

— ¿Fue grande tu dolor? — preguntó
el Guerrero.
　　　— No tanto como el gozo
de dar un nuevo hombre al mundo.
— ¿Y tu herida — dijo ella —
fue honda y torturante?
　　　— No tanto
como el gozo de dar al hombre un mundo nuevo.
— ¿Y conociste a tu hijo?
　　　　　　　　　— ¡Nunca!
— ¿Y conociste el fruto de tu lucha?
　　　　　　　　　　　　— Morí antes.
— ¿Duermes? — preguntó el Guerrero.
— Sueño — respondió la madre.

12 / Cardenal / **La hora cero**

En abril, en Nicaragua, los campos están secos.
Es el mes de las quemas de los campos,
del calor, y los potreros cubiertos de brasas,
y los cerros que son de color de carbón;
del viento caliente, y el aire que huele a quemado
　　. . .
En mayo llegan las primeras lluvias.
La hierba tierna renace de las cenizas.
Los lodosos tractores roturan la tierra.
Los caminos se llenan de mariposas y de charcos,
y las noches son frescas, y cargadas de insectos,
y llueve toda la noche. En mayo
florecen los malinches en las calles de Managua.
Pero abril en Nicaragua es el mes de la muerte.

En abril los mataron.
Yo estuve con ellos en la rebelión de abril
y aprendí a manejar una ametralladora Rising.　　　►

11 / P. A. Cuadra / The Secret of the Burning Stars

To him who fought for Liberty
Was given a star next
to the shining mother
dead in giving dawn to life.

–"Was it great, your suffering?" – asked
the Warrior.
    –"Not so great as the joy
of giving a new man to the world."
–"And your wound?" – she asked,
"Was it deep? Did it burn?"
    –"Not so much
as the joy of giving a new world to man."
–"And did you know your son?"
                    –"Never!"
–"And did you know the fruit of your battle?"
                         –"I died too soon."
–"Do you sleep?" – asked the Warrior.
The mother replied: "I dream."

12 / Cardenal / Zero Hour

In April Nicaraguan fields are dry.
It is the month when fires burn in the fields,
the hottest month, the pastures covered with hot cinders,
and the hills the color of coal;
when the winds are hot and the air smells of smoke
   . . .
In May the first rains begin to fall.
The young grass is reborn from the ashes.
Muddy tractors plow through fields.
Butterflies and puddles litter the paths,
the nights fresh and filled with insects,
and it rains all night. In May
the jacarandas bloom in Managua streets.
But April is the month of death in Nicaragua.

They murdered them in April.
I was with them in the April rebellion
and I learned how to handle a Rising machine gun.

►

Y Adolfo Báez Bone era mi amigo:
Lo persiguieron con aviones, con camiones,
con reflectores, con bombas lacrimógenas,
con radios, con perros, con guardias;
y yo recuerdo las nubes rojas sobre la Casa Presidencial
como algodones ensangrentados,
y la luna roja sobre la Casa Presidencial.
La radio clandestina decía que vivía.
El pueblo no creía que había muerto.
(Y no ha muerto.)
Porque a veces nace un hombre en una tierra
    que es esa tierra.
Y la tierra en que es enterrado ese hombre
    es ese hombre.
Y los hombres que después nacen en esa tierra
    son ese hombre.
Y Adolfo Báez Bone era ese hombre.
"Si a mí me pusieran a escoger mi destino
(me había dicho Báez Bone tres días antes)
entre morir asesinado como Sandino
o ser Presidente como el asesino de Sandino
yo escogería el destino de Sandino."
    Y él escogió su destino.
La gloria no es la que enseñan los textos de historia:
es una zopilatera en un campo y un gran hedor.

    Pero cuando muere un héroe
          no se muere:
    sino que ese héroe renace
          en una Nación.

13 / Cardenal / Epitafio para la tumba de Adolfo Báez Bone

Te mataron y no nos dijeron dónde enterraron tu cuerpo,
pero desde entonces todo el territorio nacional es tu sepulcro;
o más bien: en cada palmo del territorio nacional en que no está
                                                          tu cuerpo,
tú resucitaste.

¡Creyeron que te mataban con una orden de Fuego!
Creyeron que te enterraban
y lo que hacían era enterrar una semilla.

108

And Adolfo Báez Bone was my friend:
They hunted him down with airplanes, with armored cars,
with searchlights, with tear-gas bombs,
with radios, with dogs, with guardsmen;
and I remember the red clouds over the Presidential Palace
like bloody balls of cotton wool,
and the moon red over the Presidential Palace.
The underground radio said he was alive.
The people didn't believe he had been killed.
    (And he is not dead.)

For sometimes a man is born in a land
        who is that land.
And the earth where that man is buried
        is that man.
And the men who are later born in that land
        are that man.
And Adolfo Báez Bone was that man.
"If they forced me to choose between the fate
(Báez Bone had told me three days before)
of being murdered like Sandino
or becoming President like Sandino's murderer
I would choose Sandino's fate."
    And he chose his fate.
The history books don't teach about glory:
it's all a flock of vultures in a foul-smelling field.

    But when a hero dies
        he's not dead
    for the hero is reborn
        in a Nation.

13 / Cardenal / **Epitaph for the Tomb of Adolfo Báez Bone**

They killed you and didn't say where they buried your body,
but since then the entire country has been your tomb,
and in every inch of Nicaragua where your body isn't buried,
you were reborn.

They thought they'd killed you with their order to fire!
They thought they'd buried you
and all they did was to bury a seed.

109

Sección 4
La muerte de Anastasio I

---

1 / Rigoberto López Pérez / **Ansiedad**

La sangre germinal de Sandino
azota los tejados homicidas:
multiplicada, en torrentes
colmará los tejados vulnerables;
y en inminente, seguro apocalipsis
exterminará todos los homicidas,
y a todos los descendientes
de los homicidas.
El abrazo proditorio de Sandino
se anuncia grávido de bíblicas premoniciones:
como el crimen de Caín
y el beso de Judas.

Después reinará la paz. . .
y Nicaragua se poblará de olivos y de voces
que subirán al infinito en interminable
salmo de amor.

2 / Leonel Rugama / **Rampas y rampas y rampas. . .**

Rampas y rampas y rampas
y la línea férrea entre un polvasal.
Hacia el oeste el barrio va cambiando.
Hasta llegar a la iglesia del calvario
                              y a una cancha de volibol
donde el sábado 21 de septiembre de 1956
Rigoberto López Pérez
                              jugó hasta las seis de la tarde
y cuando se fue
                    limpiando la cara con un pañuelo
y las muchachas le hablaron
para que continuara jugando
                              él dijo:
"tengo que ir a hacer un volado"

Section 4
The Death of Anastasio I

1 / Rigoberto López Pérez / **Anxiety**

The seed of Sandino's blood
lashes the murderous rooftops
multiplied, in torrents
it will cover exposed rooftops
and in sure, inevitable apocalypse
will exterminate all the murderers,
and each and every one
of the murderers' seed.
Their treacherous embrace of Sandino
is pregnant with biblical premonitions:
like the crime of Cain
like the kiss of Judas.

And then peace will reign. . .
and Nicaragua will fill with olive branches and voices
that loft to the heavens
an everlasting psalm of love.

2 / Leonel Rugama / **Ramps and Ramps and Ramps. . .**

Ramps and ramps and ramps
and a railroad line lost in a dust storm.
Toward the west the neighborhood changes
Until reaching Calvary church
                    and a volleyball court
where on Saturday, the 21st of September, 1956
Rigoberto López Pérez
                    played until six in the evening
and when he left
                    wiping his face with a kerchief
and the young girls asked him
to keep on playing,
                    he said:
"I have to deliver a message."

111

3 / López Pérez / Carta-Testamento

San Salvador, septiembre 4 de 1956
Señora Soledad López
León, Nicaragua

Mi querida mamá:
                Aunque usted nunca lo ha sabido,
yo
  siempre
      he andado tomando parte
                 en todo
lo que se refiere
        a atacar
              el régimen funesto
              de nuestra patria
y en vista
      de que todos los esfuerzos
                 han sido inútiles
para tratar
      de lograr que
           Nicaragua
           vuelva a ser
           (o lo sea por primer vez)
una patria libre,
sin afrentas y sin manchas,
             he decidido,
                aunque
                    mis compañeros
no querían aceptarlo,
         el tratar de ser
             yo
               el que inicie
el principio del fin
de esa tiranía.

Si Dios quiere
       que perezca en mi intento,
no quiero
      que se culpe a nadie
            absolutamente,
pues todo ha sido
decisión mía.   ▶

3 / López Pérez / **Last Will and Testament**

San Salvador, September 4, 1956
Señora Soledad López
León, Nicaragua

My beloved mother:
                        Although you never knew it,
I
 have
      always taken part
                        in all
the attacks
            on
              the deadly regime
                              of our country
and since
          all our efforts
                        have been useless
in attempting
              to see that
                        Nicaragua
                         becomes once again
                         (or for the first time)
a free country
without insults and manipulations
                              I have decided,
                                        although
                                          my comrades
were not in agreement,
                        to try to be
                                  the one
                                      who initiates
the beginning of the end
of that tyranny.

If God wills
            that I perish in my purpose
I want
      absolutely
                no one to be blamed,
since it has all been
my decision.   ►

_____, que nos conoce muy bien a todos nosotros, ha quedado encargado, lo mismo que los demás paisanos residentes en ese país, de ayudarla en todo lo que usted necesite. Como antes le había contado, hace algún tiempo tomé una póliza de vida por C. 10,000.00 con doble indemnización, o sea C. 20,000.00.

_____ dará todas las vueltas para que ese dinero le sea entregado a usted, ya que está a su nombre. Hay una salvedad en esto: como usted sabe, yo siempre he vivido en casa de la familia Andrade que han sido muy buenas conmigo durante tanto tiempo, y quiero que de dicho dinero le sean entregados C. 1,000.00 a la señorita Dina Andrade para que termine sus estudios, ya que posiblemente los tenga que abandonar por falta de recursos. Con Miriam Andrade de Rivera, hermana de ella y comadre mía, puede usted entenderse, ya que usted deberá viajar a esta ciudad (San Salvador) en donde terminados los trámites legales, le entregarán el valor de dicha póliza. Como le dije anteriormente _____ y demás compañeros le darán todas las vueltas para el cobro de la mencionada póliza.

Espero
       que tomará
              todas estas cosas
                     con calma
y que debe pensar que lo que
               yo
                 he hecho
es un deber
que cualquier
nicaragüense
que de veras
quiera
a su patria
         debía
         haber llevado a cabo
         hace mucho tiempo.
Lo mío
no ha sido un sacrificio
           sino un deber
           que espero haber cumplido. ►

_____, who knows all of us very well, has been charged, like other friends still residing in this country, to help you in all that you need. As I had told you before, some time ago I took out a life insurance policy for 10,000 cordobas with double indemnization, or 20,000 cordobas.

_____ will cross over every hurdle so that you receive this money, since it's in your name. There's an exception to this. As you know, I have always lived in the house of the Andrades, who have been very good to me for so long, and I want Señorita Dina Andrade to receive 1,000 of this money so she can finish her studies, since she may have to abandon them for lack of funds. You may reach an understanding on this matter with her sister, my close friend, Miriam Andrade de Rivera, since you will have to travel to this city (San Salvador) where once the legal transactions are completed, they will hand over the value of the policy. As I said before _____ and the other comrades will work through every problem regarding payment of the aforementioned policy.

I hope
     that you will take
          all these things
               calmly
and that you will think of what
          I
          have done
as a duty
that any
Nicaraguan
who truly
loves
his country
     should
     have accomplished
     long ago.
Mine
has not been a sacrifice
        but a duty
        that I hope to have fulfilled.   ►

Si usted
      toma las cosas como
                 yo
                  lo deseo
                     le digo
                        que me sentiré feliz.
Así es que
      nada de tristeza,
            que el deber
            que se cumple
            con la patria
es la mayor satisfacción
que debe llevarse
un hombre de bien
          como
             yo
              he tratado de serlo.
Si toma
      las cosas
          con serenidad
              y con la idea absoluta de que
he cumplido
con mi más alto deber de
nicaragüense,
         le estaré
            muy agradecido.
Su hijo
      que siempre
          la quiso mucho,
               Rigoberto.

If you
     accept things as
          I
               want you to
                    I tell you
                    that you will make me happy.
Don't be sad
     I don't want sadness
               since fulfilling
               one's duty
               for one's country
is the greatest satisfaction
that a good man such
         as
        I
          have tried to be
               can possibly have.
If you take
     things
        with serenity
           and with the absolute certainty that
I have performed
my highest duty as
a Nicaraguan
     I will be
        very thankful.
Your son
     who always
        loved you very much,
             Rigoberto.

4 / Mejía Sánchez / La muerte de Somoza

La muerte de Somoza, como la del Foster,
dice Ike, es una gran pérdida ¡ay!
para el mundo libre. "Fue un gran amigo
de los Estados Unidos, en público
y en privado." Los Estados Unidos
tendrán que ampliar el cementerio
de Arlington. O adaptar el jardincillo
de la Casa Blanca para tumba de sus
íntimos amigos. Y a fé, que ya lo están
haciendo. Porque yo busqué en Nicaragua
el cadáver de Somoza, y nadie supo responder.

5 / Gordillo / Adivinanza

Dos muertos:
Uno a la vista de todos,
en el corazón de nadie;
otro a la vista de nadie,
en el corazón de todos.

6 / Mejía Sánchez / Los Somoza

Los Somozas, ¿son más fuertes que el odio de su pueblo?
No se apresure el cincel sobre la piedra o el mármol
ni el orfebre en tallar la medalla ni el poeta la elegía,
antes que mi palabra fracase en vuestros oídos
nuevos nombres se añadirán a la lista de héroes,
ángeles exterminadores como Sandino o Rigoberto, reclaman
ya su rostro a la dura materia. Que en el juicio final
de metralla o machete contra la cachorra bestia bicéfala,
mi mano no esté lejos; no lo está cuando escribe estas líneas
fervorosas, no lo estuvo el veintiuno al señalar el rumbo de las balas.

4 / Mejía Sánchez / The Death of Somoza

Somoza's death, like Foster's,
is a terrible loss, says Ike. Weep!
for the free world. "He was a great friend
of the United States, in public
and in private." The U.S. will have to
enlarge Arlington. Or fix up the
White House lawn as a tomb for their
bosom buddies. And I bet they're at it
already. Because I looked for Somoza's body
all over Nicaragua,
and nobody knew what to say.

5 / Gordillo / Riddle

Two corpses:
One for all to see
in no one's heart;
Another for none to see
in everyone's heart.

6 / Mejía Sánchez / The Somozas

Are the Somozas stronger that the hatred of their people?
Stay the sculptor's hand from stone or marble,
the goldsmith from his medals, the poet from his verse.
Before my word falls upon deaf ears,
new names will be added to the list of heroes;
they are coining the visage of exterminating angels
like Sandino or Rigoberto upon hard metal.
At the final judgment of shrapnel or machete against
the two-headed baby beast, my hand will not be distant;
it is not as I write these fervid lines, nor was it
on the twenty-first when it marked the bullets' way.

7 / Otto René Castillo / **Ay Patria**

Ay Patria
a los coroneles que orinan tus muros
tenemos que arrancarlos de raices,
colgarlos en un árbol de rocío agudo,
violenta de cóleras del pueblo.

8 / Neruda / **Salud, capitán del continente**

El labriego que pasa
de muerte en muerte,
buscando, en los cafetos,
la razón de la existencia;
el minero que arranca
a golpe de pulmón
la sortija para la dama gringa;
el pequeño que ensucia la cuartilla
en la escuela-choza
en la comarca Segoviana,
y la mujer de rosa
que lava su nezquisa
en la rosa de sus pies
todos dicen entre dientes,
Sandino, Sandino, Sandino.

7 / Otto René Castillo / **Ay Patria**

Oh, my country
the colonels who piss on your walls
we must yank them out at the roots,
hang them from a wind-torn tree
filled with the rage of the people.

8 / Neruda / **Hail, Captain of the Continent**

The peasant who goes
from death to death,
seeking his reason to be
in the coffee trees;
the miner who uproots
at the cost of his lungs
the ring for the Yankee lady;
the child who scribbles his lesson
in the school-hut
of the Segovias,
and the woman in pink
who washes her blouse
in the pink of her feet
all say under their breath,
Sandino, Sandino, Sandino.

Neruda / REVOLUCIONES

Fueron éstos
los
años
intermedios:
caía Trujillo con sus muelas de oro,
y en Nicaragua
un Somoza acribillado
a tiros
se desangró en su acequia pantanosa
para que sobre aquella rata muerta
subiese aún como un escalofrío
otro Somoza o rata
que no durará tanto.

Part 3

Neruda / REVOLUTIONS

These were
the
in between
years:
Trujillo fell with his gold teeth,
and in Nicaragua
a Somoza riddled like a sieve
bled in his swampy gutter
so that over that dead rat
could climb like a death chill
another Somoza rat
who would not last long.

The Struggle Continues (1956-1970)

The third part narrates the formative years of organized resistance to the government of Luis Somoza, who dies in 1967, and the first years in power of his younger brother, Anastasio II. These are years of increasing repression, "the in-between years," beginning with the torture and death of the men who brought Anastasio I to justice, and ending with the unbreakable determination of the people and their vanguard, the Sandinista Liberation Front, to put an end to so many years of ignominy. FREE HOMELAND OR DEATH is the slogan which expresses that will to make sacrifices for freedom. The death of Leonel Rugama, a Sandinista poet-revolutionary like so many others in this book, exemplifies the extermination tactics used by the dictatorship to break the people's will. His story provides a fitting image of how the 70s begin.

The first section portrays the fate of the small group of men who killed the dictator in full knowledge of the consequences which awaited them. Edwin Castro is the most representative example. In the midst of death, he speaks of life: "Tomorrow, my son, all will be different." His son's life, that of the new generation, will be unlike his own. His words are a premonition. The next generation, the one growing up between 1956 and 1979, is truly the generation of victory, the generation which will begin to experience liberty and life. But long before this happens, there is torture and more torture: the *Chiquita* cell, Velázquez and Narváez in the lion and panther cages where Luis and his brother Tachito sent those who opposed the tyranny. Castro is mangled and murdered by Tacho's own hand. Weary of the persistent pattern, the poets cry out to the dictator: "What have you done, Luis, with our country?" In the city, everything oozes blood and death, and more blood and more death. Life is in the mountains, in El Chaparral, in Pancasán, in Bocaycito, places where the organized popular struggle led by the Sandinistas is beginning.

The second section tells of the bloodiest figure of the entire clan, Somoza's youngest son, Tachito. The stronger the opposition, the worse the repression. Tachito's years are blood years. The National Guard imposes its own law. The list of martyrs is interminable: David Tejada Peralta, Ajax Delgado, and so many more – those unnamed, those who remain anonymous.

The third section brings us into the revolutionary process and explains what the dominant conception of revolution is. This conception encompasses every aspect of life: land, the Indian, food, books, freedom, changing reality. The idea of national reconstruction already surfaces in this early period in the vision of a transformed, democratized agriculture. We are no longer in the presence of the old, archaic agricultural structure, but rather we begin to foresee the development of the nation's wealth justly distributed. These are the formative years of the Cuban Revolution. Although it is not mentioned directly and only the representative figure of Che is presented, its image fills Nicaragua with hope.

The fourth section further intermingles revolution and repression. Whole groups join individualized heroes. Along with Casimiro Sotelo and Julio Buitrago, the peasant women of Cuá. A few years later it will be all of Monimbó. The people learn about, recognize and begin to accept the Sandinista National Liberation Front as their vanguard.

The fifth section is dedicated to Leonel Rugama, poet, ex-seminarist, Marxist. Rugama joins the urban guerrillas; his death at twenty years of age truncates a life of poetic creation. His promise was great, and in a few years he produced very much. In his poetry he contrasts the useless gestures of imperialism, its armaments and its space capsules, with the people's hunger and misery. He also relates the history of the present with the distant and not so distant colonial past. American Indian struggles against foreign invaders constitute the prehistory for more contemporary struggles in Latin America. Cardenal relates the Rugama story and other poets pay Leonel homage. In his life and death, Rugama shows that poetry is linked to struggle, and that poets can also fight. In the years to come, the unity of arms and letters will become an essential fact of national life.

Sección 1
Edwin Castro y
el régimen de Luis Somoza: 1956-67

1 / Iván Uriarte / Muelle

De pie sobre el pequeño muelle de Bluefields
tambaleante de maderas carcomidas
diviso el colorido de los barcos pesqueros y mercantes.

Me desayuno con frutas
mientras barcazas de cereales, cerdos y ganado
son mecidas por las olas del Atlántico.

Un vapor viejo y sucio lleno de carbón
se acerca volando humo
La isla del Venado se pierde a lo largo
(y recuerdo las marchas fúnebres en el entierro de Somoza
y a Edwin Castro esperando la muerte en la otra isla del Venado).

2 / Edwin Castro / Mañana, hijo mío, todo será distinto. . .

Mañana, hijo mío, todo será distinto.
Se marchará la angustia por la puerta del fondo
que han de cerrar, por siempre, las manos de hombres nuevos.

Reirá el campesino sobre la tierra suya
(pequeña, pero suya)
florecida en los besos de su trabajo alegre.
No serán prostitutas la hija del obrero
ni la del campesino;
pan y vestido habrá de su trabajo honrado.

Se acabarán las lágrimas del hogar proletario.

Tu reirás contento con la risa que lleven
las vías asfaltadas, las aguas de los ríos,
los caminos rurales. . .

Mañana, hijo mío, todo será distinto;   ►

126

Section 1
Edwin Castro and
the Regime of Luis Somoza: 1956-67

1 / Iván Uriarte / **The Dock**

Standing on the small Bluefields dock
tottering with rotten wood
I make out the colors of fishing and trading boats.

I breakfast on fruits
while Atlantic waves rock
barges of grain, pigs and cattle.

The old and dirty coal-filled stoker
draws near blowing smoke
obscuring the island of Venado
(and I recall the funeral marches at Somoza's burial
and Edwin Castro awaiting death on another Venado island).

2 / Edwin Castro / **Tomorrow, My Son, All Will Be Different. . .**

Tomorrow, my son, all will be different.
Anguish will go out the back door
which hands of new men will then shut for good.

Peasants will rejoice over their land
(small, but theirs)
flowering with the touch of their happy work.
Daughters of factory and farmworkers will not be whores;
There'll be bread and dress from honest work,

an end to tears in proletarian homes.

Content, you'll laugh with the laughter that comes from
paved roads, water in the rivers,
rural highways. . .

Tomorrow, my son, all will be different;
without whips or jails, or rifle bullets

►

sin látigo, ni cárcel, ni bala ni fusil
que repriman la idea.
Pasarás por las calles de todas las ciudades,
en tus manos las manos de tus hijos,
como yo no lo puedo hacer contigo.

No encerrará la cárcel tus años juveniles
como encierran los míos;
ni morirás en el exilio,
temblorosos los ojos,
anhelando el paisaje de la patria,
como murió mi padre.
Mañana, hijo, mío, todo será distinto.

3 / Gordillo / Circunstancia y Palabra

¿Cómo es la tortura?
No lo preguntes,
eres joven.

4 / Castro / ¿Y si no regresara?

Si algún día regreso
volveremos al campo
y marcharemos juntos
por el viejo camino
que un día recorrimos
cogidos de las manos,
en el último abril
de nuestra dicha.

Quizás será otro abril
caluroso y florido.
Se unirán nuestros pasos
en la alfombra de polvo.
Cruzaré los cercados
del pueblo vecino
para cortar racimos
de flores amarillas
que pondré en tus manos.   ►

that repress ideals.
You'll walk down the streets of all the cities,
in your hands the hands of your children,
as I can't walk with you.

Jails won't lock up your young years
as they locked up mine,
nor will you die as my father died
in exile, with tremulous eyes
craving the sight of your country.
Tomorrow, my son, all will be different.

3 / Gordillo / Circumstance and Word

What is torture like?
Don't ask,
you're young.

4 / Castro / And If I Don't Return?

If someday I return
we'll go back to the countryside
and we'll walk together
along the same road
that we once walked
hand in hand,
in the last April
of our happy time.

Perhaps it will be another April
hot and florid.
Our footsteps will join
in the carpet of dust.
I'll climb over the fences
of the neighboring town
to cut clusters
of yellow flowers
that I'll place in your hands.　　►

Le robaré al malinche
sus bellas flores rojas
que prenderé en tu pecho.
Bajaremos al río
y en sus aguas tranquilas
mojaremos las manos...

¿Y si no regresara?
¿Si no volviera nunca?
No importa. Vete al campo
y lleva a nuestro hijo
por el camino viejo
que un día recorrimos;
haz que corte al malinche
sus bellas flores rojas
para adornar tu pecho
y cruce los cercados
del potrero vecino
para llevarte ramos
de flores amarillas.
Baja, con él, al río
y mójale las manos.
¡En el agua tranquila
sentirás mi presencia
que llenará los cauces
abiertos por mi ausencia!

5 / Cardenal / Oráculo sobre Managua

'Me metieron en una celda llamada La Chiquita
frente a la planta eléctrica de la Casa Presidencial
en su parte más alta tiene 1 metro 13 cmts. de alto
y en su parte más baja se junta con el piso. Desde allí
vi las torturas. Eran de las 12 a las 2 todas las noches.
    Me apretó los testículos el Mayor Morales'
'...Me llevaron al jardín, donde había visto a Narváez en la
jaula de la pantera en piyama y descalzo
    y a otros hombres en la jaula de los leones
ahora con los leones estaba Narváez
    en la jaula de la pantera Julio Velázquez'   ►

130

From the jacaranda I'll steal
lovely red flowers
that I'll place on your breast.
We'll go down to the river
and wet our hands
in tranquil waters. . .

And if I don't return?
If I never come back?
No matter. Go to the countryside
and take our son
along the old road
where once we walked
make him cut the jacaranda's
lovely red flowers
to adorn your breast
and climb over the fences
of the nearby pasture
to bring you bouquets
of yellow flowers.
Go down with him to the river
and wet your hands.
In the tranquil waters,
you'll feel my presence
that will fill the channels
opened by my absence!

5 / Cardenal / **Oracle on Managua**

'They put me in a cell called La Chiquita
in front of the electric plant of the Presidential Palace
at its highest point it is 1 meter 13 centimeters high
and at its lowest point the ceiling touches the floor. From there
I saw tortures. They took place from 12 to 2 every night.
  Major Morales squeezed my testicles'
'. . .They carried me to the garden where I had seen Narváez in the
panther's cage in pyjamas and bare feet
  and other men in the lions' cage
now Narváez was with the lions
  and Julio Velázquez in the panther's cage'   ▶

(Era junto a la piscina, a las casetas de la piscina presidencial)

Desde mi casa se oían los rugidos en la madrugada.
Cuando tenían hambre. Cada madrugada. El zoológico de Somoza.
Entonces no sabíamos que los presos estaban con las fieras.
La pantera negra había sido regalo de Castillo Armas
lo que no era muy tranquilizador que digamos. Somoza
gordo lleno de condecoraciones como un árbol de Navidad.

6 / Anónimo / 3 Muertes

En mayo fueron tres.
Negras dalias aplicaron la muerte en sus cuerpos
. . .
La primera para Castro
la del centro para Narváez
la tercera para Silva.

7 / Luis Rocha / Treinta veces treinta

Edwin Castro salió de la cárcel, Nicaragua,
muerto.
Y Sandino del que todos sabemos por qué murió,
pero no de qué manera.
Y SANDINO y no sólo Sandino;
y el pueblo de Sandino
por todas las montañas sin patria,
en el filo de los machetes cansados,
a la sombra de los árboles viejos,
en un beso fugaz, en un tiro lejano.

(It was next to the pool, by the bathhouses of the presidential
                                                swimming pool)
From my house you could hear the roars at dawn.
When they were hungry. Every morning. Somoza's private zoo.
At the time we didn't know that the prisoners were with the beasts.
The black panther had been a gift from Castillo Armas
which did not, let us say, put us at ease. Somoza
fat, decked out with medals like a Christmas tree.

6 / Anonymous / 3 Corpses

In May there were three.
They laid black dahlias of death on their bodies.
      . . .
The first one for Castro
the center one for Narváez
the third for Silva.

7 / Luis Rocha / Thirty Times Thirty

Edwin Castro came out of the jail, Nicaragua,
dead.
And Sandino: we all know why he died,
but not how.
And SANDINO and not only Sandino;
and the people of Sandino
throughout the mountains without a country,
in the edge of tired machetes,
beneath the shade of old trees,
in a fleeting kiss, in a far off shot.

8 / Roberto Cuadra / **¿Cuándo?**

¿Qué has hecho, Luis,
con mi patria?
¿Cómo has podido escupirla
por más de treinta años?
Desde que tengo memoria
sólo SOMOZA veo en los periódicos,
en los lamentos
y en las velas de los muertos,
asesinados, Luis, por tu guardia.
¿Cuándo va a llegar la hora
en que ha de desaparecer la pesadilla
que ustedes causan
con tanto TERROR, y TORTURAS.
PERSECUCIONES y EXILIOS
y HAMBRE y CADA VEZ MÁS HAMBRE. . .

9 / David Macfield / **No hay nada en la ciudad**

No hay nada en la ciudad,
abran todos los ojos y miren por las puertas,
miren por las ventanas,
por las rendijas,
por los poros,
por donde se pueda mirar:
miren.

No hay nada en la ciudad.

Los hombres se han dormido en sus sombras,
y no hay un sólo hombre en las calles de la ciudad.
No hay quien diga esta boca es mía.
No hay quien defienda a las mujeres, del silencio.

La ciudad está muerta;
muerta,
muerta.

La ciudad está muerto del miedo:
el miedo ronda por las noches;
su bandera está izada en las casas vecinas
y sus dominios se han extendido hasta el amanecer. ▶

8 / Roberto Cuadra / When?

What have you done, Luis,
to my country?
How have you been able to spit on her
for more than thirty years?
For as long as I can remember
only SOMOZA appears in the papers,
in the laments
in the wakes for the dead,
murdered, Luis, by your Guard.
When will the time come
when the nightmare ends
the nightmare you cause
with so much TERROR and TORTURE,
with PERSECUTIONS and EXILES
and HUNGER, EVER MORE HUNGER. . .

9 / David Macfield / There is Nothing in the City

There is nothing in the city,
everyone open your eyes and look through the doorways,
look through the windows,
through the slits,
through the pores,
through wherever you can look,
look.

There is nothing in the city.

The men have fallen asleep in their shadows,
and there's not one man in the city streets.
There is no one who dares to open his mouth.
There is no one to defend the women, from the silence.

The city is dead;
dead,
dead.

The city is dead from fear:
fear stalks the night;
its flag flies on neighborhood houses
its dominion extends all the way to dawn.   ►

No hay quien levante la voz.

La voz está lejana,
detrás del horizonte,
y se ahoga en Pancasán,
en Bocaycito,
en el Chaparral,
en todas Las Segovias anda el duende de la ciudad.

Vayan a traer el fantasma de la ciudad,
la ciudad llena de luz,
llena de hombres y de niños
la ciudad con parques,
con jardines,
con casas para todos,
con bibliotecas,
con música del pueblo.
Vayan a Pancasán
Vayan a Bocaycito
a traer el himno de la ciudad,
a buscar maestros para la ciudad,
a buscar presidente para la ciudad,
la ciudad necesita presidente,
vayan a Las Segovias a buscar historiadores
para contar las hazañas de la ciudad.

Vayan las mujeres,
vayan los niños,
vayan las madres,
vayan los ancianos.
Porque esta ciudad está muerta,
están muertos los hombres,
y sólo el fantasma del miedo ronda por las calles,
izando su bandera a cada paso, izando su triunfo
y lanzando la vergüenza al viento,
porque la ciudad está muerta
muerta de silencio y no hay quien diga "esta boca es mía."

No one raises a voice.

The voice is far away,
beyond the horizon,
it drowns in Pancasán,
in Bocaycito,
in El Chaparral,
throughout the Segovias walks the ghost of the city.

Go and get the vision of the city
city filled with light
filled with men and children
city with parks,
with gardens
with houses for everyone,
with libraries,
with the people's music.

Go to Pancasán
Go to Bocaycito
to bring back the hymn of the city,
to seek teachers for the city,
to seek a president for the city,
the city needs a president,
go to the Segovias to seek historians
to tell of the city's great deeds.

Let the women go,
the children,
the mothers,
the old ones.
Because this city is dead,
the men are dead,
and only the specter of fear patrols the streets,
unfurling his flag at every step, flaunting his triumph
and hurling shame to the wind,
because the city is dead
dead with silence and no one dares to open his mouth.

10 / Beltrán Morales / **La insoportable presencia**

Por la Avenida Sandino
suenan clan clan
las cantimploras
del Batallón Somoza.
Y no sólo suenan las
cantimploras. Al ratito
sangre de ancianos y niños
sisea en cunetas y alcantarillas.

11 / Cardenal / **Kayanerenhkowa**

Un hombre saltó a media calle con los brazos abiertos:
¡¡BASTA YA!!
y lo acribillaron.
Otro Somoza será presidente.

10 / Beltrán Morales / **The Unbearable Presence**

On Sandino Avenue
the Somoza Batallion
canteens bang,
clang, clang.

And not only the canteens
bang. A bit later
the blood of old men and children
hisses in gutters and sewers.

11 / Cardenal / **Kayanerenhkowa**

A man leapt up in the middle of the street with open arms:
     ENOUGH NOW!!
     and they riddled him with bullets.
Another Somoza will be president.

Sección 2
Muerte y miseria al comenzar Tacho

1 / Rocha / Treinta veces treinta

Después de treinta años
así hablaron los enviados de Sandino:

. . .
poseemos un mismo sol. .
una misma miseria nos cobija

2 / Macfield / Zoologías para hoy

Respaldo nacional al gobierno y al ejército.
Gran homenaje a Tesorera del Distrito Nacional.
Telegrama de adhesión incondicional a Somoza:
Incondicionalmente a su disposición, para respaldarlo
y mantener siempre glorioso a nuestro Ejército Nacional.

3 / Rocha / Treinta veces treinta

Los políticos vociferaban,
suspendían las garantías
y las reclamaban
con los muertos del pueblo,
y los muertos del pueblo
eran todo el pueblo;
pero sus cadáveres eran ocultados.

4 / Macfield / A David Tejada Peralta

Los asesinos a la hora de la mesa
hablan del presupuesto
del aumento de salario y responsabilidades
de las órdenes del día
y las maravillas del general.

Section 2
Murder and Misery as Tacho's Reign Begins

1 / Rocha / Thirty Times Thirty

After thirty years
the heirs of Sandino spoke:

   . . .

   we own the same sun.
   one same misery mantles us.

2 / Macfield / Zoologies for Today

National support for the government and the army.
Great homage to the Treasurer of the National District.
Telegram of unconditional support for Somoza:
Unconditionally at his disposition, to back him
and maintain our National Army ever glorious.

3 / Rocha / Thirty Times Thirty

The politicians boasted,
they suspended guarantees
and reclaimed them
with the corpses of the people,
and the corpses of the people
were the entire people;
but they hid the bodies.

4 / Macfield / To David Tejada Peralta

The assassins at dinner
discuss the state budget
pay raises and duties
the orders of the day
and the glories of the general.

5 / Rocha / **Treinta veces treinta**

. . .Ajaz Delgado murió en la cárcel;
lo mataron y su cadáver fue devuelto
a su madre.
Y *Novedades* dijo:
"Un gesto democrático."

6 / Macfield / **A David Tejada Peralta**

El elefante habla en su casa,
a la cena
de los programas en la TV
y el estado de la liga de béisbol
y quizá
la necesidad de enviar a sus hijos a estudiar
al extranjero.

7 / Rocha / **Treinta veces treinta**

Muertos, muertos y muertos
los muertos ya inútiles
inútilmente muertos
y todo se esparce
como una mancha eterna. . .

8 / Macfield / **A David Tejada Peralta**

Por las noches sueña estar parado en arena movediza
con el mar de sangre a la garganta.

5 / Rocha / **Thirty Times Thirty**

. . .Ajaz Delgado died in jail;
they killed him and returned the cadaver
to his mother.
And *Novedades* said:
"A democratic gesture."

6 / Macfield / **To David Tejada Peralta**

At home for dinner
elephant Tacho talks
of TV shows
the baseball standings
and maybe the need
to send his kids
to study abroad.

7 / Rocha / **Thirty Times Thirty**

Corpses, corpses and corpses
corpses already useless
uselessly killed
and all splayed out
like eternal stains. . .

8 / Macfield / **To David Tejada Peralta**

At night Tacho dreams of standing in quicksand
a sea of blood at his throat.

9 / Rocha / **Treinta veces treinta**

Y los políticos persistían hablando;
prometiendo menos muertes,
construyendo grandes ciudades libres. . .
    . . .
Sergio
    José
        Mauricio
            Eric
muertos el 23 de Julio
en una calle de León.
Báez Bone, Pablo Leal, Díaz y Sotelo,
Rigoberto López, Carlos Nájar, Cornelio Silva,
Augusto César Sandino,
y más, y los ignorados, y muchos más
y los que van a morir
y Julio Romero de trece años quien protestó en otro 23 de Julio;
y así todos fuimos comprendiendo que en Nicaragua
ésta es la muerte natural.

10 / Rocha / **Sueño del optimista**

En su palacio Somoza
hace planes para el futuro
y piensa: "30 años más
se sacrificará mi familia por el pueblo". . .
y sus hijos pululan de alegría ante la herencia
mientras abajo el pueblo piensa:
"ni un año más"
"ni un año más"
"ni un año más"
porque
entre el presente y el futuro
está el destino
incluso para la vida de los tiranos
y la prolongación de las dinastías
y el destino es inexorable como la muerte
y oscuro como la noche.   ▶

9 / Rocha / Thirty Times Thirty

And the politicians kept on talking
promising fewer deaths,
building great free cities. . .
     . . .
Sergio
     José
         Mauricio
              Eric
died July 23rd
on a street in León.
Báez Bone, Pablo Leal, Díaz and Sotelo
Rigoberto López, Carlos Nájar, Cornelio Silva
Augusto César Sandino,
and more, and the unknown, and many more
and those who are going to die
and Julio Romero, thirteen years old, who protested on another
                                         July 23.
And so we all came to understand that in Nicaragua
this is the natural way to die.

10 / Rocha / The Optimist's Dream

In his palace Somoza
makes plans for the future
and thinks: "For 30 more years
my family will sacrifice itself for the people". . .
and his sons swarm with glee over the legacy
while below the people think:
"not one year more"
"not one year more"
"not one year more"
because
between present and future
destiny awaits
even the lives of tyrants
and the survival of dynasties
and destiny is as inexorable as death
and dark as night.   ▶

En mi país
llena de sombras está la vida
de los hombres que aman
y llena de sombras la de los que odian.
Que las sombras se guarden de las sombras:
El guerrillero cae como la noche
de un solo tajo
    interrumpiendo la cena del dictador.

11 / Gordillo / **Andrés**

Andrés
Tu piedra es mi esperanza.
Ha pasado un siglo y ya la ves,
todo lo mismo.
Pudo más el oro que la sangre.
Toda tu tierra, Andrés.
Desde los lagos al Coco,
desde el cabo hasta el San Juan.
Es una sola lágrima donde la patria llora.
Lanza la piedra.
Lánzala:
A un siglo de distancia, el enemigo
es el mismo.

In my country
the lives of men who love
are filled with shadows
and filled with shadows are the lives of those who hate.
Let the shadows beware of shadows:
The guerrilla falls all at once
like the night
   to break up the dictator's dinner.

11 / Gordillo / **Andrés**

Andrés
Your stone is my hope.
A century has passed and still you see,
everything the same.
Gold was more powerful than blood.
Your whole country, Andrés.
From the lakes of Coco,
from the cape to the River San Juan.
It is one great tear where the nation cries.
Throw the stone.
Throw it:
At a century's distance, the enemy
is the same.

Sección 3
La llamada a la lucha

1 / Mario Cajina Vega / **Cartel**

LA REVOLUCIÓN es la tierra,
son los arados surcando los maizales
y una familia de azadones cultivando hortalizas.

2 / Macfield / **Generacional**

Para tí,
hijo mío
el escaso pan de mi trigo
el sudor de mi frente,
la esperanza de un día claro
y este legado de treinta oscuros años de vergüenzas.

3 / Cajina / **Cartel**

LA REVOLUCIÓN es el indio

4 / Cardenal / **Canto nacional**

Ha habido domingos en que las muchachas miskitas
han ido a la iglesia (Bautista) desnudas en pelota
señoritas miskitas, por no tener nada que ponerse.
Y hay quienes han muerto de hambre
literalmente.

148

Section 3
The Call to Struggle

1 / Mario Cajina Vega / **Placard**

THE REVOLUTION is the land,
is the plow preparing the cornfields
and a family of hoes cultivating gardens.

2 / Macfield / **Generational**

For you,
my son
the scarce bread of my wheat
the sweat of my brow,
the hope of a clear day
and this legacy of thirty dark years of shame.

3 / Cajina / **Placard**

THE REVOLUTION is the Indian

4 / Cardenal / **National Song**

There have been Sundays when the Miskita girls
have gone to the (Baptist) church virtually naked
Miskita misses, because they did not have anything to wear.
And there are those who have died literally
of hunger.

5 / Cajina / Cartel

LA REVOLUCIÓN es la comida,
es una mesa servida con su pichel de agua
y el tenedor y el cuchillo
sobre el mantel a cuadros,
teniendo además otro cubierto listo
por si acaso se aparece una visita.

6 / B. Morales / Desayuno

Como el Kellogg's Corn Flakes
el Cuerpo de Paz
es penetración imperialista
en su forma más deliciosa.

7 / Cajina / Cartel

LA REVOLUCIÓN es un libro y un hombre libre

8 / Alvaro Gutiérrez / Las armas y las letras

"Con la pluma vuela el hierro
que ha de herir." Quevedo: *Marco Bruto.*

Desde César y Alejandro
hierro y letra se hermanaron.
Quevedo vio a la sangre
salir del tintero
y Montalvo mató al tirano
por correo.
(La espada, pues, tuvo marca
de lápiz o bolígrafo)
Cuando sepas contar piedras
                    poeta
sabrás que pluma es machete
en el hablar del campesino:
con ellos aprende
el oficio.

5 / Cajina / **Placard**

THE REVOLUTION is a meal,
                it is a table set with its water pitcher
                and knife and fork
                on the checkered tablecloth
                with an extra setting
                in case someone comes.

6 / B. Morales / **Breakfast**

Like Kellogg's Corn Flakes
the Peace Corps
is imperialist penetration
in its tastiest form.

7 / Cajina / **Placard**

THE REVOLUTION is a book and a free man

8 / Alvaro Gutiérrez / **Arms and Letters**

                "With the pen flies the weapon
                that must wound." Quevedo: *Marco Bruto.*

Since Caesar and Alexander
weapons and words have been brothers.
Quevedo saw blood
rise from his inkwell
and Montalvo killed the tyrant
by mail.
(The sword, then, had the stamp
of ballpoint or pencil)
When you know how to count stones
                poet
you'll find out that pen means machete
in the language of the peasant:
learn your trade
from them.

9 / Cajina / **Cartel**

LA REVOLUCIÓN es el trabajador

10 / Ricardo Morales Avilés / **Santa Bárbara**

Cuando los obreros de Procón
se fueron a la huelga
porque había que reglamentar las horas y horas
de la explotación de su trabajo
hermanos suyos morían electrocutados
por evitar que el fuego consumiera los comercios
y obtenían un editorial de *Novedades* como recompensa;
porque el comercio no sólo devora los sobrantes de la producción
y la producción misma
sino la energía y la vida de los productores,
porque el comercio siempre repercute,
de una u otra forma,
sobre la sociedad en que se desarrolla.

Por ese mismo tiempo oímos que un tal Somoza,
que amasó una inmensa fortuna
tiranizando un pueblo
y vendiendo andrapoda a Wall Street,
empezó diciendo en Santa Bárbara
una bonita cinta a colores y Panavisión
sobre las bombas constructivas,
sobre el progreso y la justicia social en Nicaragua,
mientras otros obreros con el dolor de los ayunos
penetraban por las galerías subterráneas
para arrancar las rocas que obstruían
el paso de las aguas,
cambiando a cada rato la posición de sus cuerpos
siguiendo los contornos de las rocas
y las llevaban hacia fuera
a la entrada de los túneles
y se les obligaba a trabajar a golpes redoblados
bajo la vigilancia de capataces extranjeros,
agotados de fatiga,
para cumplir los planes del gobierno y del consorcio.

9 / Cajina / Placard

THE REVOLUTION is the worker

10 / Ricardo Morales Avilés / Santa Barbara

When the Procón workers
went on strike
to protest the hour by hour
exploitation of their labor,
fellow workers died electrocuted
rather than let the shop be consumed by fire
and they got as a reward an editorial in *Novedades;*
for the Market devours not only surplus production
and production itself
but the strength and life of the producers as well;
because in one form or another
the Market always pervades
the society which fosters it.

Around the same time, we heard that someone named Somoza
who amassed a vast fortune
tyrannizing a people
and selling human forms to Wall Street,
was talking in Santa Barbara
about construction pumps,
about progress and social justice in Nicaragua
in color and Panavision,
while workers wracked with hunger pangs
probed underground galleries
to yank out the rocks
that blocked the waterways,
now and then adjusting their bodies
to the contours of the rocks
which they carried forward
to the mouth of the tunnels,
and they were made to work double time
under the watchful eyes of foreign foremen
worn out from fatigue
to meet the deadlines of the government and the consortium.

11 / Cardenal / Oraculo sobre Managua

LA REVOLUCIÓN es cambiar la realidad

      12 / Jorge Eduardo Arellano / En Rivas, Nicaragua

      En Rivas,
               Nicaragua,
                       te vi
      flaco,
           barbudo,
                maloliente
      cantando tangos
                  con otros viajeros.
      Venías de los Andes
                  fatigosos y helados
      y del Caribe
      tu mar.
          Desde una ventana
                  los chavalos te miramos
      comer arroz con pollo
               en calzoncillos.
      Luego te marchaste
             y no volvimos
                  a saber nada
                     de tí
      hasta que tu nombre
             brilló
      Che Guevara.

13 / Cajina / Cartel

LA REVOLUCIÓN es el hombre.

11 / Cardenal / **Oracle on Managua**

THE REVOLUTION is changing reality

      12 / Jorge Eduardo Arellano / **In Rivas, Nicaragua**

In Rivas,
        Nicaragua,
             I saw you
skinny,
      bearded,
           smelly
singing tangos
          with other travelers.
You came from the Andes
             frozen and steep
and the Caribbean
your sea.
       From the window
             we kids watched you
eat chicken and rice
         in your underwear.
Then you went away
          and we didn't hear
                any more
                   about you
until your name
        rang out
Che Guevara.

13 / Cajina / **Placard**

THE REVOLUTION is humanity.

Sección 4
Los que pelean: Los que caen

1 / Rugama / Biografía

Nunca apareció su nombre
en las tablas viejas del excusado escolar.
Al abandonar definitivamente el aula
nadie percibió su ausencia.
Las sirenas del mundo guardaron silencio,
jamás detectaron el incendio de su sangre.
El grado de sus llamas
se hacía cada vez más insoportable.
Hasta que abrazó con el ruido de sus pasos
la sombra de la montaña.
Aquella tierra virgen le amamantó con su misterio
cada brisa lavaba su ideal
y lo dejaba como niña blanca desnuda,
temblorosa, recién bañada.
Todo mundo careció de oídos y el combate
donde empezó a nacer
no se logró escuchar.

2 / Mario Santos / Son los muchachos

Mis hermanos esta noche ya volvieron
Mis hermanos ya están a nuestro lado
Entraron a la casa escondidos de la luna
Y mañana el viento sur
les soplará sus cabellos
y el viento norte llorará al no verlos.
Han vuelto mis hermanos
Y aunque la montaña los reclame con sus rifles
los labios de mi mamá vuelven a ser como flor
y en sus ojos hay un brillo de vidrio de color.
El retorno de mis hermanos
alivia el vacío de nuestra casa
y borra pesadillas en el sueño de mi mamá. ▶

Section 4
The Fighters: The Fallen

1 / Rugama / **Biography**

His name never appeared on
the old walls of the school john.
When he left the classroom for good
no one noticed his absence.
The sirens of the world remained silent,
they never detected the fire in his blood.
The heat of his flames
grew more and more unbearable,
until the sound of his footsteps embraced
the shadow of the mountain.
That virgin land nurtured him with its mystery.
Every breeze cleansed his ideals
leaving him naked
trembling and newly bathed.
The whole world was deaf
and failed to hear when
the battle began to be born.

2 / Mario Santos / **It's the Boys**

Tonight my brothers returned
My brothers are now at our side
They entered the house hidden from the moonlight
and tomorrow the south wind
will ruffle their hair
and the north wind will cry not to see them.
My brothers have returned
And though the mountains reclaim them and their rifles
my mother's lips flower once more
and a lustre like stained glass shines in her eyes.
The return of my brothers
fills the void in our house
and wipes out the nightmares in my mother's dreams. ►

Han vuelto mis hermanos
Y me han cargado en sus hombros
y he sentido en sus barbas el olor de los montes
y les he sacado de sus ropas migaja de pan
y bastantes pedacitos de hojas secas.

3 / Cardenal / **Las campesinas del Cuá**

Voy a hablarles ahora de los gritos del Cuá
      gritos de mujeres como de parto
María Venancia de 90 años, sorda, casi cadáver
      grita a los guardias no he visto muchachos
la Amanda Aguilar de 50 años
      con sus hijitas Petrona y Erlinda
      no he visto muchachos
como de parto
– Tres meses en un cuartel de montaña –
Angela García de 25 y siete menores
      La Cándida de 16 años amamanta una niñita
      muy diminuta y desnutrida
Muchos han oído estos gritos del Cuá
      gemidos de la Patria como de parto
Al salir de la cárcel Estebana García con cuatro
      menores
dio a luz. Tuvo que regalar sus hijos
      a un finquero. Emelinda Hernández de 16
      las mejillas brillantes de llanto
      las trenzas mojadas de llanto. . .
Capturadas en Tazua cuando venían de Waslala
      la milpa en flor y ya grandes los quiquisques
      las patrullas entraban y salían con presos
      A Esteban lo montaron en el helicóptero
y al poco rato regresaron sin él. . .
      A Juan Hernández lo sacó la patrulla
una noche, y no regresó más
      Otra noche sacaron a Saturnino
      y no lo volvimos a ver. . . a Chico González
      también se lo llevaron
      ésto casi cada noche
a la hora que cantan las cocorocas   ►

My brothers have returned
they've lifted me onto their shoulders
and I've smelled the mountains in their beards
and from their clothes I've taken breadcrumbs
and lots of bits of dry leaves.

3 / Cardenal / The Peasant Women of Cuá

Now I'll tell you about the cries of Cuá
    cries of women like pangs of birth
María Venancia, 90 years old, deaf, half dead
    shouts at the soldiers, I haven't seen any boys.
Amanda Aguilar, 50 years old
    with her daughters Petrona and Erlinda
    I haven't seen any boys
like pangs of birth
– Imprisoned three months straight in a mountain barrack –
Angela García, 25 years old and seven children
    Cándida, 16 years old, suckles a baby girl
    very tiny and underfed
Many have heard these cries of Cuá
    wails of the native land like pangs of birth
On leaving her house, Estebana García, mother of four
gave birth to another. She had to give up her children
    to a landowner. Emelinda Hernández, 16 years old
        her cheeks shiny with tears,
    her braids wet from crying. . .
They were captured in Tazua as they came from Waslala
    the cornfields in flower and the yucca full-grown
    the patrols came and went with prisoners
    They sent Esteban up in a helicopter
and soon after returned without him. . .
    They carried off Juan Hernández
one night, and he never came back again
    Another night they took Saturnino
and we never saw him again. . . Then they took
    Chico González
    It's the same almost every night
   when the *cocorocas* sing
even people we didn't know.   ▶

ₔente que no conocimos también
La Matilde abortó sentada
cuando toda una noche nos preguntaron por los
guerrilleros
A la Cándida la llamó un guardia
vení lavame este pantalón
pero era para otra cosa
(Somoza sonreía en un retrato como un anuncio
de Alka-Seltzer)
Llegaron otros peores en un camión militar
A los tres días que salieron parió la Cándida
Esta es la historia de los gritos del Cuá
triste como el canto de las cocorocas
la historia que cuentan las campesinas del Cuá
que cuentan llorando
como entreviendo tras la neblina de las lágrimas
una cárcel
y sobre ella un helicóptero
"Nosotras no sabemos de ellos"
Pero sí han visto
sus sueños son subversivos
barbudos, borrosos en la niebla
rápidos
pasando un arroyo
ocultos en la milpa
apuntando
(como pumas)
¡saliendo de los pajonales!
pijeando a los guardias
viniendo al ranchito
(sucios y gloriosos)
la Cándida, la Amanda, la Emelinda
en sueños muchas noches
— con sus mochilas —
subiendo una montaña
con cantos de dichoso-fui
la María Venancia de 90 años
los ven de noche en sueños
en extrañas montañas
muchas noches
a los muchachos.

160

Matilde aborted sitting down
when they questioned her all night long
about the guerrillas
A guardsman called Cándida,
come here and wash my pants
but he wanted something else
(Somoza smiled in a picture like
an Alka-Seltzer ad)
Worse ones came in an army truck
Three days after they left Cándida gave birth
This is the story of the cries of Cuá
sad as the *cocoroca's* song
the story that the peasant women of Cuá tell
that they tell in tears,
as though glimpsing a jail behind the mist of tears
and above the jail a helicopter
"We know nothing about them"
But they have seen
their dreams are
bearded subversives hazy in the mist
quickly
fording a stream
concealed in the cornfields
taking aim
(like pumas)
springing from the tall grass!
beating the guardsmen
coming to the farm
(dirty and triumphant)
Cándida, Amanda, Emelinda
so often, at night, in dreams,
– with their knapsacks –
climbing a mountain
with happy-go-lucky songs
María Venancia, 90 years old
on distant mountains
so often at night
in dreams,
they see the boys.

4 / Horacio Bermúdez / **Los guerrilleros**

Desde los campamentos
en la otra costa del pantano,
fieras en acecho
los guerrilleros se deslizan en callejones
de luces borrosas por la lluvia,
asaltando el cuartel.

Al amanecer
el paisaje se había empañado.
En lo profundo cantan los pájaros.

Suenan bombas distantes.
Las nubes de ceniza
forman un túnel de sombra.

Mientras,
marchitos por la fiebre
esperan entre los pajonales.

5 / Arellano / **Pesadilla y/o realidad**

Estábamos cercados por los reflectores
El grito de un coronel amenazaba nuestras vidas
¿Qué pensábamos hacer?
No lo recuerdo.
Yo vi venir a los guardias con sus garands y metralletas
Oí las balas en dirección a nosotros
Cayeron Julio Ramón y Alberto
Y otros más que no conocía.

Sólo luchábamos por el bien de nuestros hermanos
Sólo pedíamos justicia por nuestro pueblo
Sólo queríamos ser libres.

4 / Horacio Bermúdez / **The Guerrilla Fighters**

From the encampments
on the swamp's outer edge
wild beasts on the prowl
the guerrillas slip into alleyways
the streetlights blurred by rain
assaulting the barracks.

At dawn
the countryside is misted.
Birds sing from its depths.

Bombs blast in the distance.
Clouds of debris
form a tunnel of darkness.

Meanwhile,
withered by fever
amidst the reeds
they wait.

5 / Arellano / **Nightmare and/or Reality**

Searchlights surrounded us
The colonel's cry threatened our lives
What did we intend to do?
I don't remember.
I saw the guards come with their garands and machine guns.
I heard bullets come our way
Julio Ramón and Alberto fell
and others I didn't know.

We only fought for the good of our brothers
We only urged justice for our people
We only wanted to be free

6 / Anónimo / A la muerte de mi amigo Orlando Narváez

Recuerdo aquella tarde en que gozamos
con las bellezas de los verdes campos. . .
por las tranquilas calles de Managua;
el sol se hundía en el dorado cielo.
Y tú me hablabas de la "revolución"
del asesinato de tu hermano de las
torturas, encarcelamiento y exilio.
Y me hablabas de proyectos,
de conquistar al mundo,
con riquezas y placeres. . .
mas no pensabas nunca,
lo incierto del futuro.

Ah. . . recuerdo tu voz,
y tu mirar sincero.
Pero llegó el día funesto.
Una tarde tranquila como aquella
pasó tu vida como toda pasa,
como mueren las flores en los campos
y las luces tranquilas del poniente.
Tú pasastes como pocos pasan,
con la frente pura y el alma fija en Dios.
Al caer la tarde yo recuerdo,
aquel hermano fiel que me quería,
que en placer y en el dolor me comprendía.

7 / R. Morales Avilés / Tres veces Casimiro

Casimiro Sotelo,
amigo, camarada,
alma rojinegra,
caminar de estrella.

Nos prometimos plantar un mundo nuevo
a partir de nuestros sueños
y tú marchaste primero al duelo necesario
        . . .
Aire te vestiste
para andarte clandestino por la calle
con tu pasión y tus sandalias de siempre,   ►

6 / Anonymous / To the Death of my Friend Orlando Narváez

I remember that evening when we enjoyed
the beauty of the green fields. . .
along the quiet streets of Managua;
the sun sinking into the golden sky.
And you talked to me about the "revolution"
about your brother's assassination
about torture, jail and exile.
And you talked to me of your plans
to conquer the world,
with its wealth and pleasures. . .
but you never considered
the uncertainty of the future.

Oh. . . I remember your voice,
and your sincere eyes.
But the dreadful day arrived.
One peaceful evening like that other one
your life ended as all lives end,
like the flowers of the fields
and the soft lights of the setting sun.
You died as very few do,
untainted brow and soul turned toward God.
At sunset, I remember
that loyal brother who loved me,
who understood me in pleasure and in pain.

7 / R. Morales Avilés / Casimiro Three Times Over

Casimiro Sotelo,
friend, comrade,
red and black soul,
walking in the stars.

We promised ourselves to sow a new world
based on our dreams
and you left first for the inevitable battle

    . . .

You clothed yourself in air
to walk hidden along the streets
with your passion and your customary sandals   ►

camina que camina agitando gente.
Y digo que vuelas
y te agitas
y gritas
y rondas la tristeza de los niños
y rondas el corazón de tu novia urbana-campesina
y rondas el hombre y la ira de los hombres
como ávido peregrino de dolores
y quejas.

Yo no te pienso
solo en el espacio
no preguntando rumbos de galaxias
ni acumulando pájaros en tu cabeza
ni siquiera plantando besos a las estrellas.

Casimiro Sotelo,
amigo, camarada,
mezcla de barro nuevo,
recuerdo bien el fuego de tus ojos.

8 / Cardenal / **Oráculo sobre Managua**

Y ahora pretenden con bazukas
                    detener la historia
En verdad, en verdad os digo
                    la revolución está en medio de vosotros.'

9 / Carlos José Guadamuz / **Julio Comandante**

Con fuego sonó un día una voz:
. . .Esta humanidad ha dicho basta y ha echado a andar. . .

y empezaste a caminar,
nuevo, pero seguro de no parar.
Y después alguien te dijo
. . .El deber de todo revolucionario es hacer la revolución. . .   ►

walking, walking stirring up the people.
And I say that you fly
and you stir yourself
and you cry
and you haunt the children's distress
and you haunt the heart of your citified country bride
and you haunt men's hunger and wrath
an avid pilgrim of pain
and protest.

I don't think of you
as alone in space
or asking which way to the galaxies
or with birds perched on your head
or even planting a kiss on the stars.

Casimiro Sotelo,
friend, comrade,
mixture of new clay,
I well remember your eyes' fire.

8 / Cardenal / **Oracle on Managua**

And now they try to
                    halt history with bazookas
'In truth, in truth I tell you
                    the revolution is in your midst.'

9 / Carlos José Guadamuz / **Commander Julio**

One day a voice rang out with fire:
. . .Humanity has said *enough* and begun to move. . .

and you began to walk,
new, but determined not to stop.
And then someone told you
. . .The duty of every revolutionary is to make revolution. . .   ►

y no preguntaste cómo hacerla
sino que comenzaste a hacerla
Y en una noche de octubre oíste:
. . .En una revolución, si es verdadera, se triunfa o se muere. . .

y dijiste
          Moriré peleando
Y escuchaste un canto:
                    . . .De pie América Latina. . .
y pensaste: ya vamos marchando.

Y el amigo en un abril te susurré:
. . .Crear dos, tres, muchos Viet Nam
                          es la consigna. . .
y respondiste
          En eso estamos

Una tarde de julio musitó tu hermano:
. . .En cualquier lugar que nos sorprenda la muerte
                              bienvenida sea. . .
y disparaste
. . .Siempre que ese, nuestro grito de guerra, haya llegado
                              hasta un oído receptivo. . .
y te hirieron
. . .Y otra mano se tienda para empuñar nuestras armas. . .
y lanzaste una granada
. . .Y otros hombres se apresten a entonar los cantos luctuosos. . .
y sentiste el primer rugido de la tanqueta
. . .Con tableteos de ametralladoras. . .
y seguiste disparando
. . .Y nuevos gritos de guerra y de victoria. . .
y seguiste disparando
   y seguiste. . .
     y seguiste. . .hasta la victoria. . .
                        . . .siempre. . .
                        . . .siempre. . .

168

and you didn't ask how to do it
instead you began to do it
And one October night you heard:
. . .In a true revolution, you win or die. . .

and you said
        I will die fighting
And you heard a song:
                . . .Rise up Latin America. . .
and you thought: now we're marching.

And a friend one April whispered:
. . .Create two, three, many Viet Nams
                that's the watchword. . .
and you answered
        That's what we're about

One July afternoon your brother whispered:
. . .Wherever death finds us
               be it welcome. . .
and you fired back
. . .So long as our war cry reaches
              a receptive ear. . .
and they wounded you
. . .And another hand reached out to grasp your weapons. . .
and you flung a grenade
. . .And other men readied to intone laments. . .
and you heard the first rumblings of the tank
. . .With the rattling of machine guns. . .
and you kept firing
. . .And new cries of war and victory. . .
and you kept firing
  and you kept on. . .
    and kept on. . .until victory. . .
                . . .forever. . .
                . . .forever. . .

10 / Rugama / **Las casas quedaron llenas de humo**

A los héroes sandinistas:
Julio Buitrago Urroz
Alesio Blandón Juárez
Marco Antonio Rivera Berrios
Aníbal Castrillo Palma

Yo ví los huecos que la tanqueta Sherman
abrió en la casa del barrio Frixione.
Y después fui a ver más huecos
en otra casa por Santo Domingo.
Y donde no había huecos de Sherman
había huecos de Garand
o de Madzen
o de Browning
o quién sabe de qué.
Las casas quedaron llenas de humo
y después de dos horas
Genie sin megáfono gritaba
que se rindieran.
Y antes hacía como dos horas
y antes hacía como cuatro horas
y hacía como una hora
gritaba
y gritaba
y grita.
Que se rindieran.
Mientras la tanqueta y las órdenes
Las Browning
las Madzen
las M-3
los M-1
y las carretas
las granadas
las bombas lacrimógenas. . . . .
y los temblores de los guardias.

NUNCA CONTESTÓ NADIE

Porque los héroes nunca dijeron
que morían por la patria,
sino que murieron.

10 / Rugama / **The Houses were Filled with Smoke**

To the Heroes of the *Frente Sandinista:*
Julio Buitrago Urroz
Alesio Blandón Juárez
Marco Antonio Rivera Berrios
Aníbal Castrillo Palma

I saw the holes the Sherman tank
opened in the house of the Frixione barrio.
And later I went to see more holes
in another house in Santo Domingo.
And where there weren't any Sherman tank holes
there were rifle holes
from Madzens
or Brownings
or who knows what.
The houses were filled with smoke
and after two hours
Genie, without a megaphone, screamed
at them to surrender.
And almost two hours later
and almost four hours later
and almost one hour
he shouted
and shouted
and shouts
at them to surrender.
Meanwhile the tank and the commands
The Brownings
the Madzens
the M-3s
the M-1s
and the bullet rounds
the grenades
and tear-gas bombs. . . . .
and the thundering of the guards.

NO ONE EVER ANSWERED

Because the heroes never said
they would die for their country,
they just died.

La historia se repite.
Las traiciones se repiten.
El enemigo es el mismo.
La muerte se repite. "Sólo quedaron las casas llenas de humo. . ."
dijo el prisionero desde la cárcel
y *Novedades* como un eco sórdido:
>"Un triunfo más del gobierno que preside
>nuestro excelentísimo General de División
>Anastasio Somoza Debayle"

y el jesuita ex-rector de la UCA asentía:
>"Es la única forma de acabar con estos. . ."

y el pueblo esperaba que el humo se disipara
para ir a recoger sus cadáveres y no vieron nada
sólo supieron que todavía iban vivos
que eran tres hombres
y una mujer
y pensaba:
>"Nunca hubo tal despliegue militar de tantos
>para matar a tan pocos"

y sentía dolorosamente
que algo dentro de ellos comenzaba a florecer.

Envueltas en humo como fantasmas ruinosos
las casas cañoneadas y ametralladas
aparecían ante los ojos del pueblo:
>"La juventud de Nicaragua está siendo asesinada"

denunciaron los poetas
y sus libros fueron prohibidos
y desde entonces nunca como antes
apareció tanto la huella, la sigla,
apuntada, escrita, presurosa
en paredes y calles:
>FSLN
FSLN
>fren. . .   ▶

11 / Rocha / Today's Communique

History repeats itself.
Treason repeats itself.
The enemy is the same.
Death repeats itself.
            "Only the houses filled with smoke remained. . ."
said the prisoner in his jail
and like a dull echo *Novedades* said:
            "One more triumph for the government
            headed by our super-excellent Division General
            Anastasio Somoza Debayle"
and the Jesuit ex-rector of the Central American U. agreed:
            "It's the only way to finish with these. . ."
and the people waited for the smoke to clear
to gather up their dead and they saw nothing
but they knew three men
and a woman
were still living
and they thought:
            "Never were so many soldiers
            sent to kill so few."
And they felt, pained,
that something within them began to grow.

Wreathed in smoke like ruined ghosts
the cannon-blasted machine-gunned houses
appeared before the eyes of the people:
            "The youth of Nicaragua is being murdered"
the poets cried
and their books were forbidden
and since then as never before
there appeared the mark, the initials,
etched, written, with haste
on the walls and on the streets:
                        FSLN

      F S L N
                  fren. . .   ►

"Los Sandinistas están en todas partes"
"El frente le aparece hasta en la sopa al dictador"
decía el pueblo y Somoza:
            "This is a stupid situation:
            I am a friend of the United States"
y entonces Somoza saluda a Mr. Shelton
y Mr. Shelton les hace una señita
los asesores militares norteamericanos
y el Mr. President U.S.A. está pendiente
de que todo salga bien:
300 alistados de la Guardia Nacional
equipados con el más moderno armamento made in usa
y con severas y prolongadas prácticas de "contra-insurgencia,"
rifles garand, máuseres, 30-30, M-1, carabinas, bombas,
gases, escudos, máscaras, pistolas Smith & Wesson de 9 mm,
tres tanquetas, ametralladoras de todo calibre, basookas,
equipo móvil, demoledoras, radios, ambulancias y 1 tanque Sherman
"combatieron heroicamente durante cuatro horas"
contra tres hombres y una mujer del
Frente Sandinista de Liberación Nacional.

Al final del "encuentro"
dieron muerte a los hombres
e hicieron prisionera a la mujer.

Según el parte los "bandoleros" o "delincuentes"
murieron en la acción
pero según la mujer ella fue ultrajada
golpeada vejada violada
y logró ver a sus compañeros
hechos prisioneros aún con vida.
Nuevos rótulos aparecen en Colegios y Universidades:
            "El Che vive en nuestras conciencias"
        "¡Viva el P. Camilo Torres!"
                "Patria libre o morir"   ▶
        "Sandino es siempre libertad"

"The *Sandinistas* are everywhere"
"The *Frente* appears even in the dictator's soup"
the people said and Somoza:
> "This is a stupid situation:
> I am a friend of the United States"

and then Somoza welcomes Mr. Shelton
and Mr. Shelton briefs
the North American military advisors
and Mr. President U.S.A. expects
that all will turn out well:
300 enlistees of the National Guard
equipped with the most modern weapons made in usa
and with prolonged and rigorous training in "counter-insurgency,"
garand rifles, mausers, 30-30s, M-1s, carbines, bombs,
gas, shields, masks, Smith & Wesson 9 mm. pistols,
three tanks, machine guns of every caliber, bazookas
mobile demolition equipment, radios, ambulances and 1 Sherman tank
"battled heroically for four hours"
against three men and a woman of the
Sandinista National Liberation Front.

At the end of the "incident"
they killed the men
and took the woman prisoner.

According to the communique, the "bandits" or "delinquents"
died in the encounter
but the woman said she was reviled,
beaten humiliated raped
and succeeded in seeing her comrades
taken prisoner still alive.
New slogans appear in the high schools and universities:
> "Che lives in our consciences"
> "Long live Father Camilo Torres"
> "Free Homeland or Death"
> "Sandino means liberty forever" ▶

Los G.N. siguen combatiendo
y otras casas quedan llenas de humo.
El pueblo contempla la escena:
"Pero, ¿qué sucederá cuando el humo se disipe?
Mr. Somoza bebe un trago con Mr. Embajador:
el pueblo contempla la escena.
La oficina de Leyes y Relaciones de la G.N.
emite un comunicado dando cuenta de que
"el movimiento subversivo ha sido sofocado"
y que "el pueblo de Nicaragua debe de agradecer
al General de División Anastasio Somoza Debayle
la forma en que mantiene la paz."
El pueblo contempla la escena
y la miseria se acurruca como un gruñido
en sus entrañas.

La pobreza produce un silencio estruendoso
mientras
              "La juventud de Nicaragua está siendo asesinada"
y el pueblo contempla la escena
y las casas quedan llenas de humo
y otra vez el Frente reaparece
y Mr. Somoza bebe más tragos con Mr. Embajador
y las casas vuelven a quedar llenas de humo
y el pueblo contempla la escena
y los corazones laten presurosos
y las conciencias estallan
como granadas.

The National Guards continue fighting
and other houses are filled with smoke.
The people observe the scene:
"But what will happen when the smoke clears?"
Mr. Somoza has a drink with Mr. Ambassador:
the people observe the scene.
The National Guard Office of Laws and Relations
sends a communique claiming that
"the subversive movement has been wiped out"
and that the "Nicaraguan people should give thanks to
Division General Anastasio Somoza Debayle
for the way he keeps the peace."
The people observe the scene
and misery wraps itself like a groan
around their entrails.

Poverty creates a deafening silence
while
                    "The youth of Nicaragua is being murdered"
and the people observe the scene
and the houses are filled with smoke
and again the *Frente* reappears
and Mr. Somoza has another drink with Mr. Ambassador
and the houses are filled with smoke again
and the people observe the scene
and hearts beat fast
and consciences explode
like grenades.

Sección 5
Vida y muerte de Leonel Rugama

1 / Rugama / Los paniquines están vacíos

Los paniquines están vacíos
esperando alimentos. *Life*
les toma fotos a colores.
Los astronautas del Apolo VIII
envían un mensaje de amor
desde la luna: "En la tierra paz
a los muertos de buena voluntad."

2 / Cardenal / Oráculo sobre Managua

Por eso vos Leonel Rugama poeta de 20 años
te metiste a la guerrilla urbana:
Ex-seminarista, marxista, decías
en la Cafetería La India que la revolución
es la comunión con la especie.

Por eso peleaste toda la tarde en aquella casa.
. . .
Por eso diste tu vida vos
en el quinto planeta de una estrella mediana de la Vía Láctea

3 / Rugama / La tierra es un satélite de la luna

El apolo 2 costó más que el apolo 1
el apolo 1 costó bastante.

El apolo 3 costó más que el apolo 2
el apolo 2 costó más que el apolo 1
el apolo 1 costó bastante.

El apolo 4 costó más que el apolo 3
el apolo 3 costó más que el apolo 2
el apolo 2 costó más que el apolo 1
el apolo 1 costó bastante.

►

Section 5
The Life and Death of Leonel Rugama

1 / Rugama / The Bowls are Empty

The bowls are empty
waiting for food. *Life*
takes color photos of them.
The astronauts of Apollo VIII
send a message of love
from the moon: "Peace on earth
and good will to the dead."

2 / Cardenal / Oracle on Managua

That is why you Leonel Rugama 20 year-old poet
joined the urban guerrillas:
Ex-seminarian, Marxist, you said
in the India Cafeteria that the revolution
is communion with the species.

That is why you fought in that house all afternoon.
. . .
That is why you gave your life
on the fifth planet of a middling star of the Milky Way.

3 / Rugama / The Earth is a Satellite of the Moon

Apollo 2 cost more than Apollo 1
Apollo 1 cost quite a bit.

Apollo 3 cost more than Apollo 2
Apollo 2 cost more than Apollo 1
Apollo 1 cost quite a bit.

Apollo 4 cost more than Apollo 3
Apollo 3 cost more than Apollo 2
Apollo 2 cost more than Apollo 1
Apollo 1 cost quite a bit.

►

El apolo 8 costó un montón, pero no se sintió
porque los astronautas eran protestantes
y desde la luna leyeron la Biblia,
maravillando y alegrando a todos los cristianos
y a la venida el Papa Pablo VI le dió la bendición.
El apolo 9 costó más que todos juntos,
junto con el apolo 1 que costó bastante.
Los bisabuelos de la gente de acahualinca tenían menos hambre
que los abuelos.
Los bisabuelos se murieron de hambre.
Los abuelos de la gente de acahualinca tenían menos hambre
que los padres.
Los abuelos se murieron de hambre.
Los padres de la gente de acahualinca tenían menos hambre
que los hijos de la gente de allí.
Los padres se murieron de hambre.
La gente de acahualinca tiene menos hambre que los hijos de la
gente de allí.
Los hijos de la gente de acahualinca no nacen por hambre,
y tienen hambre de nacer, para morirse de hambre.
Bienaventurados los pobres porque de ellos será la luna.

4 / Cardenal / Oráculo sobre Managua

La revolución es a veces rutinaria y sin gloria.
También conoció esa lucha el Che
                 – leche condensada y gato podrido –
Y cuando fuiste acólito en el manicomio: los locos cagados
         y la misa oliendo a mierda
                 Y también la humillación
de llevar, con este calor, una túnica negra de saduceo
cuando iban en fila a Acahualinca a ver las huellas.
Quien no odia a su padre y a su madre y a muchachas pijudas. . .
El celibato, una Sierra Maestra o la Larga Marcha.
Por eso podías predicar después (Cafetería La India)
'la liberación es nuestra MUERTE pero con ella damos VIDA'
o: ". . .el temor a entregarnos a una vida sacrificada. . ."
'el deber de hacer la revolución aun sin esperar ver el triunfo'

                                                      ▶

Apollo 8 cost a bundle, but no one minded
because the astronauts were Protestant
and read the Bible from the moon,
inspiring awe, infusing joy in every Christian
and on their return Pope Paul VI gave them his benediction.

Apollo 9 cost more than all of them together,
including Apollo 1 which cost quite a bit.

The great-grandparents of the people of Acahualinca were less
                              hungry than their grandparents.
The great-grandparents died of hunger.
The grandparents of the people of Acahualinca were less hungry
                              than their parents.
The grandparents died of hunger.
The parents of the people of Acahualinca were less hungry than
                              the children of the people of that place.
The parents died of hunger.
The people of Acahualinca are less hungry than the children of
                              the people of that place.
The children of the people of Acahualinca are not born because
                              of hunger,
and hunger to be born, to die of hunger.
Blessed are the poor for they shall inherit the moon.

4 / Cardenal / Oracle on Managua

The revolution is at times routine and without glory.
Che also knew that struggle
                              – canned milk and rotten cat meat –
And when you were an altar boy in the insane asylum: the luna-
                              tics all shitty
              and the mass smelling like shit
                      And also the humiliation
of wearing, in this heat, a black Sadducean tunic
when you walked single file to see the footprints of Acahualinca.
Who doesn't hate their father and their mother and filthy little
                              girls. . .
Celibacy, a Sierra Maestra or the Long March.
That's why you were able to preach later on (the India Cafeteria)
'liberation is our DEATH but with it we give LIFE'

▶

El Che conoció esa lucha más arrecha
"pedos, vómitos, y diarrea"
dice el diario. Sin gloria, cagado en una hamaca
le prestaron un pantalón
"pero sin agua hiedo a mierda a una legua"

5 / Rugama / El libro de la historia del "Che"

El libro de la historia del "Che"
hijo de Augusto
hijo de Lautaro:
Lautaro
        "Inche Lautaro
        apubim ta pu huicán"
        (Yo soy Lautaro que acabó con los españoles)
casado con Guaconda
y hermano a su vez de Caupolicán (El flechador del cielo)
y de Colocolo
engendró a Oropello;
Oropello engendró a Lecolón
y a sus hermanos;
Lecolón engendró a Cayeguano;
Cayeguano engendró a Talco;
Talco engendró a Rengo;
Rengo engendró a Túpac-amaru;
Túpac-amaru engendró a Túpac-yupanqui;
Túpac-yupanqui engendró a Tucapel;
Tucapel engendró a Urraca de Panamá;
Urraca engendró a Diriangén de Nicaragua
y éste se suicidó
en las faldas del volcán Casitas
para nunca ser capturado.
Diriangén engendró a Adiact
y éste fue colgado
en un palo de tamarindo que está en Subtiaba
"Aquí murió el último jefe indio"   ▶

or: ". . .the fear of committing ourselves to a life of sacrifice. . ."
'our obligation to make revolution even without hope of seeing
victory'
Che knew the filthiness of that struggle
"farts, vomit and diarrhea"
he writes in his journal. Without glory, lying shitcovered in a
hammock
they lent him a pair of pants
"but without water I stink from shit a mile away"

5 / Rugama / **The Book of "Che"**

The book of the story of "Che"
son of Augusto
son of Lautaro:
Lautaro
"*Inche Lautaro*
apubim ta pu huicán"
(I am Lautaro who vanquished the Spaniards)
married to Guaconda
and brother in turn of Caupolicán (the celestial archer)
and of Colocolo
begat Oropello;
Oropello begat Lecolón
and his brothers;
Lecolón begat Cayeguano;
Cayeguano begat Talco;
Talco begat Rengo;
Rengo begat Túpac-amaru;
Túpac-amaru begat Túpac-yupanqui;
Túpac-yupanqui begat Tucapel;
Tucapel begat Urraca of Panama;
Urraca begat Diriangén of Nicaragua
and the latter took his own life
on the slope of the Casitas volcano
so that he might never be captured.
Diriangén begat Adiact
and the latter was hanged
from a tamarind branch that is in Subtiaba.
"Here died the last Indian chief"   ►

183

y la gente de otras partes lo llega a ver como gran cosa
Adiact engendró a Xochitl Acatl (Flor de la Caña);
Xochitl Acatl engendró a Guegue Miquistl (Perro Viejo)
Guegue Misquistl engendró a Lempira;
Lempira engendró a Tecún-Umán;
Tecún-Umán engendró a Moctezuma Iluicamina;
Moctezuma Iluicamina engendró a Moctezuma Zocoyotlzin;
Moctezuma Zocoyotlzin engendró a Cuauhtémoc;
Cuauhtémoc engendró a Cuauhtemozin
y éste fue ahorcado por los hombres de Cortés
y dijo:
> "Así he sabido
> lo que significa confiar
> en vuestras falsas promesas
> ¡oh Malinche! (Cortés)
> yo supe desde el momento
> en que no me di muerte
> por mi propia mano
> cuando entrasteis a mi ciudad
> de Tenochtitlán
> que me tenías reservado ese destino."

Cuauhtemotzin engendró a Quaupopoca;
Quaupopoca engendró a Tlacopán;
Tlacopán engendró a Huáscar;
Huáscar engendró a Jerónimo;
Jerónimo engendró a Pluma Gris;
Pluma Gris engendró a Caballo Loco;
Caballo Loco engendró a Toro Sentado;
Toro Sentado engendró a Bolívar;
Bolívar engendró a Sucre;
Sucre engendró a José de San Martín;
José de San Martín engendró a José Dolores Estrada;
José Dolores Estrada engendró a José Martí;
José Martí engendró a Joaquín Murrieta;
Joaquín Murrieta engendró a Javier Mina;
Javier Mina engendró a Emiliano Zapata;
Emiliano Zapata engendró a Pancho Villa;
Pancho Villa engendró a Guerrero;
Guerrero engendró a Ortíz;
Ortíz engendró a Sandino;
Augusto César Sandino
hermano de Juan Gregorio Colindres ▶

and people from other places come to see it as a wondrous thing
Adiact begat Xochitl Acatl (Cane Flower)
Xochitl Acatl begat Guegue Miquistl (Old Dog)
Guegue Miquistl begat Lempira;
Lempira begat Tecún-Umán;
Tecún-Umán begat Moctezuma Iluicamina;
Moctezuma Iluicamina begat Moctezuma Zocoyotlzin;
Moctezuma Zocoyotlzin begat Cuauhtémoc;
Cuauhtémoc begat Cuauhtemotzin
and the latter was hanged by the men of Cortés
and he said:
    "Thus have I learned
    what it means to believe
    your false promises
    oh Malinche! (Cortés)
    I knew from the moment
    that I did not take my life
    with my own hand
    when you entered my city
    Tenochtitlán
    that this was the fate
    you had assigned me."
Cuauhtemotzin begat Quaupopoca;
Quaupopoca begat Tlacopán;
Tlacopán begat Huáscar;
Huáscar begat Geronimo;
Geronimo begat Gray Feather;
Gray Feather begat Crazy Horse;
Crazy Horse begat Sitting Bull;
Sitting Bull begat Bolívar;
Bolívar begat Sucre;
Sucre begat José de San Martín;
José de San Martín begat José Dolores Estrada;
José Dolores Estrada begat José Martí;
José Martí begat Joaquín Murieta;
Joaquín Murieta begat Javier Mina;
Javier Mina begat Emiliano Zapata;
Emiliano Zapata begat Pancho Villa;
Pancho Villa begat Guerrero;
Guerrero begat Ortíz;
Ortíz begat Sandino;
Augusto César Sandino   ►

y de Miguel Angel Ortez
y de Juan Umanzor
y de Francisco Estrada
y de Sócrates Sandino
y de Ramón Raudales
y de Rufus Marín
y cuando hablaba decía:
       "Nuestra causa triunfará
       porque es la causa de la justicia
       porque es la causa del amor."
y otras veces decía:
       "Yo me haré morir
       con los pocos que me acompañan
       porque es preferible
       hacernos morir como rebeldes
       y no vivir como esclavos."
Sandino engendró a Bayo;
el esposo de Adelita
del cual nació el "CHE"
que se llama Ernesto.
       leonel rugama
       gozó de la tierra prometida
       en el mes más crudo de la siembra
       sin más alternativa que la lucha.

6 / Cardenal / **Oráculo sobre Managua**

       Sin más alternativa que la muerte.
Entraste a la clandestinidad
       o como vos dijiste, las Catacumbas.
Las noches en que todas las luces son sospechosas
noches durmiendo vestido en el piso de una casa vacía
con la M-3 al lado
atisbar de puntillas tras la persiana con la pistola montada
       (se ven fantasmas por todos lados decía Julio)
y es sólo una pareja haciendo el amor dentro de un carro.
       También Julio dijo
¿Vos crees que me dejaré coger vivo de esos hijoeputas?
Alguna vez tal vez guerrilleras con radio oyendo rock.
       Fue después del asalto al Banco de América.
Selim Shible, Silvio, Casimiro, Julio, habían caído.

brother of Juan Gregorio Colindres
and of Miguel Angel Ortez
and of Juan Umanzor
and of Francisco Estrada
and of Sócrates Sandino
and of Ramón Raudales
and of Rufus Marín
and when he spoke he said:
"Our cause will prevail
for it is the cause of justice,
for it is the cause of love."
and other times he said:
"I will seek death
with the few who go with me
for it is better to die as rebels
than to live as slaves."
Sandino begat Bayo;
husband of Adelita
to whom was born "CHE"
who is called Ernesto.
leonel rugama
rejoiced in the promised land
in the cruelest month of planting
with no choice but to join the struggle.

6 / Cardenal / **Oracle on Managua**

With no choice but to die.
You joined the underground
or as you put it, the Catacombs.
The nights when every light is suspect
nights sleeping dressed on the floor of an empty house
with the M-3 at your side
to peek tiptoeing behind the venetian blind with the pistol cocked
(one sees ghosts everywhere Julio said)
and it's only a couple making love in a car.
Julio also said
Do you think I'll let the motherfuckers catch me alive?
Sometime perhaps guerrilla women with a radio listening to rock.
Then came the assault on the Bank of America.
Selim Shible, Silvio, Casimiro, Julio, had fallen.

7 / Francisco Santos / Leonel Rugama

Una tarde Leonel me recomendó
 – para la flacura – hacer ejercicios
aclarándome que no se trataba de
   "ejercicios espirituales"
hablamos acerca de las muchachas
que iban o venían del trabajo o del colegio
de las que entraban o salían de una tienda
de zapatos
de otra que pasaba vendiendo chancho
también me leyó un poema sobre una guerrillera Vietnamita
Ahora – otra tarde – que veo su cuerpo acribillado
por la G.N. en la foto de un diario
recuerdo que José Coronel Urtecho
una vez me dijo: "los poetas no sirven para nada"

8 / Cardenal / Oráculo sobre Managua

NIDO SANDINISTA DEMOLIDO A METRALLA Y CAÑONAZOS
Eran tres. 18, 19 y 20 años.
El mayor eras vos. Agentes de Seguridad llegaron
a la casa celeste frente al Cementerio Oriental
la mamá de Efrén gritó: "¡La guardia!"
    la primera ráfaga y caen dos guardias
más patrullas, y más ráfagas de ametralladoras guerrilleras
y caen más guardias, fuego de rifles garand
              empiezan a llegar refuerzos
jeeps buses de la Jefatura del Tránsito jeepone
del Batallón de Combate carros de oficiales camiones
de la Seguridad más guardias con rifles o ametralladoras
cienes de espectadores viendo el combate como en un cine
una avioneta volaba sobre la casa, más alto un helicóptero
el sonido de las balas contra las paredes de la casa
adentro vivas a Sandino
a las 4 llega una tanqueta disparando cañonazos
nube de polvo sobre la casa cuando disparaba la tanqueta
    algo comenzó a humear
. . .
    Las balas de la avioneta contra el techo de zinc
las balas haciendo volar las hojas de los árboles   ►

7 / Francisco Santos / **Leonel Rugama**

One afternoon Leonel told me
to build myself up with exercises
adding that he didn't mean "spiritual" ones
we talked about the girls
who came or went from work or school
of those who entered or left a shoestore
of another who passed by selling food
and then he read me a poem about
    a guerrilla fighter from Vietnam
Now, another afternoon, seeing
a newsphoto of his body
bullet-torn by the National Guard
I remember José Coronel Urtecho once
saying to me: "poets are good for nothing."

8 / Cardenal / **Oracle on Managua**

SANDINISTA NEST DEMOLISHED BY GUNFIRE AND HEAVY
                                     ARTILLERY
There were three. 18, 19, and 20 years old.
The eldest was you. Security Agents arrived
at the sky-blue house across from the East Cemetery
Efrin's mother yelled "The Guard!"
    the first round of fire and two guards fall
more patrols, and more rounds of fire from the guerrilla machine
                                      guns
and more guards fall, shots from garand rifles
                 reinforcements begin to arrive
jeeps busses from Traffic Control Headquarters big jeeps
from the Combat Batallion carloads of officers trucks
from Security more guards with rifles or machine guns
hundreds of spectators watching the fighting as one might at a movie
a small plane flying over the house, higher up a helicopter
the sound of bullets against the walls of the house
inside Long Live Sandino!
at 4 p.m. a tank arrives firing its guns
clouds of dust over the house whenever the tank fired
    something began to smoke
   . . .

                                        ▶

ambulancias con sus aullidos como de animal herido
los soldados tras jeeps plomos, tras jeeps kakis
tirando a las ventanas, la casa esquinera recién pintada
color celeste, tirando y gritando que se entregaran
nuevos refuerzos por la Ave. del Cementerio Oriental
y los muchachos gritaron *Patria Libre o Morir!*
        . . .
Los chavalos gritaban a los guardias hijo-de-la-verga
y ellos los seguían con la bayoneta calada
        otros les gritaban atrás y se volvían
y vos fuiste también chavalo que jugó chibolas
que jugaba a la taba en las esquinas, ladrillete
en los ladrillos del parque, sin traer las tortillas
        – Otro cañonazo más y más disparos adentro.
La tuya fue la 1ª etapa" (destrucción)
        que tiene siempre, decías, un "matiz" de dolor
Suenan tiros del interior, más
balazos de rifles garand contra la casa
pasa otra vez la avioneta
        otra vez el traca-traca de las ametralladoras
        sin más alternativa que la muerte
cerca de tu plazuela de chavalo donde jugabas chibolas
        . . .
Otro cañonazo de la tanqueta del Batallón Blindado
        casi sin contestación del interior
Allá están los reportajes y las fotos
la canción de gesta fue un periódico que se llevó el viento.
        La casa ya toda acribillada a balazos y cañonazos
ahora tiroteo esporádico
        tiros desde el interior (débiles)
Plap. . . Plap. . . Plap. . . Silencio. Otra granada
        Y grita un militar: "¡Ríndanse que están cercados!"
allí fue que gritaste dicen
        Que se rinda tu madre!
y ya eran miles los espectadores viendo la película
pueblo, montón de pueblo, el pueblo por el que morían
"La avioneta señor bañaba la casita de arriba abajo"
Los muchachitos de Chola Paz corrieron desnuditos a la calle
        Y la otra que dijo que creyó que eran triquitracas
pero vio la guardia. . .
        . . .

The bullets from the small plane against the zinc roof
the bullets making the leaves of the trees fly
ambulances screaming like a wounded animal
the soldiers behind lead-grey jeeps, behind khaki jeeps
shooting at the windows, the corner house recently painted
sky-blue, shooting and yelling for them to surrender
new reinforcements through Cementerio Oriental Avenue
and the young men yelling *Free Homeland or Death!*
        . . .
the young kids yelled at the guards son-of-a-bitch
and they followed them with fixed bayonets
        others yelled at them from behind and they turned back
and you too were a kid who played marbles
and who pitched pennies on the corners, hopscotch
on the tiles in the park, forgetting to bring the tortillas
        — Another tank shell more and more shots from within.
Yours was the "1st stage" (destruction)
        that had always, you would say, been "colored" by pain
One hears shots from within, more
shots from garand rifles against the house
the small plane flies over again
        again the rat-tat-tat-tat-tat of the machine guns
                with no choice but to die
near the little plaza of your youth where you played marbles
        . . .
Another shell from the tank of the Armored Batallion
        almost without response from within
There are the articles and the photographs
the epic song — a newspaper blown away in the wind
        The house already torn apart by bullets and shells
now sporadic shooting
                shots from within (weak)
Bang. . . Bang. . . Bang. . . Silence. Another grenade
        And a soldier yells out: "Surrender! We have you sur-
                                        rounded!"
which is, they say, when you yelled back
        Let your mother surrender!
And finally there were thousands of onlookers watching the movie
people, tons of people, the people for whom they died
"The plane sir it bathed the house from head to toe"
Chola Paz's kids went running out into the street stark naked   ▶

Hasta el atardecer la guardia ocupó la casa
. . .
Los centenares de guardias comenzaron a guardar sus armas
Puertas destrozadas hierros retorcidos techo de zinc
perforado por la avioneta las paredes con grandes huecos
sangre en el patio un colchón ensangrentado en el baño
pedazos de camisas calzonetas pañuelos llenos de sangre
sangre en la cocina los frijoles regados tapas de porras
con goterones de sangre en el patio la casa llena de humo —

9 / Octavio Robleto / **Elegía por el guerrillero**

Al siguiente día de tu muerte
yo anduve por las calles de Managua muy apesarado
me fijaba bien en los rostros que encontraba
y a todos los veía indiferentes
como si nada hubiera sucedido.

Y pensar que tu vida era para el pueblo!

Para las muchachas que platican
para los hombres en las calles
para los policías que dirigen el tránsito
y para los guardias nacionales!

Conversé con algunos profesores y estudiantes
y me dijeron haberte conocido
¡Ah, sólo eso,
y tal vez alguna anécdota trivial!

En verdad, de tu persona sabíamos muy poco:
un muchacho tímido, un estudiante que escribía
y de tu poesía es menos lo que se conoce!

Sin embargo tu figura irá creciendo
tus puños se irán poniendo duros
y tu poesía será esparcida como maíz en tierra fertil.

And the other woman who said she thought it was firecrackers
but she saw the Guard. . .
    . . .
        Until sundown the Guard occupied the house
    . . .
The hundreds of guards began to stack their weapons
Smashed doors twisted iron bars zinc roof
perforated by the plane big holes in the walls
blood in the patio a bloody mattress in the bathroom
bits of shirts underpants handkerchiefs soaked in blood
blood in the kitchen the beans full of it the greens too
gobs of blood in the patio the house filled with smoke —

9 / Octavio Robleto / Elegy for the Guerrilla Fighter

The day after your death
I rushed through the streets of Managua
I stared hard at the faces I met
and found them all indifferent
as if nothing had happened.

And to think that your life was for the people!

For the girls who talk together
for the men in the streets
for the police directing traffic
and for the national guards.

I talked with some professors and students
they told me they had known you
Just that
and maybe some small anecdote.

The truth is, we knew so little about you:
a shy kid, a student who wrote poems,
and of your poetry what's known is even less!

But word of you, your grip on us,
will grow
And your words will spread
like grain in fertile ground.

10 / Michele Najlis / **A Leonel Rugama**

Sólo el tamaño de tu palabra que comenzaba a ser sabíamos.
Nada sabíamos entonces de la línea que trazaría tu muerte.
Ahora pienso que es inútil evocar las tertulias en La Prensa o en
La India donde apenas nos vimos, o la única vez que llegaste a
enseñarme tus primeros poemas. Un día nos contaste de un tío
tuyo que terminó trastornándose, y que vivía en Macondo con
algún Momotombo al fondo. Luego supimos que contestaste
¡QUE SE RINDA TU MADRE! y que ya herido seguías
disparando.

11 / Najlis /
Ahora que andas por los caminos de la Patria

Ahora que andas por los caminos de la Patria
con el corazón en todo el cuerpo.
Ahora,
con las piernas en el barro
y el fusil — más tarde arado —
junto a tu espalda fuerte.
Ahora,
tal vez de día
tal vez de noche,
piensa que el pueblo es tu victoria
y lucha contigo.

12 / Roberto Vargas /
Homenaje a la tercera manifestación de Delano

Con el Espíritu de Che y Sandino
Manifestándonos ya contra la explotación
Manifestándonos ya contra la mierda y la frustración

194

10 / Michele Najlis / **To Leonel Rugama**

We knew only the size of your word which was beginning to be.
We knew nothing then of the line your death would draw. Now
I think it useless to evoke the get-togethers at *La Prensa* or *La
India* where we hardly saw each other, or the one time you
finally showed me your first poems. One day you told us about
an uncle of yours who wound up going mad, and who lived in
Macondo with the Momotombo Volcano in the background.
Then we found out that you answered LET YOUR MOTHER
SURRENDER! and that, wounded, you kept firing.

11 / Najlis /
Now as You Walk Along the Roads of Your Country

Now as you walk along the roads of your country,
heart bursting out of your body.
Now,
with your legs in the mud
and your rifle – someday a plow –
borne on your strong back.
Now,
perhaps by day
perhaps by night,
remember that the people are your victory
and your fight is theirs.

12 / Roberto Vargas /
Homage to the Third March on Delano

With the Spirit of Che and Sandino
Now Marching Against Exploitation
Now Marching Against Shit and Frustration

13 / Macfield / **Uníos**

Unámonos
juntemos brazos para dar el golpe
juntemos fuerzas para alzar la voz.

Juntemos cenizas
y hagamos cuenta de todo lo perdido.

Han pasado frente a nuestras puertas
ante nuestros ojos
hacia la muerte
solos, solos,
tristes, muertos ya de soledad
y tristes.

Unámonos
juntemos ilusiones
y ansias de tempestad.

Que todos seamos como un hormiguero.

Juntemos ponzoña con ponzoña
dolor con dolor
duelo con duelo;
y afinemos el hocico,
afinemos el oído
afinemos la puntería de nuestras palabras.

Unámonos.

Están alzando paredes hasta el cielo contra nosotros.

Nos han cercado el paso por todos lados
y es contra nosotros que apuntan sus armas.

Cabalgan por las noches acechándonos, fichándonos,
pinchándonos, visitándonos inesperadamente,
inoportunamente, calladamente.
Han afilado sus colmillos contra nosotros
presupuestándonos, educándonos, amaestrándonos,
amonestándonos, acariciándonos, violándonos,
y a costa de nuestro dolor
están haciendo sus fiestas.

Yo busco luz en la noche,   ►

Unite
join arms to strike the blow
join forces to raise our voice.

Join ashes
and measure all that we have lost.

They have passed before our doors
before our eyes
toward death
alone, alone,
desolate, already dead in their loneliness
and sad.

Unite
together we will forge our dreams
and our longing for the storm.

Let us live together like an anthill.

Mixing venom with venom
pain with pain
mourning with mourning;
and sharpening our teeth,
sharpening our ears
sharpening the arrows of our words.

Unite.

They are raising walls to the sky against us.

They have cut off the pass on every side
and it is against us that they aim their arms.

They ride through the night stalking us, watching us,
harrassing us, visiting us unexpectedly,
without warning, silently.
They have sharpened their fangs against us
budgeting us, educating us, taming us,
threatening us, caressing us, raping us,
and with the wages of our pain
they pay for their parties.

I search for light in the night,

▶

gritos para amanecer;
sólo una llama que arde
otra llama que se enciende
otra llama que se apaga.

Yo busco luz en la noche.

Unámonos.

Juntemos brazo para dar el golpe
juntemos fuerza para alzar la voz.

Un grano de arena, y otro grano de arena,
un grano de arena más, y otro grano de arena,
y otro grano de arena y otro y otro y otro.

Una luz en la noche y otra luz en la noche y otra luz
y otra y otra y otra.
Yo he querido valor
y harto miedo me han dado,
harto miedo y soledad,

> una llama y otra llama que pasan como fantasmas
> pasan frente a nuestras puertas
> frente a nuestros ojos. Solos. Muertos de soledad.

Una llama y otra llama.

Encendamos la noche
pongamos el llano en llamas
pongamos el llanto en llamas
pongamos la noche en llamas. . .
y por güevo tiene que amanecer.

Un grano de arena. . . Otro grano de arena.
Otro grano de arena.
Y otro y otro y otro.

Unámonos
granos de arena,
chispas sueltas por Sodoma.

Juntemos brazos para dar el golpe.
Juntemos fuerzas para alzar la voz.

cries to awaken;
just one burning flame
here a flame is lit
there another is dying.

I search for light in the night.

Unite.

Join arms to strike the blow
join forces to raise our voice.

One grain of sand, and another grain of sand,
one more grain of sand, and another grain of sand,
and another grain of sand and another and another and another.

One light in the night and another light in the night and another
light
and another and another and another.
I wanted courage
and they filled me with fear,
with fear and loneliness,

> one flame and another flame that pass by like ghosts
> that pass in front of our doors
> in front of our eyes. Alone. Dead from loneliness.

One flame and another flame.

Let us set fire to the night
let the plain burst into flames
the wailing rise up in flames
the night crackle with flames. . .
and by god the dawn must break.

One grain of sand. . . Another grain of sand.
Another grain of sand.
And another and another and another.

Unite
grains of sand,
sparks scattered throughout Sodom.

Join arms to strike the blow.
Join forces to raise our voice.

14 / Cardenal / Canto nacional

Decía que desovan las iguanas. . . Es el proceso. Ellas
(o las ranas) en el silencioso carbonífero
        emitieron el primer sonido
    la primera canción de amor sobre la tierra
    la primera canción de amor bajo la luna
        es el proceso
El proceso viene desde los astros
    Nuevas relaciones de producción: eso
también es el proceso. Opresión. Tras la opresión, la liberación.
La Revolución empezó en las estrellas, a millones
    de años de luz. El huevo de la vida
        es uno. Desde
el primer huevo de gas, al huevo de iguana, al hombre nuevo.
Sandino se gloriaba de haber nacido del 'vientre de los oprimidos'
        (el de una indita de Niquinohomo)
Del vientre de los oprimidos nacerá la Revolución.
Es el proceso.
Entre los alcatraces el macho hincha el buche para el cortejo
    luego coge a la hembra.
El proceso es más todavía:
el Che después de muerto sonreía como recién salido del Hades.

"El Paraíso de Mahoma" que dijo Gages
    les cuento que el Paraíso ha sido vendido.

15 / Neruda / Salud, capitán del continente

Hay un suspiro prolongado
en la tierra del banano
suspiro de retorno. . .
porque ha vuelto el guerrillero
a musitar un nombre:
Sandino, Sandino, Sandino.

200

14 / Cardenal / **National Song**

I said that iguanas spawn. . . It's the process. They
(or the frogs) in the carboniferous silence
        emitted the first sound
        the first love song over the earth
        the first love song under the moon
        it's the process
The process emanates from the stars
        New relations of production: that
too is the process. Oppression. After oppression, liberation.
The Revolution began in the stars, millions
        of light years away. The egg of life
        is one. From
the first gaseous egg, to the egg of the iguana, to the new man.
Sandino boasted of having been born from 'the belly of the
                                                oppressed'
        (from a Niquinohomo Indian woman)
From the belly of the oppressed will be born the Revolution.
It's the process.
Among the pelicans the male's chest swells in courtship
        afterwards he takes the female.
There's more to the process yet:
in death Che smiled as if he had just left Hell.

"Mahoma's Paradise" said Gages
        I tell you that Paradise has been sold out.

15 / Neruda / **Hail, Captain of the Continent**

A deep sigh heaves
throughout banana lands
a sigh of return. . .
for the guerrilla has begun again
to murmur a name:
Sandino, Sandino, Sandino.

201

Cardenal / ORÁCULO SOBRE MANAGUA

Entramos a la Pascua de la Revolución.
Tras el bombardeo de palabras y de bombas
   la lenta venta de vidas (horas/meses/años)
saboteada la fecundidad y la belleza saboteada
tras el terror en las calles llenas de radiopatrullas
   la Central Intelligence Agency
   anquilostomiasis y equisistomosis
la United Fruit frondosa como un cedro del Líbano
incendio de ranchos, la bota sobre el vientre encinta
   y base-ball para que olvide el pueblo
(éste es el misterio pascual de la revolución)
renaceremos juntos como hombres y como mujeres.
   Se vuelve crisálida y a la
      crisálida le salen alas

Part 4

Cardenal / ORACLE ON MANAGUA

We are approaching the Easter of the Revolution.
After the avalanche of words and bombs
      the slow sale of lives (hours/months/years)
sabotaged fertility and beauty sabotaged
after the terror of streets filled with patrol cars
        the Central Intelligence Agency
      anquilostomiasis and equisistomosis
the United Fruit fruitful like a cedar of Lebanon
ranch burnings, the boot in the pregnant belly
      and baseball so the people will forget
(this is the Easter mystery of the revolution)
we will be reborn together as men and women.
      We become chrysalis and from the
              chrysalis burst forth wings

The March Toward Victory
Cannot Be Stopped (1970-1979)

Part Four takes us into the final stage of the revolutionary struggle. The poetry of this period is evidence of the faith in victory and the blending of poetic activity with the writing of proclamations and the waging of war. We see the emergence of revolutionary women who, in many cases, are also poets. Doris María Tijerino, a fighter, and Michele Najlis, a poet-activist, are already important figures in the '60s; to this list must be added numerous Sandinista women, some in positions of leadership, as well as women poets like Gioconda Belli, Judith Reyes and Christian Santos. The active presence of the women is symptomatic of a broadening of the base and of the revolutionary perspective which will ultimately lead to victory.

At the same time that the nexus between revolutionary dream and reality is being forged, a paradox emerges; these poems, together with Cardenal's early epigrams and almost all of Pablo Antonio Cuadra's work, are the most intensely lyrical ones in the entire collection. It is a lyricism of a special kind, blending revolutionary fervor and longing for the future, with a pragmatic assessment of everyday problems and a consciousness of military tactics.

The first section tells of the persecution and imprisonment of those who did not die in the repression of 1969 and 1970. Ricardo Morales Avilés writes poetry centered on the figure of Doris María Tijerino. Morales speaks of the pain of their separation, the imminence of his death, and of international solidarity. These are poems written in jail on bits of paper, probably between torture sessions and certainly under the cover of darkness. In these conditions, he reaffirms his unity with Doris María, with Nicaragua, with the millions who, like them, believe in liberation.

The second section describes the earthquake of 1972 and compares it with the decades of social catastrophe resulting from the Somoza regime. In a series of word-plays, Cardenal shows us Pepsi Cola on the ground, the American embassy on its knees, the Security Building toppling. Carlos Mejía Godoy invents an Everyman out of the dispossessed masses and calls him Panchito Rubble. All the poets allude to the overseas aid monopolized by Somoza and divided up between the National Guard and the politicians. Pablo Antonio Cuadra dramatizes the robbery with a poem in the form of a dialogue between a mother and her son.

The third section develops the theme of family relations conditioned by the dictatorship. It concentrates on the separations of parents in exile from their children, and the responsibility of the parents to change reality so that they may give successive generations the legacy of a better world. Nicaragua means pain. Belli borrows a metaphor from Cardenal to speak of cries of pain, "like pangs of birth." Exploitation continues; torture continues. But the will of the people becomes stronger as Edwin Castro's "tomorrow" becomes Francisco de Asís Fernández's "today."

The fourth section returns to the fury of the struggle in order to denounce the military tactics of imperialism and its aggression against the people of Nicaragua. First CONDECA, then Operation Eagle Z. The poets write to honor their fallen comrades. Belli remembers Eduardo Contreras (Comandante Marcos), who seemed indestructible. Then Carlos Fonseca Amador falls, and after the Sandinista uprisings of 1977, the whole community of Solentiname. But Carlos Fonseca and the spirit of Pancasán live on, as new leaders come forward. Everywhere a word, a concept, emerges: VENCEREMOS. As Carlos Mejía Godoy says, "the cornfields are blooming, and it's harvest time."

In the fifth section, the opposition to Somoza becomes a universal clamor. Pedro Joaquín Chamorro is assassinated; the massacre of Monimbó takes place. The guards attack, but the Front counterattacks; fire is answered with fire. The poets sing of revolutionary tactics, of protracted struggle against interminable terror, until finally we see the expression of the people's will in Belli's beautiful poem urging a massive general strike against the regime.

The poetry of section six brings us to the very threshold of victory. The excitement and longing to move forward pulse against the need to look back and remember the fallen comrades. "We will go wake the dead," cries Belli, and together they will share in the new Nicaragua, a free Nicaragua. The revolutionaries write proclamations urging the people onward; the proclamations are poetry. Cardenal gives us his vision of the great peasant cooperatives, the literacy campaign, and everyone sharing in the fruit of their labor. The spirit of Sandino has prevailed. A new dawn is beginning.

Sección 1
Prisión y tortura, muerte y esperanza:
Los sobrevivientes de los años 60

1 / R. Morales Avilés / **Doris María, Camarada**

Vengo, camarada, con las manos llenas
del polvo de esta tierra, sobre los hombros
cargando los dolores de este pueblo.
Vengo hasta tí
con el alma sudando todo el odio
porque alguien inventó la esclavitud,
cogió su arma
y alguien más tuvo hambre y frío
y se empezaron a morir nuestros hermanos,
nuestros padres y nuestros hijos.

Vengo cantando
y hay dolores trenzados con la piel de mi cuerpo.
Tú me comprendes, camarada,
porque también te pesan estos crepúsculos
que nos han echado encima.

Vengo jubiloso
para juntar a tu cruzada
la audacia de mi brazo fuerte.
La lucha está difícil. Y hay que seguir
adelante y cuesta. Cuesta arriba.
Todo el que anda derecho
tiene en su haber una sonrisa y una onza de plomo.
No hay otra manera de contar la historia.

El fusil para todos,
lágrimas, flores y recuerdos para todos.
Hay que seguir entonces,
la historia tiene un solo sentido.
Y hay siempre y cada vez nuevas espadas
y una vieja manera de levantar la frente.

Section 1
Prison and Torture, Death and Hope:
Those Who Survived the 1960s

1 / R. Morales Avilés / **Doris María, Comrade**

I come, comrade, with my hands full
of the dust of this land, carrying on my shoulders
the sorrows of this people.

I come to you
with my soul sweating hatred
because someone invented slavery,
took up his weapon
and left someone else hungry and cold
and our brothers, our parents,
our children began to die.

I come singing
and there are sorrows braided with the skin of my body.
You understand me, comrade
because these twilights which they threw
on our shoulders also weigh on you.

I come joyfully
to join the daring of my strong arm
to your crusade.
The struggle is hard. We have to keep moving ahead,
and it's an uphill struggle.
Whoever walks straight has in his power
a smile and an ounce of lead.
There's no other way to tell the story.

A rifle for all,
tears, flowers and memories for all.
So we have to keep moving,
history has only one direction.
And each and every time there are new swords
and the old way of holding our head high.

2 / Najlis / **Nos persiguieron en la noche**

Nos persiguieron en la noche,
nos acorralaron
sin dejarnos más defensa que nuestras manos
unidas a millones de manos unidas.
Nos hicieron escupir sangre,
nos azotaron,
llenaron nuestros cuerpos con descargas eléctricas
y nuestras bocas las llenaron de cal.
Nos dejaron noches enteras junto a las fieras,
nos arrojaron en sótanos sin tiempo,
nos arrancaron las uñas.
Con nuestra sangre cubrieron hasta sus tejados,
hasta sus propios rostros,
pero nuestras manos
siguen unidas a millones de manos unidas!

Los inocentes alzaron los fusiles y los cuerpos caídos;
los inocentes se alzaron como un sol que no se oculta;
los inocentes clamaron
y su clamor fue oído por multitud de pueblos,
sangraron
y su sangre regó toda la tierra;
los inocentes despertaron de la muerte, y se despertar
fue el comienzo de la vida:
volvieron a crecer los ríos con el agua que acumula cada vida,
el aire llegó hecho canción de amor
y canción de cuna,
las madres tejieron los combates de sus hijos,
las esposas salieron frente al alba para ver nacer al pueblo,
los niños amasaron con fuego sus cuerpos de barro
y lucharon con sus cuerpos y con los de sus padres
y en cada victoria nació un hijo
y cada hijo engendró una nueva victoria
y las victorias y los hijos retoñaron en el árbol de las generaciones.

2 / Najlis / **They Pursued Us in the Night**

They pursued us in the night,
they surrounded us
leaving us no more defense than our hands
united to a million united hands.
They made us spit up blood,
they whipped us;
they racked our bodies with electric charges
and filled our mouths with lime.
They left us whole nights with wild beasts
they cast us into dark timeless cellars
they tore out our fingernails.
They covered the rooftops, even their own faces
with our blood,
but our hands
remain united to millions of united hands.

The innocents raised their rifles and their fallen comrades;
the innocents rose up in arms like a sun that can't be concealed;
the innocents cried out
and their cry was heard by a multitude of peoples,
they bled
and their blood irrigated the entire land;
the innocents awoke from death, and their awakening
was the beginning of life:
the rivers began to rise with the water each life accumulates
the air became a song of love
a cradle song,
the mothers embroidered the battles of their children
wives came out at dawn to see a people born
children molded clay bodies with fire
and fought with their bodies and with the bodies of their fathers
and each victory gave birth to a son
and each son engendered a new victory
and the victories and the sons blossomed again in the tree of gen-
                                                                erations.

3 / Guadamuz / **Cinco años de cárcel**

Cinco años en la cárcel
son cinco años de no ver
               no oír
               no hablar.
De aprender a tragar saliva
de mil formas diferentes.
De no ver nunca una puesta de sol
               o una salida
               una luna llena
               o la estrella polar.
Cinco años en los que el sexo se vuelve un misterio
               un cuerpo de mujer un sueño
               un beso algo imposible
y hasta se olvida cõmo se hace el amor.
Cinco años teniendo como universo una celda.
Cinco años con la mochila al hombro
               − siempre lista −
Cinco años de saber esperar.

4 / R. Morales Avilés / **Nos-otros**

Qué importancia pueden tener el tiempo y el espacio.
La distancia entre uno y otro punto.
Los otros que nos siguen, los lazos que nos unen a ellos
la certidumbre de la lucha el amor la vida,
otros verán el movimiento del futuro
otros verán el nacimiento de otras islas
               grandes y pequeñas
de aquí a cincuenta años
a la luz del sol rojo que acaba de salir
o quizás sean cien o doscientos o muchos más años
otros contemplarán el crecimiento de las espigas.
Nosotros otros una y muchas generaciones.
Así que no importan el tiempo y el espacio
si de un punto a otro los recorre el movimiento.

3 / Guadamuz / **Five Years in Jail**

Five years in jail
are five years without seeing
           without hearing
           without speaking.
Of learning how to gulp down your saliva
in a thousand different ways.
Of never seeing a sunset
           or a way out
           a full moon
           or the north star.
Five years in which sex becomes a mystery
           a woman's body a dream
           a kiss something impossible
and you even forget how to make love.
Five years in which your cell becomes the whole universe.
Five years with a knapsack on your back
           – always ready –
Five years of knowing how to wait.

4 / R. Morales Avilés / **We-others**

What do time and space matter,
the distance between one point and another.
The others who follow us, the ties that unite us to them
the certainty of the struggle, love, life
others will see the movement of the future
others will see the birth of other islands
           large and small
fifty years from now
in the red sunlight of a new dawn
or perhaps a hundred, two hundred, many years away
others will contemplate the growing stalks of grain
We-others, one and many generations.
So time and space don't matter
if the movement flows from one point to another.

5 / R. Morales Avilés / **Poema para los dolores de tu cuerpo**

. . .no existe significación para la calumnia
ni para las ofensas a tu cuerpo
robado,
ultrajado,
pero sí la caliza de tu ejemplo que construye
no sólo a un pueblo, sino
da cuerpo a la esperanza.
Doris María,
recuérdate que vamos a seguir juntando tristezas
y allegándonos dolores.
Recuérdame que aún nos falta caminar de noche
para llegar en la mañana sobre la luz cantando,
y es bueno estar despiertos
y dar la bienvenida al dolor para gritar
y tener prisa
y darnos crecimiento.

6 / R. Morales Avilés / **Carta mínima a mi mujer**

Si me matan, quiero que sepan que he vivido
en lucha por la vida y por el hombre.
Un mundo de todos para todos.

Si me matan, una rosa roja
modelo de mi corazón
es el amor que te dejo.

Si me matan, es igual.
No veré el maíz a la orilla de todos los caminos
ni el rastro de ternura para los pies descalzos
pero sé que vendrá.

Si me matan, no importa
nuestra causa seguirá viviendo
otros la seguirán.

El porvenir es brillante.

5 / R. Morales Avilés / Poem for the Aches of Your Body

. . .there is no meaning in slander
nor in the violations of your body
raped,
outraged,
but there is meaning in the force of your example that
not only builds a people,
but embodies hope.
Doris María,
remember that we will continue to gather up sorrows
and to collect pain.
Remind me that we must still walk in the night
in order to reach the morning light singing,
and it's good to be awake
and to welcome pain in order to shout
and to hurry
and to grow.

6 / R. Morales Avilés / Brief Letter to My Wife

If they kill me, I want them to know that I lived
struggling for life and humanity.
A world of all for all.

If they kill me, a red rose
model of my heart
is the love I leave you.

If they kill me, it's all the same.
I won't see the corn bordering all the roads
or the tender furrow for the naked feet
but I know it will come.

If they kill me, it doesn't matter
our cause will live on
others will rally to it.

The future is bright.

7 / Francisco de Asís Fernández / **A sangre fría**

Llamaba a Nicaragua una página blanca sin cumplir,
datada y cifrada
escriturada sobre la crueldad y el martirio,
sombradía y montaraz.
Sobre la letra lo prometido para el que pueda leerla:
familia, barrio, periódico, fauce de bestia.
Atrévete tú compañero:
a él lo mataron a sangre fría.

8 / Carlos Mejía Godoy / **No se me raje mi compa**

Me contaba el otro día
el que torturó a Ricardo
me daban miedo las chispas
de sus grandes ojos claros
jamás pudimos sacarle
más palabras que las mismas:
"Soy y seré militante
de la causa Sandinista"

9 / R. Morales Avilés / **Doris María, Camarada**

Somos muchos, camarada. Somos millones.
Nuestro grito recorre la piedra vertebral
de nuestra América,
piedra del mundo para juntarse después de la
montaña.
Este país se levantó con el sol del mediodía
y le damos la bienvenida a la mañana guerrillera.

Somos millones, Doris María de Nicaragua,
muchacha combatiente del pueblo,
geografía de nuestros campos, de nuestras costas
y de nuestros ríos.
Somos millones y desde pequeños estamos soñando
y la insistencia vuelve otra vez a retoñarnos.

Somos millones y tú eres bandera y escudo,
chispa y camino,
ejemplo y llave,
Doris María, camarada.

7 / Francisco de Asís Fernández / In Cold Blood

He called Nicaragua a blank page falling due,
dated and coded
notarized by cruelty and martyrdom
darkness and bestiality.
Above the signature, the promise for whoever can read it:
family, *barrio,* newspaper, jaw of the beast.
Risk it, comrade:
Him they killed in cold blood.

8 / Carlos Mejía Godoy / Don't Let Me Down, Comrade

The one who tortured Ricardo
told me the other day
I was frightened by the sparks
that flew from his large bright eyes
we could never get from him
any words but these:
"I am and always will be
a militant *Sandinista.* "

9 / R. Morales Avilés / Doris María, Comrade

We are many, comrade. We are millions.
Our cry runs through the spinal rock
of our America.
Rock of the world, joining together beyond the
mountain.
This country rose up with the noonday sun
and we welcome the dawn of the guerrilla fighter.

We are millions, Doris María of Nicaragua,
fighting woman of the people,
geography of our fields, of our coasts,
and of our rivers.
We are millions and we have been dreaming since childhood
and tenacity makes us blossom again.

We are millions and you are flag and shield,
spark and path,
example and key,
Doris María, comrade.

Sección 2
El terremoto

1 / Cardenal / **Viaje a Nueva York**

. . ."Nuestra Sistema
Señor, que agrava esas catástrofes. . ." (Y pienso: Los Somoza
un terremoto de 40 años). . .

2 / P. A. Cuadra / El hermano mayor

María, hermana, te cuento
¡fué el acabóse! Se vino
al suelo todo
      y quedamos
en la calle con lo puesto.
Los doce hermanos temblando
y mamá
queriéndose hacer brazos
para rodearnos a todos.
A esa hora, ahogándonos
en polvo, oyendo
el estertor del mundo.

3 / Rogelio Sinán / Acertijo nicaragüense

Señor Vicario, dígame, si le cuadra,
¿nuestro gran terremoto
no fue algo más jodido
que el bíblico pasaje
de Somoza y Gomorra?

Section 2
The Earthquake

1 / Cardenal / Journey to New York

...."Our System
Lord, that agravates these catastrophes..." (And I think: The Somozas
a 40-year-long earthquake)...

2 / P. A. Cuadra / The Older Brother

María, my sister, I tell you
it was the limit! Everything
fell to the ground
        and we were left
in the street with the clothes on our back.
The twelve brothers trembling
and mother
wanting to put her arms
around all of us.
In that moment, we drowned
in dust, hearing
the death rattle of the world.

3 / Rogelio Sinán / Nicaraguan Riddle

Tell me, Mr. Vicar,
if you please,
wasn't our great earthquake worse
than the Biblical story
of Somoza and Gomorrah?

4 / Cardenal / **Oráculo sobre Managua**

Ahora desde el seminario se mira otra Managua
unos segundos y todo el orgullo se fue a la mierda
cascarones de casas como huevos podridos y quemados
paredes ahumadas
         ventanas como cuencas sin ojos
rodeada de inmensa alambrada de campo de concentración
su cadáver en descomposición que se deshace en pedazos
     zopilotes sobre el City Bank
Otra Managua: manzanas y manzanas y manzanas ¡planas!
     "He aquí que hago nuevas todas las cosas"
pisos pegados unos con otros como naipes
sobre escombros de un nightclub un resto de rótulo
                     LA DIVERSIÓN - - -
un gran anuncio de televisor sobre otras ruinas
     Aquí estuvieron las vitrinas llenas de jugetes
        . . .un olor como a ratón muerto. . .
. . .
el rascacielo del Banco de América era una antorcha en la noche
     la Pepsi Cola en el suelo
el Gran Hotel como bombardeado por las tanquetas Sherman
la cárcel de La Aviación sin paredes ni presos ni guardianes
     la embajada de USA de rodillas
el Luis Somoza hueco tumbado en tierra hecho tucos
como un cadáver más desenterrado de las ruinas
     Allá arriba, "La Loma," ya inhabitable
la Seguridad tambaleándose sobre la laguna de Tiscapa
las salas de tortura resbalaron hacia la laguna. Rodó
hasta el agua de la laguna el gran torreón. Con una
tajada menos el pastel de bodas del Palacio Presidencial
los mensajes de Somoza en el suelo, hojeándolos el viento, con
añicos de la vajilla, la que tanto aparecía en "Novedades"
al fondo arrasados los cuarteles del Batallón de Combate
y el Batallón Blindado: aplastadas bajo concreto las tanquetas
y "Novedades" quedó hecha polvo
esa madrugada Hughes huyó
como muerciélago al que se ha jincado su escondrijo, sin
     organizar la cadena de casinos
Algo más que un movimiento de acomodación de capas terrestres.
     En la acera el 5º piso de Comunicaciones (era
                                             ►

4 / Cardenal / **Oracle on Managua**

Now from the seminary one can see another Mangua
a few seconds and all the pride turned to shit
carcasses of houses like scorched, rotten eggs
smoky walls
       windows like eye sockets without eyes
surrounded by the immense barbed wire fence of a concentra-
                          tion camp
its decomposing cadavers falling apart
       vultures over City Bank
Another Managua: blocks and blocks and blocks. Flattened!
   "Herewith I make all things new"
Floors stacked together like playing cards
over the rubble of a night club the fragment of a sign
                 ENTERTAINMENT - - -
a billboard for a television set over the ruins
       here where there were shop windows full of toys
        . . .an odor of dead mice. . .
  . . .
the skyscraper of the Bank of America was a torch in the night
       Pepsi Cola tumbled to the ground
the Grand Hotel as if bombarded by Sherman tanks
La Aviacion prison without walls without prisoners without guards
       the U.S. embassy on its knees
the statue of Luis Somoza hollow knocked down dashed to pieces
like one more cadaver unearthed from the ruins
       Over there *"La Loma,"* no longer inhabitable
la Seguridad trembling over Tiscapa Lagoon
the torture rooms fallen into the lagoon. The big tower
slid into the lagoon. One slice
gone from the wedding cake of the Presidential Palace
Somoza's speeches on the floor with the wind thumbing through
                        them,
turning the pages, with the shattered pieces of that china
which appeared so often in *Novedades*
in the background the leveled headquarters of the Combat Batallion
and the Armored Battallion: the tanks crushed under concrete
and *Novedades* now dust
that dawn Hughes flew off
like a bat poked out of its cave, without   ►

el de la censura telefónica)
partera geológica o como se llame
    esa noche los presos sandinistas salieron libres
el Palacio de Justicia oblicuo y quebrado
        los bancos dinamitados, caídos
todos los colegios religiosos − eran sólo para ricos −
los templos ¡todos! allí se celebraban ritos falsos
liturgias que a Dios le juegan el estómago.
   . . .
perdieron todas sus casas los caseros
todos igual ahora
    el subsuelo liberó su energía
        ninguno de sus amantes la consuela
ay la ciudad amada, la de la propiedad privada
tus profetas anunciaron para tí falsedad y babosadas
siguen echando al lago ladrillos televisores cajas de hierro
(los pagarés carbonizados) muebles rotos carros
todas las cosas que fabricaron los trabajadores
floreros alfombras trajes licuadoras
pero les eran vendidas como si fueran de otro
todo lo que sigue llevando el tractor tocadiscos los juguetes
imposibles de comprar registradoras caviar pesebres
    velocidad pasmosa de la evolución, esto es
un preludio telúrico de la revolución
El cuento del agrónomo que llevó a su hijita a ver el centro
   "ve hija para que no creás jamás en estas cosas"
Para Faraón y sus técnicos eran sólo 'reveses económicos'
    Y todavía nos dicen no profeticen
Estamos bajo Ley Marcial, no profeticen
Y vendrán más horrores todavía
Horas antes unos jóvenes iniciaron un ayuno en Catedral
pancartas "Comida para la gente de Acahualinca" y
    "Una nochebuena sin presos políticos"
    Dos maneras de ver una plaga:
el punto de vista de Egipto
        y el de los hebreos
  . . .
El pueblo se fue en camiones con sus trastes, sus roperos
cogió las carreteras
el pueblo nunca muere
        "Partieron en medio de lágrimas   ▶

220

putting together his chain of casinos
Something more than just an accomodating movement of terres-
trial layers.
On the sidewalk the 5th floor of Communications
(department of telephone censorship)
geologic midwife or whatever it's called
that night the *Sandinista* prisoners were free
the Palace of Justice leaning and cracked
the banks dynamited, all
the religious schools fallen — they were only for the rich —
the temples! All of them! there where they celebrated false rites
liturgies that make God sick to his stomach.
. . .
the landlords lost all of their houses
all equal now
the substrata liberated its energy
none of its lovers to console it
Oh beloved city, city of private property
your prophets prophesized falseness and stupidity
and they continue throwing bricks tv sets iron safes
(the burned up IOUs) broken furniture cars into the lake
all the things made by the workers
flowerpots carpets suits blenders
but they were sold to them as though they belonged to others
all that the tractors continue taking away record players toys
items impossible to buy cash registers caviar cribs
amazing velocity of evolution, this is
a tellurian prelude to the revolution
The story of the agronomist who took his little daughter downtown
"Child, see for yourself, so that you will never believe in
these things"
For Pharaoh and his technicians it was simply an 'economic reverse'
And they still tell us not to prophesize
We are under Martial Law, do not prophesize
And more horrors will follow
A few hours earlier some young people had started a fast in the
Cathedral
picket signs "Food for the people of Acahualinca" and
"A Christmas Eve without political prisoners"
Two ways to look at a plague:
the point of view of Egypt ►

pero los hago regresar contentos"
– Y el simbolismo de estas tiendas de campaña.
Condiciones propicias ¿para qué? (Signo de interrogación).
Con el sismo el capitalismo se hundió más en el capitalismo
La diversión de unos guardias, hacer correr a la
gente tras los camiones de alimentos, lanzando
de vez en cuando unas cuantas latas al suelo.
Medios de producción no en manos de los pocos cabrones.
¿Van a parar la marcha hacia la sociedad de promisión?
A una clase salvaré
y a otra clase perderé. Oráculo de Yavé.
Nadie sabe cuándo se realizará, dijo Lenín (el paraíso)
El pueblo está intacto
limpian los escombros y transforman la ciudad macabra
constructores de la ciudad trabajando sólo por la comida
van ya muy noche a dormir a las afueras, unas horas después
a formar otra vez los pelotones y marchar a los escombros.
Uno de 15: sólo por la comida – y le cayó la marquesina de cine.
Pero el pueblo es inmortal. Sale sonriente de la morgue.
Los vendedores de chicles de diarios los cuidadores de coches
pepenadores afiladores están en todas partes, son la *base*
si se sacuden caen los rascacielos.

5 / C. Mejía Godoy / **Panchito Escombros**

En el alboroto
de este terremoto
todo lo perdí,
perdí mi casita
que era tan bonita
de la Tenderí.   ►

and that of the Hebrews
          . . .
The people left in trucks with their belongings, their clothesracks
hit the highways
the people never die
          "They left amid tears
          but I will have them return in joy"
— And the symbolism of those camping tents.
Propitious conditions for what? (Question mark)
With the quake capitalism sank more deeply into capitalism
     The entertainment of a few guards to make people run
     after the trucks carrying food, throwing
     a few cans on the ground now and again.
The means of production not in the hands of a few sons of bitches.
Are they going to stop the march to the promised society?
          One class I shall save
               and another class I will let perish. Oracle of Yaweh.
No one knows when it shall come to pass, Lenin said (of paradise)
          The people remain whole
they clean up the ruins and transform the macabre city
builders of the city working solely for food
going to sleep late at night on the outskirts, a few hours later
back to form the platoons and march to the ruins.
One 15-year-old; solely for food — and the movie marquee fell
                                                  on him.
But the people are immortal. Leaving the morgue smiling.
Everywhere the chiclet vendors newspaper boys parking attendants
rag pickers knife sharpeners they are everywhere, they are the *base*
          if they are shaken skyscrapers fall.

5 / C. Mejía Godoy / **Panchito Rubble**

In the panic
of this earthquake
I lost everything,
I lost my little house
that was so pretty
in the town of Tenderí.   ►

223

Me puse contento
cuando supe el cuento
que iban a venir
muchas toneladas
de carne enlatada
para mi país,
pero siempre a la sardina
se la come el tiburón
y el que tiene más galillo
siempre traga más pinol.

6 / P. A. Cuadra / Letanía de los aviones

Madre, sobre el humo de los incendios desciende un avión azul. Es la ayuda del mundo. Ya llega, madre!

Hijo, el avión azul es para los señores que gobiernan.

Madre, sobre la polvareda de los escombros desciende un avión rojo. Es la ayuda del mundo. Ya llega, madre!

Hijo, el avión rojo es para los señores ministros de los señores que gobiernan.

Madre, entre las cenizas que el viento eleva baja un avión amarillo. Es la ayuda del mundo. Ya llega, madre!

Hijo, el avión amarillo es para los señores militares que guardan a los señores que gobiernan.

Madre, sobre el cielo opaco veo descender un avión verde. Es la ayuda del mundo. Ya llega, madre!

Hijo, el avión verde es para los señores funcionarios de los señores que gobiernan.

Madre, en el cielo limpio veo bajar un avión morado. Es la ayuda del mundo. Ya llega, madre!

Hijo, el avión morado es para los señores partidarios de los señores que gobiernan.

Madre, sobre el cielo del barrio veo bajar la sombra.

¡Duerme, hijo! ¡la ayuda del mundo para el pobre, es la noche!

I felt better
when they told me
they were sending
tons and tons
of canned meat
to my country,
but finders keepers
losers weepers
it's always the shark
that eats the sardine.

6 / P. A. Cuadra / Litany of the Planes

Mother, above the smoke of the fires a blue plane descends.
It is help from the world. Here it comes, mother!

Son, the blue plane is for the men who govern.

Mother, above the dust clouds of the ruins a red plane descends.
It is help from the world. Here it comes, mother!

Son, the red plane is for the ministers of the men who govern.

Mother, amidst the ashes raised by the wind, a yellow plane is
landing. It is help from the world. Here it comes, mother!

Son, the yellow plane is for the military men who guard
the men who govern.

Mother, beyond the opaque sky I see a green plane descending.
It is help from the world. Here it comes, mother!

Son, the green plane is for the officials of the men who govern.

Mother, in the clear sky I see a purple plane landing.
It is help from the world. Here it comes, mother!

Son, the purple plane is for the supporters of the men who govern.

Mother, over the sky of the *barrio* I see a shadow fall.

Sleep, my son. The help of the world for the poor is the night.

Sección 3
De las cenizas renace la esperanza

1 / Gioconda Belli / **¿Qué sos Nicaragua?**

¿Qué sos
sino dolor y polvo y gritos en la tarde,
—"gritos de mujeres, como de parto"—?

¿Qué sos
sino puño crispado y bala en boca?

¿Qué sos, Nicaragua
para dolerme tanto?

2 / Héctor Vargas / **Collage sobre despale**

¿Qué país, hijas mías, recibiréis de herencia?
¿Cómo será vuestra vida en esta tierra que avanza
sin cesar
    hacia la muerte,
sin importar a nadie su cotidiana destrucción
fecunda?
Quizás no viviré para saber la respuesta.

3 / Belli / **Ya van meses, hijita**

que no te veo.
Meses en que mi calor
no ha arrullado tu sueño.
Meses en que sólo
hemos hablado por telélfono
  — larga distancia, hay que hablar aprisa —
¿Cómo explicarte, mi amor,
la revolución a los dos años y medio? ▶

Section 3
The Rebirth of Hope out of the Ashes

1 / Gioconda Belli / **What Are You Nicaragua?**

What are you
but aches and dust and cries in the evening
– "cries of women, like pangs of birth" – ?

What are you
but clenched fist and a bullet in the mouth?

What are you
to make me ache so much?

2 / Héctor Vargas / **Wasteland Collage**

What country, my daughters, will you inherit?
What will your life be in this land that moves
incessantly
    towards death,
with no one to care about its deep daily
destruction?
Perhaps I shall not live to know the answer.

3 / Belli / **It's Been Months, My Daughter**

since I last saw you.
Months in which my warmth
has not lulled your sleep.
Months in which we've only
talked by phone
– long distance, you have to talk fast –
How can I explain the revolution to you,
my love, when you're only two and a half years old?

▶

¿Cómo decirte: Las cárceles están llenas de gente,
en las montañas el dolor arrasa poblados enteros
y hay otros niños que no escucharán ya la voz de sus madres?
¿Cómo explicarte que, a veces,
es necesario partir
porque el cerco se cierra
y tenés que dejar tu patria, tu casa, tus hijos
hasta quien sabe cuando
(pero siempre con la fe en la victoria)
¿Cómo explicarte que te estamos haciendo un país nuevo?
¿Cómo explicarte esta guerra contra el dolor,
la muerte, la injusticia?
¿Cómo explicarte tantas,
pero tantas cosas,
mi muchachita...?

4 / H. Vargas / Collage sobre despale

Por ello, flores de mi sangre, os cuento que alguna
vez hubo aquí un paraíso:
buenas aguas – decía el cronista –
maíz y legumbres
vinos que duraban un año
         . . .
tigres negros y leones y lobos
zorras y zorrillos
dantas y venados
puercos y osos hormigueros
liebres y conejos ni más ni menos como los de
España
         pero más pequeños
muchas perdices volando sobre los llanos. . .

How can I tell you: The jails are full of people,
in the mountains the pain razes whole towns
and there are other children who will never hear their mother's
                                                    voice again?
How can I explain to you that sometimes
it's necessary to go away
because the siege is closing in
and you must leave behind your country, your home, your children
until who knows when
(but always with faith in victory)
How can I explain that we're making a new country for you?
How can I explain to you this war against pain
against death and injustice?
How can I explain so many,
so many things,
my little girl. . .?

4 / H. Vargas / Wasteland Collage

That is why, flowers of my blood, I tell you that once
here there was a paradise
good waters – the chronicler said –
corn and vegetables
wines that lasted a year
        . . .
black tigers and lions and wolves
foxes and skunks
tapirs and deer
hogs and anteaters
hares and rabbits not more nor less than those of
Spain
        but smaller
many partridges flying over the plains. . .

5 / Belli / **El tiempo que no he tenido el cielo azul**

El tiempo que no he tenido el cielo azul
y sus nubes gordas de algodón en rama,
sabe que el dolor del exilio
ha hecho florecer cipreses en mi carne.
Es dolor el recuerdo de la tierra mojada,
la lectura diaria del periódico
que dice que suceden
cada vez más atrocidades,
que mueren y caen presos los amigos
que desaparecen los campesinos
como tragados por la montaña.

6 / H. Vargas / **Collage sobre despale**

Mientras tanto
la United Fruit Co. y las desmontadoras de Occidente arrasan
        los manglares del Pacífico
los jefes políticos despalan el Norte y secan el lago
de
    Apanás
los diputados y los alcaldes y demás poderosos
nos saquean el clima y el paisaje y el futuro. . .
        mientras tanto
la profesora comenta en su ancho corredor:
        "Se ha fijado que aquí todavía hay pájaros"
cuando leemos en el diario, esa misma tarde, la
exportación
            insaciable:
"12 millones 564 mil pies superficiales de pino,
166 mil pies de caoba, 421 mil pies de cedro real,
164 mil pies de guayacán, nambar y cocobolo
y 684 mil pies de otras maderas en sólo cuatro
meses,
lo que significó para las compañías una entrada de
    2 millones 719 mil dólares. . ."

230

5 / Belli / **The Time I Haven't Seen the Blue Sky**

The time I haven't seen the blue sky
and its fat cotton wool clouds
knows how the pain of exile
has made cypresses flower in my flesh.
The memory of the damp earth is pain,
and the daily reading of the newspaper
which says that more and more
atrocities take place,
that my friends are killed or captured
that the peasants disappear
as if swallowed by the mountains.

6 / H. Vargas / **Wasteland Collage**

Meanwhile
the United Fruit Co. and the bulldozers from the West wipe out
            Pacific Ocean mangrove swamps
politicos strip the North and dry out the lake
of
    Apanás
deputies and mayors and other powerful men
ransack climate and countryside and future. . .
        meanwhile
the professor comments in her narrow corridor
            "Have you noticed that there are still birds"
and that same afternoon, we read in the papers
about insatiable
            exportation:
"12 million 564 thousand surface feet of pine
166 thousand feet of mahogany, 421 thousand feet of royal cedar
164 thousand feet of guayacán, namblar and cocobolo
and 684 thousand feet of other woods in only four
months,
which for the companies meant an income of
    2 million 719 thousand dollars. . ."

7 / Fernández / En tierra propia y ajena

Detenerse y decir:
"Mañana, hijo mío, todo será distinto"
sería engañarte y detenernos.
Detenerte hoy con la promesa.
Detenernos hoy para soñar con el mañana.
Hoy es nuestro mañana.

8 / Belli / Hasta que seamos libres

Ríos me atraviesan,
montañas horadan mi cuerpo
y la geografía de este país
va tomando forma en mí,
haciéndome lagos, brechas y quebradas,
que me está abriendo como un surco,
llenándome de ganas de vivir
para verlo libre, hermoso,
pleno de sonrisas.

Quiero explotar de amor
y que mis charneles acaben con los opresores
cantar con voces que revienten mis poros
y que mi canto se contagie;
que todos nos enfermemos de amor,
de deseos de justicia,
que todos empuñemos el corazón
sin miedo de que no resista
porque un corazón tan grande como el nuestro
resiste las más crueles torturas
y nada aplaca su amor devastador
y de latido en latido
va creciendo,
más fuerte,
más fuerte,
más fuerte,   ►

7 / Fernández / **In One's Own and Foreign Land**

To stop and say:
"Tomorrow, my son, all will be different"
is to deceive you and stop us.
To stop you with a promise today.
To stop us today to dream about tomorrow.
Today is our tomorrow.

8 / Belli / **Until We're Free**

Rivers run through me
mountains bore into my body
and the geography of this country
begins forming in me
turning me into lakes, chasms, ravines
earth for sowing love
opening like a furrow
filling me with longing to live
to see it free, beautiful,
full of smiles.

I want to explode with love
and finish off my oppressors with my guts
to sing with voices that burst through my pores
and let my song be contagious;
let's all get sick with love,
with longings for justice,
let's all brandish our heart
never fearing that it will burst
for a heart the size of ours
resists the cruelest tortures
and nothing can placate its devastating love
which grows
beat by beat
stronger,
stronger,
stronger,   ►

ensordeciendo al enemigo
que lo oye brotar de todas las paredes,
lo ve brillar en todas las miradas
lo va viendo acercarse
con el empuje de una marea gigante
en cada mañana en que el pueblo se levanta
a trabajar en tierras que no le pertenecen,
en cada alarido de los padres que perdieron a sus hijos,
en cada mano que se une a otra mano que sufre.

9 / Fernández / En tierra propia y ajena

No. No debemos decir:
"Mañana, amor mío, todo será distinto"
Digamos:
"Hoy nadie podrá seguirnos,"
"no llevaremos nada en los bolsillos que pueda comprometernos"
"no hablaremos más de la cuenta"
"no hay que saber más de lo debido"
"cumpliremos por hoy lo que se nos ha encomendado."

10 / Belli / El tiempo que no he tenido el cielo azul

Es dolor,
pero se crece en canto
porque el dolor es fértil como la alegría
riega, se riega por dentro,
enseña cosas insospechadas,
enseña rabias
y viene floreciendo en tantas caras
que a punta de dolor
es seguro que pariremos
un amanecer
para esta noche larga.

deafening the enemy
who hears it break through all the walls
sees it shine in every eye
sees it coming closer
with the force of a great tide
in every morning when the people arise
to work on lands that don't belong to them,
in every wail of parents who have lost their sons,
in every hand that unites with another hand that suffers.

9 / Fernández / In One's Own and Foreign Land

No. We shouldn't say:
"Tomorrow, love, everything will be different."
We should say:
"They can't follow us today,"
"don't carry anything in your pockets that could endanger us"
"don't say more than is necessary"
"there is no reason to know more than you have to"
"let's finish today the task we've been given."

10 / Belli / The Time I Haven't Seen the Blue Sky

It's painful,
but it turns into song
because pain is fertile like joy
it nurtures the spirit within,
teaching unexpected things,
it teaches fury
and blossoms in so many faces
that it is certain
we will bring forth in pain
a dawn
to end this long night.

Sección 4
La lucha se prolonga

1 / Negor Len / **Canto con mi corazón**

Ayer llegué a Somoto,
puerta y frontera del frío y miedo.
Sólo miré fusiles.
Sólo miré tanques.
Se me abrió la puerta
y ahora vivo en Nicaragua.

2 / Cardenal / **La llegada**

Bajamos del avión y vamos nicaragüenses y extranjeros
revueltos hacia el gran edificio iluminado − primero
Migración y Aduana − y voy pensando al acercarnos
pasaporte en mano: el orgullo de llevar yo
el pasaporte de mi patria socialista, y la satisfacción
de llegar a la Nicaragua socialista − "Compañero"...
me dirán − un compañero revolucionario bien recibido
por los compañeros revolucionarios de Migración y Aduana
− no que no haya ningún control, debe haberlo
para que no regresen jamás capitalismo y somocismo −
y la emoción de volver otra vez al país en revolución
con más cambios cada vez, más decretos de expropiaciones
que me cuenten, transformaciones cada vez más radicales
muchas sorpresas en lo poco que uno ha estado fuera
y veo gozo en los ojos de todos − los que quedaron
los otros ya se fueron − y ahora entramos a la luz
y piden el pasaporte a nacionales y extranjeros
pero era un sueño y estoy en Nicaragua somocista
y el pasaporte me lo quitan con la cortesía fría
con que me dirían en la Seguridad "pase usted"
y lo llevan adentro y ya no lo traen (seguramente
estarán telefoneando − seguramente a la Seguridad
a la Presidencial o quién sabe a quién) y ahora ▶

Section 4
The Struggle is Protracted

1 / Negor Len / **I Sing With My Heart**

Yesterday I arrived at Somoto,
gate and border of cold and fear.
I only saw rifles.
I only saw tanks.
The door opened before me
and now I live in Nicaragua.

2 / Cardenal / **The Arrival**

We get off the plane and we go Nicaraguans and foreigners
scrambled together towards the large lit-up building – first
Immigration and Customs – and I am thinking as we approach
passport in hand: how proud I am, me, to be carrying
the passport of my socialist country, and the satisfaction
of arriving at a socialist Nicaragua – "Comrade"...
they will say to me – a revolutionary comrade made welcome
by his revolutionary comrades of Immigration and Customs
– it's not that there wouldn't be any control, there has to be
so that capitalism and *somocismo* never return –
and the emotion of returning to a country in revolution
always more changes, more expropriation decrees
that they tell me about, increasingly radical transformations
many surprises during the little time one has been away
and I see joy in everyone's eyes – the ones who stayed
the others have already gone – and now we come into the light
and they ask for the passports of nationals and foreigners
but it was all a dream and I am in Somoza's Nicaragua
and they take my passport with the same cold courtesy
with which they would say to me "come in" at Security Headquarters
and they take it inside and don't bring it back (of course
they must be phoning – of course to Security Headquarters
to the Presidential Palace or who knows where) and now   ►

todos los pasajeros se fueron y no sé si voy a caer preso
pero no: regresan con mi pasaporte al cabo de 1 hora
la CIA sabría que esta vez yo no fui a Cuba
y estuve sólo un día en el Berlín Oriental
por fin yo ya puedo pasar al registro de Aduana
sólo yo de viajero en la Aduana con mi vieja valija
y el muchacho que me registra hace como que registra
sin registrar nada y me ha dicho en voz baja "Reverendo"
y no escurca abajo en la valija donde encontraría
el disco con el último llamado de Allende al pueblo
desde La Moneda entrecortado por el ruido de las bombas
que compré en Berlín Oriental o el discurso de Fidel
sobre el derrocamiento de Allende que me regaló Sergio
y me dice el muchacho: "Las ocho y no hemos cenado
los empleados de aduana también sentimos hambre"
y yo: "¿A qué horas comen?" "Hasta que venga el último avión"
y ahora voy a ir hacia la tenebrosa ciudad arrasada
donde todo sigue igual y no pasa nada pero he visto
los ojos de él y me ha dicho con los ojos: "Compañero."

3 / Belli / **Me seguían**

con sus miradas de perros mal pagados,
me seguían
del amanecer al amanecer
espiaban
ambulaban por la acera de mi casa
estacionaban sus carros en la esquina
y andaban tras de mí por toda la ciudad,
por todas sus calles, sus esquinas y semáforos.
Me seguían
con sus caras llenas de displicencia y torturas y crímenes.
Se me quedaban viendo
seguros de mi miedo
pretendiendo que el sueño me dejara
que mis convicciones me dejaran
que dejara la lucha y mis hermanos.

all of the passengers have gone and I don't know if I am going to
                                                          be taken
prisoner but no: they come back with my passport at the end of
                                                          an hour
the CIA would know that I didn't go to Cuba this time
and I only spent a day in East Berlin
at last I am allowed to check through Customs
the only traveller in Customs with my old bag
and the boy who searches me pretends to search
without searching anything and he has said to me softly "Reverend"
and he doesn't dig beneath in my bag where he would find
the record with Allende's final call to the people
from La Moneda broken up by the noise of the bombs
that I bought in East Germany or Fidel's speech
about the overthrow of Allende that Sergio gave me
and the boy says to me: "It's eight o'clock and we haven't eaten
we customs workers get hungry too"
and me: "What time do you eat?" "Not until after the last plane"
and now I'm going to go towards the razed and shrouded city
where everything is the same and nothing has changed but I
                                                          have seen
his eyes and he has said to me with his eyes: "Comrade."

3 / Belli / They Followed Me

with the shifty eyes of hired watchdogs,
they followed me
from dawn to dawn
spying on me
pacing the sidewalk in front of my house,
they parked their cars at the corner
and citywide they dogged my tracks,
through all the streets, on all the corners, at every traffic light.
They followed me
their faces filled with hatred and torture and crimes.
They stood there watching me
confident of my fear
expecting hopes and convictions
to abandon me
and that I would abandon the struggle   ►

239

Yo sentía con cada madrugada
un odio cada vez más feroz
inventándome entrañas
en donde acomodarse.
Un odio que fue deseando balas, rifles y ametralladoras,
un odio del que nunca me habría creído capaz,
con el que podría haberlos matado
a sangre fría.
Y seguían persiguiéndome,
— me intervinieron el teléfono
— me vigilaron el trabajo
— me mandaron amenazas
y yo que nunca me había creído muy valiente
sentía que cada vez más me llenaba de coraje, de fuerza
para seguir luchando
como seguí luchando

> y que se rindan sus madres!

4 / Len / Canto con mi corazón

Los gorilas malditos se han unido en Guatemala.
En El Salvador están templando el acero,
para morder el corazón de tu Nicaragua.
CONDECA pestilencia de mierda asesina.
Buitre del tormento y deshonra.
Culebra que muerdes gentes infelices.
Párpado de flecha devoradora.
Madre, bota sombría, cementerio de Somoza.
Cruz ingrata que adormeces el futuro
yo te maldigo por puta y cobarde,
perros militares, dientes de dolor y muerte.

and my brothers.
With each dawn I felt
a more ferocious hatred
creating a hollow inside me
in which to nest.
A hatred that began wanting bullets and rifles and machine guns,
I had not believed myself capable of such hatred
and I could have used it to kill them
in cold blood.
And they kept on following me,
— they tapped my phone
— they watched me at work
— they sent me threats
and I who had never thought myself brave
felt myself filled each time with courage and strength
to keep on fighting
so I kept on fighting

    and let their mothers surrender!

4 / Len / I Sing With My Heart

The damned gorillas have gathered in Guatemala
In El Salvador they are tempering the steel
to tear at the heart of your Nicaragua.
CONDECA pestilence of murderous shit.
Vulture of torment and dishonor.
Snake that bites the unfortunate people.
Eyelid of the devouring arrow.
Bitch, filthy boot, Somoza's cemetery.
Ungrateful cross that numbs the future,
I curse you for a coward and a whore,
military scum, teeth of pain and death.

5 / Belli / **Operación Águila Z**

(Los ejércitos miembros de CONDECA, acordaron en su última reunión efectuada en Managua, realizar la operación militar ÁGUILA Z en Nicaragua en el mes de noviembre, con la participación de Guatemala, El Salvador, Honduras, y como observadores, Panamá y Costa Rica.)

"Las águilas. . . sacándonos los ojos."

Vendrán en noviembre,
amado mío,
unirán sus fusiles contra tus pies descalzos,
contra lo moreno de tu piel,
contra tus milpas.

Vendrán en noviembre,
amado mío,
han unido su odio para agrandar el odio del tirano,
juntarán en sus manos
garras para desbaratarte las entrañas asoleadas.
Vos que no has hecho más que pedir lo que te corresponde,
soportarás el peso de cinco ejércitos sobre tu lomo adolorido.

Vendrán en noviembre,
amado mío,
hasta entonces tenemos tiempo para cavar trincheras,
para multiplicarnos y nacernos en ríos, en árboles,
en manos que engendren otras manos.

Vendrán en noviembre,
amado mío,
alzaremos nuestro grito de guerra
por toda la centroamericana geografía.
Clamaremos para que los pueblos bloqueen sus fronteras
y no permitan que ejércitos hermanos nos asesinen en nuestro
propia tierra.

¿Vendrán en noviembre,
amado mío?
¿Cargará América Central el dolor de Nicaragua en su conciencia?
¿Permitirán los pueblos que los gobiernos nos asesinen en sus
nombres?

¿Vendrán en noviembre,
amado mío?

242

5 / Belli / **Operation Eagle Z**

(In their most recent meeting, held in Managua, the member armies of CONDECA agreed to carry out the military operation Eagle Z in Nicaragua during the month of November, with the participation of Guatemala, El Salvador, Honduras, and as observers, Panama and Costa Rica.)

"The eagles. . . tearing out our eyes."

They'll come in November,
my love,
they'll join their rifles against your naked feet,
against the darkness of your skin,
against your cornfields.

They'll come in November,
my love,
they have merged their hatred to enlarge the hatred of the tyrant,
they will join claws to their hands
to dismember your sunbaked entrails.
You who have done no more than to ask for what is rightfully yours,
you will bear the weight of five armies on your back.

They'll come in November,
my love,
till then we have time to dig trenches,
to multiply and be reborn in rivers, in trees,
in hands that engender other hands.

They'll come in November,
my love,
we'll raise our cry of war
all over the map of Central America
We'll call on the people to barricade their borders
and not let brother armies kill us in our own land.

Will they come in November,
my love?
Will Central America carry the pain of Nicaragua
on its conscience?
Will their people allow their governments
to murder us in their name?
Will they come in November,
my love?

6 / Luis Mejía Godoy / La herencia

Ya verás hijo que todo
llegará con el invierno
y el nombre de los caídos
cantarán los clarineros
florecerán los malinches
donde cayó el compañero
y sembraremos de amor
la cicatriz del recuerdo
Ya verás. . .

7 / Belli / Al Comandante Marcos

El ruido de la metralla nos dejó con la puerta en las narices.
La puerta de tu vida cerrada de repente
en la madera que te duerme y acurruca en el vientre de la tierra.

No puedo creer tu muerte,
tan sin despedida,
– sólo ese lejano presentimiento de aquella noche, ¿te acordás? –
en que lloré rabiosamente viéndote dormido,
sabiéndote pájaro migratorio
en rápia fuga de la vida.

Después,
cuando partiste,
cuando agarraste el peligro por las crines
y te sabía rodeado de furiosos perros,
empecé a creer que eras indestructible.
¿Cómo poder creer en el final de tus manos,
de tus ojos, de tu palabra?
¿Cómo creer en tu final cuando vos eras todo
principio?

6 / Luis Mejía Godoy / **The Inheritance**

You'll see, son, everything
will come with winter
the bugle birds will call out
the names of the fallen
the jacarandas will flower
where our comrades fell
and we'll sow with love
the scar of memory.
You'll see. . .

7 / Belli / **To Commander Marcos**

The machine gun roar left us with the door slammed in our face.
The door of your life closed suddenly
in the wood that cuddles and cradles you in the belly of the earth.

I can't believe you're dead,
so soon with no goodbye,
– only a vague foreboding that night, do you remember? –
when I cried from rage watching you asleep,
knowing you to be a migratory bird
in rapid flight from life.

Later,
when you went away,
when you grasped danger by the horns
and I knew you to be surrounded by rabid dogs,
I began to believe you were indestructible.
How could I believe in the end of your hands,
of your eyes, of your words?
How could I believe in your end when you were all
beginning?

8 / Carlos Fonseca Amador / Días amargos

Días amargos para la revolución
no son aquéllos
en que los fusiles liberatorios
fueron derrocados,
sino aquéllos
en que fueron derrocados
porque no había nadie
que los empuñara.

9 / Belli / Dios dijo:

Ama a tu prójimo como a tí mismo.
En mi país
el que ama a su prójimo
se juega la vida.

**10 / Cardenal / Lo que fue Solentiname
/ C. Mejía Godoy / Misa campesina** *(bastardillas)*

Ahora en nuestra comunidad todo ha terminado.

Llegué con otros dos compañeros hace doce años a Solentiname
para fundar allí una pequeña comunidad contemplativa.
Contemplación quiere decir
        unión con Dios y, en primer lugar,
        unión con los campesinos.
La contemplación
nos llevó después a un compromiso político;
la contemplación
nos llevó a la revolución;
y así tenía que ser
porque en América Latina
el contemplativo no podía estar ajeno
a las luchas políticas.

> *Vos sos el Dios de los pobres*
> *el Dios humano y sencillo*
> *el Dios de rostro curtido*
> *por eso es que te hablo yo*   ►

8 / Carlos Fonseca Amador / **Bitter Days**

The bitter days for a revolution
are not those
when liberating rifles
are routed,
but those
when they are routed
because there is no one
to take them up.

9 / Belli / **God Said:**

Love thy neighbor as thyself.
In my country
to love your neighbor
is to risk your life.

10 / Cardenal / **The Meaning of Solentiname**
  / C. *Mejía Godoy* / **Peasant Mass** *(italics)*

Now everything has come to an end in our community.

Twelve years ago I went to Solentiname with two brothers in Christ
to found a small contemplative community.
Contemplation means
        union with God and, in the first place,
        union with the peasants.
Contemplation
brought us, later, to political commitment;
contemplation
brought us to the revolution;
and thus it had to be
because in Latin America
a man of contemplation cannot turn his back
on political struggle.

> *You are the God of the poor*
> *the human and simple God*
> *the God with a work-hardened face*
> *that's why I talk to you,*

▶

así como habla mi pueblo
porque sos el Dios obrero
El Cristo trabajador.

Lo que más nos radicalizó políticamente fue
el Evangelio.
En la misa comentábamos con los campesinos
en forma de diálogo
el Evangelio, y ellos
comenzaron a entender la esencia del mensaje evangélico:
el anuncio del reino de Dios.
Esto es: el establecimiento en la tierra de una sociedad justa,
sin explotadores ni explotados,
como la sociedad que vivieron los primeros cristianos.
Y los campesinos de Solentiname que profundizaban
este Evangelio
se sentían solidarios con sus hermanos campesinos
que en otras partes del país
padecían la persecución y el terror:
los estaban encarcelando,
            torturando,
            asesinando,
les violaban sus mujeres,
les quemaban sus ranchos,
los arrojaban desde los helicópteros.
También tenían que sentirse solidarios con todos aquellos
que por compasión al prójimo
estaban ofrendando sus vidas.
Y esta solidaridad,
para ser real
significa que uno también tiene que comprometer
            su seguridad
            y su vida
si uno quería poner en práctica la palabra de Dios.
Al principio nosotros habíamos preferido una revolución
con métodos de lucha no violenta.
Pero después nos fuimos dando cuenta que
en Nicaragua, actualmente,
la lucha no violenta no es practicable.
En Solentiname
se sabía
que la hora del sacrificio iba a llegar,
y esa hora ya llegó.   ►

just as my people do
because you are the worker God
and the laborer Christ.

What most radicalized us politically were
the Gospels.
At mass, we discussed the Gospels
with the peasants
in the form of a dialogue,
and they began to understand the essence of the divine message:
the heralding of God's kingdom.
Which is: the establishment on earth of a just society,
without exploiters and exploited,
like the society of the early Christians.
And the peasants of Solentiname who delved deeply into
 this Gospel
felt solidarity with their brothers
who in other parts of the country
suffered persecution and terror:
they were jailed
            tortured,
            killed,
their women raped,
their farms burned,
they were thrown out of helicopters.
And they felt solidarity with all those
who, out of compassion for their brothers,
offered up their lives.
And for this solidarity
to be real
means that we too must risk
            our security
            and our lives
if we want to put God's word into practice.
At first we had preferred to make
a non-violent revolution.
But later we came to understand that
right now, in Nicaragua,
non-violent struggle is not possible.
In Solentiname
we knew the time for sacrifice would come,
and that time did come.   ►

Gloria al que sigue la luz del Evangelio,
al que denuncia sin miedo la injusticia.
Gloria al que sufre la cárcel y el destierro
y da su vida combatiendo al opresor.

Ahora en nuestra comunidad todo ha terminado.

Sucedió que un día
un grupo de muchachos y también muchachas
de Solentiname se resolvieron a tomar las armas.
¿Por qué lo hicieron?
Lo hicieron por una razón:
       por su amor al reino de Dios,
       por el ardiente deseo de que
se implante una sociedad justa,
un reino de Dios
       real
       y concreto
aquí en la tierra.

Yo creo en vos, compañero,
Cristo humano, Cristo obrero,
de la muerte vencedor,
con el sacrificio inmenso
engendraste el hombre nuevo
para la liberación.

Cuando llegó la hora,
los muchachos y muchachas combatieron con mucho valor,
pero también lo hicieron cristianamente.
Esa madrugada en San Carlos,
trataron de razonar con los guardias
para no tener que disparar un solo tiro.
Pero los guardias
respondían con metralla a sus razonamientos,
y muy a su pesar,
tuvieron que disparar ellos también sus armas.
Iban a pegar fuego al cuartel
para que no quedara duda del éxito del asalto,
pero no lo hicieron por consideración a los guardias heridos. ►

Glory unto the man who follows the light of the Gospel,
who fearlessly cries out against injustice.
Glory unto the man who suffers jail and exile
and who gives his life to fight the oppressor.

Now everything has come to an end in our community.

It happened that one day
a group of young men and women
from Solentiname
decided to take up arms.
Why did they do it?
They did it for one reason:
        for love of the kingdom of God,
        from a burning desire
to establish a just society,
a kingdom of God
        real
        and concrete
here on earth.

                I believe in you brother,
                the human Christ, the worker Christ,
                who triumphed over death,
                who, with immense sacrifice,
                gave life to a new man
                for liberation.

When the time came,
they fought bravely,
but they fought as Christians.
That morning in San Carlos,
they tried to reason with the guards,
so they would not have to fire a single shot.
But the guards
answered them with bullets,
and they, against their wishes,
also had to fire their weapons.
They were going to set the outpost on fire,
so that there would be no doubt as to the success of their assault,
but, out of consideration for the wounded guards,
they did not.   ►

Ahora la represión ha llegado también a Solentiname.
Muchos campesinos han sido llevados presos,
muchos han tenido que huir.
Pero pensaron en el prójimo, y en el país entero.
Este es un ejemplo para todos.
Ahora en nuestra comunidad todo ha terminado.

Solentiname
tenía una belleza paradisíaca,
pero en Nicaragua
no es posible ningún paraíso todavía.
No pienso
en la reconstrucción de nuestra pequeña comunidad
de Solentiname.
Pienso en la tarea mucho más importante
que tendremos todos:
la reconstrucción del país entero.

11 / C. Mejía Godoy / La tumba del guerrillero

Guerrillero, vos surgís en ríos
montes y praderas
en el viento que mece el chinchorro
del hijo de Juan
en las manos humildes y toscas
de la vivandera
en la milpa donde el campesino
busca y busca el pan.

12 / Judith Reyes / Soy del Frente Sandinista

Honor a Carlos Fonseca
lo gritaré sin parar
soy del Frente Sandinista
de Liberación Nacional.

Now repression has come to Solentiname as well.
Many peasants have been imprisoned,
many have had to flee.
But they thought of their brothers, and of the whole country.
This is an example for everyone.

Now everything has come to an end in our community.

Solentiname
was like a paradise,
but in Nicaragua
paradise is not yet possible.
I have given no thought
to the reconstruction of our little community
of Solentiname.
I think
of the far more important task,
the task for us all:
the reconstruction of the whole country.

11 / C. Mejía Godoy / The Guerrilla's Tomb

Warrior, you surge from rivers
mountains and prairies
in the breeze that rocks
the peasant's hammock
in the humble coarse hands
of the peddler
in the cornfield where the peasant
searches and searches for bread.

12 / Judith Reyes / I Belong to the Sandinista Front

Honors to Carlos Fonseca
I'll shout forever more
I belong to the Sandinista Front
of National Liberation.

13 / R. Morales Avilés / Pancasán

Es la decisión tomada por el pueblo
que no sabe qué hacer con la palabra sola.
Es la decisión y la palabra del Basta Ya!
Coreada como golpeando la cosa titular
y con estridente furia:
La ciudad y el campo caminando hacia el sol
hasta los alcances de la necesidad;
modo de caminar con maldiciones, ademanes violentos.
Agujas en los ojos, en el cuerpo, en el vientre.
No una palabra sola, tal vez el incendio
definitivo en nuestras manos,
las vacilaciones se sujetan al mediodía
cuando nos quedamos frente a la verdad,
frente a la bestia rubia cargada de dinero,
frente a la mula criolla en la calle dando la noticia
y seguimos adelante sin la piel que teníamos
      hace un momento
como si la muerte se hiciera extraña en nosotros
y alguién nos dijera que al final está el principio de todo. . .

14 / C. Mejía Godoy / No se me raje mi compa

No se me raje mi compa
no se me ponga chusmón
que la patria necesita
su coraje y su valor
no se me raje mi hermano
no me vuelva a ver pa atrás
la milpa está reventando
y es tiempo de cosechar.

13 / R. Morales Avilés / **Pancasán**

It is the decision made by the people
who will not be satisfied by words alone.
It is the decision and the word *Enough!*
spoken in unison, with strident fury, as
if striking out against authority.
City and country marching toward the sun,
toward the achievement of necessity;
a way of walking with curses, violent gestures,
needles in the eyes, in the body, in the stomach.
Not any single word, perhaps the definitive
fire in our hands,
hesitation is overcome at midday
when we stand facing the truth,
facing the blond beast weighed down with money,
facing the creole mule in the street shouting the news,
and we go forward shedding the skin
    that just a moment ago was ours,
as if death were alien to us
and someone told us that at the end is the beginning of everything. . .

14 / C. Mejía Godoy / **Don't Let Me Down, Comrade**

Don't let me down, comrade
don't lag behind me now
your country needs
your courage and valor
so don't let me down, brother
don't turn your back on us
the cornfields are blooming
and it's harvest time.

15 / Daniel Ortega / Los frutos sean

Cuando los sembradores se decidieron
a cultivar el campo
previeron que tendrían que apartar
las piedras
las espinas
las malas hierbas.
Que les sangrarían las manos
y se les cortarían los pies.
Que habría que cuidarse
del gusano roedor
y de la langosta
y de las ratas.
Que la limpia iba a ser dura
pero que al fin y al cabo
contra fuego y alambre
la cosecha se daría. . .

16 / C. Mejía Godoy / La consigna

Ya nadie detiene la avalancha
de un pueblo que tomó su decisión
esta es la guerra desatada
la guerra prolongada contra el opresor.

¿Cuál es la Consigna?
El pueblo no se detiene
¿Cuál es la Consigna?
F. S. L. N.

15 / Daniel Ortega / **The Fruits**

When the sowers decided
to cultivate the fields
they knew that they would have to clear
the stones
the thorns
the weeds.
That they would bloody their hands
and cut their feet.
That they would have to be careful
of the gnawing worm
of the locusts
and the rats.
That the cleanup would be hard
but that finally
against all odds
they would reap a harvest. . .

16 / C. Mejía Godoy / **The Watchword**

Now no one can stop the avalanche
of a people that's decided
this is the unleashed war
the protracted war against the oppressor.

What is the watchword?
The people won't be stopped
What is the watchword?
F. S. L. N.

Sección 5
Matanza y levantamiento

1 / HuGós / Los miércoles en Los Angeles

Noches tensas y alertas,
como de sitio.

Por avión llegan las terribles noticias,
y Edna sigue oyendo "Radio Habana"
mientras Silvio va a recoger los muertos
que se esperan
en la primera página de *La Prensa.*

Los recuerdos alegres
de la tierra de la infancia
tropiezan con 10,000 lamentos.

En "El Nica,"
se tienden los cuerpos,
como naipes,
sobre una mesa rodeada por beisbolistas
y botellas vacías de cerveza.

43 años de dictadura
irrumpen en mi mente.

2 / José Arauz Mairena / Una canción para Pedro J. Chamorro

El diez de enero por la mañana,
mi Patria entera se estremeció
Porque en las ruinas de mi Managua
Sangre inocente se derramó.

. . .

Pedro Joaquín, era un gran hombre
y con su pluma allá en LA PRENSA
él era enemigo de los honrados
y destapaba al sinvergüenza.

Section 5
Slaughter and Uprising

1 / HuGós / Wednesdays in Los Angeles

Tense and wakeful nights
as though under siege.

The terrible news arrives by plane,
and Edna stays, listening to "Radio Havana"
while Silvio goes to gather up the dead
who are waiting
on the front page of *La Prensa*.

Joyful memories
of the childhood land
come up against 10,000 laments.

In *"El Nica,"*
they lay out the bodies,
like playing cards,
on a table surrounded by baseball players
and empty beer bottles.

43 years of dictatorship
erupt in my mind.

2 / José Arauz Mairena / A Song for Pedro J. Chamorro

On January tenth in the morning
the whole country was shaken
because innocent blood was spilled
in the midst of Managua's ruins.

   . . .

Pedro Joaquín was a noble man
and there in *LA PRENSA* with his pen,
he befriended honorable men
and unmasked professional frauds.

...nunca
respetaron a nadie
y esta vez se saltaron las trancas
matando a Pedro Joaquín
el impacto
fue gigantesco
demoledor!
y su gente
rajándose el vestido
y arrancándose los cabellos
se desbordó a lo largo
y ancho
de las calles
por las quebradas
y los caminos
llorando protestando
a grito partido!
...

Bombas de fragmentación
tiros de metralleta
escopetas de perdigón
aviones y tanquetas
bombas de intoxicación
ay Dios mío
si parece
un ejército invasor
contra su
propio pueblo!
que sigue protestando
con las manos vacías
y una conciencia
recién
parida!
Genocidio
en Monimbó
Genocidio en Nicaragua!

◄

3 / Christian Santos de Praslin / Barren the Landscape

. . .they never respected
  a soul
and this time they went too far
killing Pedro Joaquín
    the impact
      was immense
      devastating!
    and his people
      tearing at their clothes
      tearing at their hair
poured through the length
      and breadth
of the streets
    the alleyways
and the roads
    crying protesting
    in heart-rending wails!
      . . .
Fragmentation bombs
    machine gun fire
scatter guns
planes and tanks
    poison gas bombs
oh my God
    it looks like
an enemy army
invading
    its own people!
who keep on protesting
    with empty hands
and a consciousness
      newly
      born!
Genocide
    in Monimbó
Genocide in Nicaragua!   ►

LLANTO. . .
LLANTO
LLAANTOO. . .
ALARIDOS DE DOLOR!
Seco el paisaje
triste y seco
lleno de incertidumbre y desolación

4 / El Indio Fernando / **Llanto Indio**

Que lo sepan todos,
que lo sepa el mundo
que en Nicaragua
mataron un barrio
en las Rinconadas
de mi Monimbó.

5 / Robleto / **Monimbó**

Decíme, en Monimbó
¿Qué pasó?

Pasó todo, hambre, guerra, violaciones,
persecución, vejaciones.

Llegaron muchos aviones,
helicópteros, tanquetas,
rifles, bombas, metralletas
que herían a montones.

Y los guardias que tiraban,
¿No tenían compasión?
¡Qué va, ni apuntaban
pues tiraban al monton!

¿Y Uds. se defendieron?
Sí, con palo, machete y piedra.
Pero como nuestra suerte es negra
ellos más duro nos dieron!

►

CRY. . .
      CRY
      CRYYYY. . .
HOWLS OF PAIN!
Barren the landscape
      barren and sad
filled with uncertainty and wretchedness

4 / El Indio Fernando / Indian Lament

Tell the world
let everyone know
that in Nicaragua
they butchered the barrio
of las Rinconadas
in my Monimbó.

                    5 / Robleto / Monimbó

Tell me, what happened
in Monimbó?

Everything happened, hunger, war, rape,
persecution, humiliation.

Many planes came,
helicopters, tanks,
rifles, bombs, machine guns
that wounded so many.

And the guards that did the shooting,
had they no mercy?
Fat chance, they didn't even bother to aim
they just shot into the crowd!

And did you defend yourselves?
Yes, with sticks, machetes and stones.
But just like our bad luck
they gave it to us worse!   ►

¿Y qué clase de soldados eran?
Iguales a nosotros hermano,
si no hubieran ido equipados
a cualquiera le dan la mano.

Lo que pasó en Monimbó
no tiene comparación
por todos lados hubo bala
Hubo masacre y agresión
El corazón se entristece
al recordar la traición.
. . .
Quebraban nuestros comales
botaban nuestro pinol
no dejaron en las ollas
ni una gotita de atol.
Para darle a nuestros tiernos
llorando de hambre y dolor.
. . .
Y tanta sangre inocente
que por las calles corrió
tanta miseria e injusticia
que el pueblo padeció
algún día mi marimba
aprenderá esta canción:
"Lo que pasó en Monimbó
¿Quién lo ordenó?
¡¡Jodido!!
¿Quién lo ordenó?"

6 / Raúl Javier García / **Exortación fraternal**

No lo apuntes con tu *garand,* hermano;
no golpees con el yatagán su espalda trabajada,
no hundas tu bayoneta en su sufrido pecho.
Abrirías tu misma carne;
derramarías tu misma sangre, hermano.

264

And what kind of soldiers were they?
The same as us, brother,
if they hadn't been armed
you'd want to shake their hand.

What happened in Monimbó
is absolutely unspeakable.
Bullets were flying everywhere
There was massacre and brutality
Remembering the treachery
our hearts grow sad.
. . .
They broke our grinding stones
they kicked over all the flour,
not a drop of porridge
did they leave in the pots
to give to our young ones
crying in hunger and pain.
. . .
And so much innocent blood
that ran down the streets,
so much misery and injustice
that the people suffered,
some day my marimba
will learn this song:
"What happened in Monimbó,
Who ordered it?
Sonuvabitch!!
Who ordered it?"

6 / Raúl Javier García / **Fraternal Exortation**

Don't point your *garand* at him, brother;
don't use your blade to whip his beaten back,
don't sink your bayonet into his wounded breast.
You would be opening your own flesh;
shedding your own blood, brother.

7 / Belli / Empezamos amando y siendo transigentes

Cuántas veces oímos decir: Pobres guardias, si ellos
  sólo obedecen órdenes. . .
pero cúantas veces vemos caer a nuestros compañeros
bajo el fuego de los "pobres guardias". . .

8 / Fernández / Perdimos el miedo

Verlos venir no es tarea ya de la imaginación
Sabíamos desde hace muchísimos años
que tarde o temprano vendrían por nosotros,
y en la espera
tuvimos tiempo de meternos todo el veneno acumulado
dentro de las cicatrices
y de amarnos más entre nosotros.

Siempre vimos cómo venían
y cómo, cuando venían por otros,
se acercaba más nuestro turno.
Los sangraban
por los cuatro costados cardinales
de nuestro amor impotente.
Estamos listos.
Ahora vienen por nosotros
pero también nosotros venimos por ellos.

9 / Belli / La marcha hacia la victoria no se detiene

Compañero,
la Guerra es popular y prolongada,
desafía el cansancio,
la inmediatez, el triunfo fácil,
la claudicación.
Es un secreto a voces
que corre por las venas de nuestro pueblo
con el sonido cadencioso de una locomotora
que alegra con pitazos − la guerrilla −
su transcurrir seguro
sobre los rieles firmes
de una correcta
apreciación de la realidad.   ►

266

7 / Belli / We Begin by Loving and Compromising

How many times have we heard it said: Poor guards, they're
    only following orders. . .
but how many times have we seen our comrades fall
from the fire of the "poor guards". . .

8 / Fernández / We Lost Our Fear

We no longer have to imagine seeing them coming for us.
We knew a long time ago
that sooner or later they would come for us,
and while we waited
we had time to inoculate our scars
with all the accumulated poisons
and to learn to love one another more.

We used to watch how they came
and how, when they came for others,
the time when they would come for us drew nearer.
They bled our comrades
through the four cardinal points
of our impotent love.
So we are ready.
Now they are coming for us,
but we are also coming for them.

9 / Belli / There is No Holding Back the March Toward Victory

Comrade,
the War is popular and protracted,
it defies fatigue,
spontaneity, the easy triumph,
the backing down.
The guerrilla fighter is a secret that shouts,
that runs through the veins of our people
like the cadence of a locomotive
whose joyful whistle
heralds its steady passage
over the firm rails
of a correct reading
of reality.   ►

Nuestro pueblo ha sufrido,
compañero,
han sido asesinados sus hijos
despiadamente,
ha sufrido un enfrentamiento
de cuerpo blando y generoso
contra duro cuerpo de metal.
Por eso, hermano, la guerrilla:
tirar la piedra y esconder la mano,
emboscar,
salir de entre la selva,
refugiarse en el calor de su sombra,
en el frío de su abrazo
para comer, dormir un poco y volver,
atacar por donde menos lo piensan,
recuperar armas,
subir y volver a bajar
dispersar al enemigo,
que no conozca de dónde viene
el tiro que lo mata.
. . .
Que se queden otros a mitad del camino
recibiendo vítores sospechosos,
nosotros sabemos trabajar en el silencio,
sabemos forjar la tormenta,
preparar el rayo,
en el yunque que nos dejó Sandino.
Sabemos que en la montaña, compañero,
enterraremos el corazón del enemigo.

10 / Fernández /
A Tomás Borge: El amanecer dejó de ser una tentación

Los pétalos
empiezan a descubrir estambres y pistilos
y los chachorros sentimos en las encías inflamadas
el filo de los dientes prontos a brotarse.

Somos jornaleros de los hondos tiempos modernos;
hechos de carne, amor, huesos,
de hermanos imperecederos
desaparecidos con una bala en la espalda. ▶

Our people have suffered,
comrade,
their children have been murdered
without remorse,
they have suffered the confrontation
of their tender and giving bodies
against the hard corpse of metal.
Thus the need, comrade, for guerrilla war:
to throw the stone and hide the hand,
to ambush,
to come from the jungle
to seek refuge in the heat of its shade,
in the cold of its embrace,
to eat, sleep a little and return,
to attack where they least expect it,
to recapture arms,
to rise and then fall back
to disperse the enemy,
who does not know where
the shot comes from that kills him.
          . . .
Let others remain at the halfway point
receiving suspicious cheers,
we know how to work in silence,
we know how to forge the storm,
hammer out the lightning
on the anvil Sandino left us.
We know, comrade, that in the mountains,
we will bury the heart of the enemy.

10 / Fernández /
To Tomás Borge: Dawn Ceased to be a Dream

The flower petals
begin to bring forth stamens and pistils
and young cubs feel in their inflamed gums
a line of teeth ready to break through.

We are the day shift in the deep mines of these modern times;
made out of flesh and love and blood,
out of deathless brothers and sisters
who disappeared with a bullet in the back.   ►

Ahora se ha puesto a caminar el contenido del corazón
Estamos reinventando
el mínimo y dulce sentido de la puerta,
de la mesa, del pan,
empuñando las letras de palabras entrañables:
Monimbó, Matagalpa, Subtiava, Estelí,
hermano.

11 / Belli / **Huelga**

Quiero una huelga donde vayamos todos.
                    Una huelga de brazos, de piernas, de cabellos,
Una huelga
naciendo en cada cuerpo.
Quiero una huelga de obreros
                    de técnicos
                    de choferes
                    de médicos
                                        de palomas
                                        de flores
                                        de niños
                                        de mujeres
Quiero una huelga grande
                    − que hasta el amor alcance −
Una huelga donde todo se detenga:
                    el reloj
                    el plantel
                    la fábrica
                    la iglesia
                                        el bus
                                        la carretera
                                        los colegios
                                        los puertos
Una huelga de ojos, de manos y de besos.
Una huelga donde respirar no sea permitido.
Una huelga donde nazca el silencio
                    para oír los pasos
                    del tirano que se marcha.

Now all that is in our hearts rises up, begins to walk
We are reinventing
the least and sweetest meanings of the door,
of the table, of bread,
raising a clenched fist of unforgettable words:
Monimbó, Matagalpa, Subtiava, Estelí,
brother.

11 / Belli / Strike

I want a strike we're all in.
                An arms, legs, hair strike,
A strike
born of each one's flesh.
I want a strike of workers
              technicians
              drivers
              doctors
                            of doves
                            and flowers
                            and children
                            and women
I want a huge strike
                  − that strikes all the way to love −
A strike where everything stops:
              the clock
              the personnel
              the factory
              the church
                            the bus
                            the road
                            the schools
                            the ports
An eyes, hands and kiss strike.
A nobody breathe strike.
A strike in which silence is born
              so that we can hear the tyrant's footfalls
              as he flees.

Sección 6
El comienzo

1 / HuGós / Dentro de mí

Soy,
dentro de mí
una mujer pariendo
un pueblo atormentado.

Y desde el vientre que habitara
en mis años fetales
desciende hasta tu vagina
un dolor que cercena
la vida en dos mitades.

Siento,
gritos puntiagudos
surcándome el cerebro;
helados sudores
brotándome en la espalda.

Es Nicaragua
que nace de tu herida,
desgarrando tus tiernas entrañas,
como una rosa que florece ensangrentada.

Section 6
The Beginning

---

1 / HuGós / **Within Me**

I am,
within me,
a woman giving birth
to a tormented people.

And from the womb where I lived
in my fetal years
an ache descends
to your vagina
and cuts life in two.

Sharp-pointed shrieks
plow my mind;
cold sweat
breaks out
on my back.

Nicaragua grows
from your wound,
tearing your tender entrails
like a blood-stained rose in bloom.

2 / Belli / Seremos nuevos

Seremos nuevos, amor,
limpiaremos con sangre lo antiguo y depravado,
los vicios, las tendencias,
los asquitos pequeño burgueses.

Seremos nuevos
con ojos claros y bocas transparentes,
con palabras sencillas como pan de pueblo,
como rosquillas de Jinotepe
o quesillo de la Paz Centro.

Sencillos y valientes
se alzarán nuestros hijos
nacidos en petates, en esteras,
en medio de una fiesta de guitarras.

Nuevos, amor, ¿te das cuenta?
                    nuevecitos.
Como lunas y soles de constelaciones recién nacidas.
con el pelo lavado y la sangre lavada
y el silencio lavado.

Seremos nuevos, amor,
con ese olor a limpio de la ropa tendida
y ese enorme reto de lanzar la libertad al aire
como una bandada de pájaros.

3 / C. Mejía Godoy / La consigna

Hermano, dame tu mano
y unidos marchemos ya
hacia el sol de la victoria
trayectoria de la libertad
Hermano de la montaña
hermano de la ciudad
juntos unidos lucharemos
y unidos lograremos
llegar al fin.

2 / Belli / We'll Be New

We'll be new, love,
we'll wash away what is old and depraved
the putrid petty bourgeois tendencies and vices
with blood.

We'll be new
with clear eyes and shiny mouths
with simple words like the people's bread
like hard rolls from Jinotepe
or Paz Centro's creamy cheese.

Sturdy and plain
our children will rise up
born on straw mats and pallets
in the midst of a fiesta of guitars.

New, love, do you understand?
                    bright, shiny new.
Like the moons and the suns of newly born stars,
with our hair washed and our blood cleansed
and our silence bathed.

We'll be new, love,
with that clean fresh smell of clothes on the line
and the enormous challenge of liberty hurled in the air
like a flight of birds.

3 / C. Mejía Godoy / The Watchword

Brother, give me your hand
and we'll march united now
towards the sun of victory
on the road to liberty
Brother of the mountain
brother of the city
together united we'll fight
and united we'll succeed
in reaching the journey's end.

4 / Uriarte / **Los muchachos**

ELLOS fueron los que prendieron el fuego
los que se tiraron a la calle en Masaya
Estelí
León
Matagalpa
con un pañuelo amarrado al cuello y una escopeta mapachinera
cuando mucho
De riflitos de madera hechos por ellos mismos
pasaron sin transición a las armas
todavía con zapatos tenis modelo americano
(o descalzos)
bluyines desteñidos y camisetas con un corazón dibujado y la
palabra "love" en el centro.
Muchos no habían emplumado todavía
zipotones, mocosos alelados
dando una improvisada lección de historia
y sólo desde allí — desde las barricadas — el pueblo inicia su propia
ciencia
— el verdadero corte epistemológico —
dándole al lenguaje un nuevo espesor.
Pero no es lo mismo verla venir que platicar con ella
a Ricardo Contreras de 13 años en Jinotepe antes de matarlo
le cortaron uno por uno los dedos de la mano
a Oto lo tiraron vivo desde un helicóptero
A Celia en sus primeros 16 años la violaron y después la hicieron
pedacitos a bayoneta limpia
a Manuel primero lo desnudaron y después le engrasaron los
testículos para que un mastín entrenado se los devora. . .
Susan Maicelas que estuvo en las barricadas de Masaya con ellos
divulgó por el mundo sus fotos,
de rodillas con una pistolita 22 en la mano,
la visera de la cachucha vuelta para atrás,
concentrados en esa tarea de observar por la mira como el biólogo
observa atentamente a través del microscopio los nocivos
microbios que viven sagrándonos, destruyéndonos y
minándonos el organismo.
"Somos una generación dispuesta a morir por una Nicaragua mejor"
es su grafitti de batalla (y desde entonces las escuelas
los colegios y las universidades se han ido vaciando). ▶

276

4 / Uriarte / The Boys

THEY were the ones who lit the fire
who threw themselves into the streets of Masaya
Estelí
León
Matagalpa
bandanas around their necks and a coon-gun at best
without any transition they went
from handmade rifles to arms
still wearing made in USA tennis shoes
                                        (or barefoot)
faded bluejeans and t-shirts with a heart saying "love" in the middle.
Many of them still wet behind the ears
raw, snotnose kids,
giving makeshift history lessons
and only from their classroom — the barricades — did the people
                                launch their own knowledge
— the true epistemological break —
bringing new weight to the language
But it's not the same way to say it as it was to see it
Ricardo Contreras 13 years old in Jinotepe: before they killed
                        him they cut off his fingers one by one.
Oto: they threw him alive out of a helicopter
Cecilia, sweet 16: they raped her and then sliced her to pieces
                                        with a bayonet.
Manuel: first they stripped him and then larded his testicles
                        so a trained mastiff would devour them.
Susan Maicelas, with them in the Masaya barricades
sent their photos around the world,
crouching on their knees, their hands gripping 22 caliber pistols,
their baseball caps' visors facing backwards
concentrating on their homework, studying their sights just
    like a biologist who through a microscope attentively
    studies the noxious microbes that attack our organism to
    bleed, undermine and destroy us.
"We are a generation ready to die for a better Nicaragua"
— their battle grafitti (and since then the grade schools
high schools and universities have been emptying).
The Spanish priest Laviana before he fell in Peñas Blancas told
                                        a reporter:

                                        ►

277

El curita español Laviana antes de caer en Peñas Blancas le dijo
a un periodista:
"Nosotros estamos ganando; en el pueblo en el que entraron 20
sandinistas han salido 500. La juventud se va con nosotros."
Y la guardia los persigue indiscriminadamente.
A diario aparecen tirados en las carreteras, en los basureros,
debajo de los puentes, a la orilla de los criques. . .
Aunque la rebelión de los muchachos (que fue uno de los factores
que convirtió al FSLN en un movimiento de masas) se
inició en septiembre pasado
en realidad se entronca a uno de los más genuinos brotes del
sandinismo:
EL CORO DE ÁNGELES: grupos de niños que acompañaban
las columnas de Sandino en Las Segovias
haciendo ruido, gritando, cantando, similando ser un numeroso
ejército.
Verdadero coro de guerra.
Y los marinos norteamericanos se ensañaron con ellos cuando
los descubrieron.
Todos eran muchachitos haraposos, descalzos, esmirriados
apenas – como los pájaros – alimentados de frutas.

"We are winning; 20 young *Sandinistas* entered a town, and 500
left. The young people go with us."
And the guards pursued them without distinction.
Every day they turned up dead on the roads,in the garbage
dumps, under the bridges, on the banks of creeks. . .
Although the rebellion of the youth (which helped change the
FSLN into a mass movement) began last September
it really revives one of the most genuine sources of *Sandinismo:*
THE CHORUS OF ANGELS: flocks of kids who went into
Sandino's columns into the Segovias
making noise, shouting, singing, making themselves out to be
a vast army.
True chorus of war.
And the American Marines took bloody revenge when they
found them out.
All of them kids in rags, barefoot, all skin and bones,
barely living – like birds – on fruit.

5 / PROCLAMA

Pueblo heroico de Nicaragua, la hora del derrocamiento de la dictadura oprobiosa ha llegado.

La gran ofensiva del Frente Sandinista de Liberación Nacional (FSLN) se ha desatado para aplastar a las fuerzas asesinas del tirano. Los frentes de guerra en todo el territorio patrio, desde el norte, desde el oriente y el occidente, desde el sur, marchan hoy combatiendo victoriosos.

La hora del tirano está cerca.

Es el momento para alcanzar la patria libre.

Todos los nicaragüenses dignos al combate.

Viva la insurreción de todo el pueblo de Nicaragua.

El Frente Sandinista llama a la huelga general. Reclama a toda la ciudadanía honesta a sumarse a la huelga general, para que con el esfuerzo de la nación entera, la dictadura somocista sea destruida.

El lunes 4 de junio es el día a partir del cual deberán cerrar todos los establecimientos industriales y comerciales y cesar toda actividad económica y social. El día lunes 4 de junio, la huelga general de nuestro heroico pueblo juntará fuerzas con la ofensiva general armada sandinista que culminará con el aplastamiento de la criminal y cobarde dictadura de los Somoza, lo que ya está en marcha.

Nicaragüenses a la huelga, a las armas, la insurrección de todo el pueblo triunfará.

PATRIA LIBRE O MORIR

Frente Sandinista de Liberación Nacional

Daniel Ortega Saavedra	Jaime Wheelock R.
Humberto Ortega Saavedra	Luis Carrión Cruz
Víctor Tirado López	Carlos Núñez
Tomás Borge Martínez	Henry Ruiz Hernández
Bayardo Arce Castaño	

5 / PROCLAMATION

Heroic people of Nicaragua, the hour of the downfall of the hateful dictatorship has arrived.

The great offensive of the Sandinista National Liberation Front (FSLN) has been unleashed to crush the assassin forces of the tyrant. The war fronts throughout the homeland, from North, South, East and West, march today in victorious combat. The hour of the tyrant is near. The moment to reach the goal of a free homeland has arived. All decent Nicaraguans arise! Long live the insurrection of the Nicaraguan people! The Sandinista Front is calling for a general strike. It appeals to all honest citizens to join this general strike so that, through the efforts of the entire nation, the Somoza dictatorship will be destroyed.

As of Monday, June 4, all industrial and commercial establishments should close and all economic and social activity should cease. On Monday, June 4, the general strike of our heroic people will join forces with the Sandinista armed offensive. Their efforts will culminate in the total collapse of the criminal and cowardly Somoza dictatorship, which is now on the way out.

Nicaraguans, strike! Bear arms! The insurrection of the entire people will triumph!

FREE HOMELAND OR DEATH

Sandinista National Liberation Front

Daniel Ortega Saavedra	Jaime Wheelock R.
Humberto Ortega Saavedra	Luis Carrión Cruz
Víctor Tirado López	Carlos Núñez
Tomás Borge Martínez	Henry Ruiz Hernández
Bayardo Arce Castaño	

6 / Belli / Hasta que seamos libres

Entonces,
iremos a despertar a nuestros muertos
con la vida que ellos nos legaron
y todos juntos cantaremos
mientras conciertos de pájaros
repitan nuestro mensaje
en todos
los confines
de América.

7 / Cardenal / Canto nacional

Vienen las grandes cooperativas campesinas
ya va a empezar la campaña de alfabetización
van a estudiar ballet los muchachos en Muy-Muy
teatro en Tecolostote, en Telpaneca. Ah la visión
de una tierra con la explotación
abolida!
Repartida la riqueza nacional todos por igual
el producto nacional bruto, toditos por igual.
Nicaragua sin Guardia Nacional, veo el nuevo día!
Una tierra sin terror. Sin tiranía dinástica. Cantá
cantá zanate clarinero.

8 / Neruda / Salud, capitán del continente

Todo está en la luz de un hombre,
repitido nombre de la montaña:
Sandino, Sandino, Sandino.

6 / Belli / Until We're Free

And then,
we'll go wake our dead
with the life they bequeathed us
and one and all we'll sing
while concerts of birds
repeat our message
throughout
the length and breadth
of America.

7 / Cardenal / National Song

The great peasant cooperatives are starting up and
the literacy campaign is ready to begin
at Muy Muy the boys are going to study ballet
theatre in Tecolostote, in Telpaneca. Ah vision
of a land with exploitation
abolished!
The nation's wealth distributed everyone his share
the gross national product, each and every one his share.
Nicaragua without a National Guard, I see a new day!
Land without terror. Without a dynastic tyrant. Sing out
sing out oh lark, the bugle call.

8 / Neruda / Hail, Captain of the Continent

Everything shines in the light of one man,
name echoing in the mountains:
Sandino, Sandino, Sandino.

Epílogo

"Carlos, hoy el amanecer dejó de ser una tentación."
— Tomás Borge a Carlos Fonseca Amador

1 / Cardenal / Luces

Aquel vuelo clandestino de noche.
Con peligro de ser derribados. La noche serena.
El cielo lleno, llenísimo de estrellas. La Vía Láctea
clarísima tras el grueso vidrio de la ventanilla,
    masa blancuzca y rutilante en la noche negra
con sus millones de procesos de evoluciones y revoluciones.
Íbamos sobre el mar para evitar la aviación somocista,
    pero cerca de la costa.
El pequeño avión volando bajo, y volando lento.
Primero las luces de Rivas, tomada y retomada por los sandinistas,
    ahora a medias en poder de los sandinistas.
Depués otras luces: Granada, en poder de la Guardia
    (sería atacada esa noche).
Masaya, totalmente liberada. Tantos cayeron allí.
Más allá un resplandor: Managua. Lugar de tantos combates.
(El Bunker). Todavía el bastión de la Guardia.
Diriamba, liberada. Jinotepe, con combates. Tanto heroismo
relumbra en esas luces. Montelimar — nos señalaba el piloto —:
la hacienda del tirano junto al mar. Al lado, Puerto Somoza.
La Vía Láctea arriba, y las luces de la revolución de Nicaragua.
Me parece mirar más lejos, en el norte, la fogata de Sandino.
    ("Aquella luz es Sandino")
Las estrellas sobre nosotros, y la pequeñez de esta tierra
pero también la importancia de ella, de estas
pequeñitas luces de los hombres. Pienso: todo es luz.
El planeta viene del sol. Es luz hecha sólida.
La electricidad de este avión es luz. El metal es luz. El calor
    de la vida viene del sol.
        "Hágase la luz."
También están las tinieblas. ▶

284

Epilogue

"Carlos, today the dawn is no longer a dream."
— Tomás Borge to Carlos Fonseca Amador

1 / Cardenal / **Lights**

> *That clandestine night flight.*
> *Running the risk of being shot down. The night, silent.*
> *The heavens filled, so filled with stars. The Milky Way*
> *so clear beyond the thick glass of the window,*
> > *a whiteish and shimmering mass in the black night*
> *with its millions of processes of evolutions and revolutions.*
> *We were flying over the sea to avoid the Somoza airforce,*
> > *but near the coast.*

The little plane flying low, and flying slow.
First the lights of Rivas, taken and retaken by the Sandinistas,
> *now halfway in the Sandinistas' hands.*
Then other lights: Granada, in the hands of the Guard.
> *(it would be attacked that night).*
Masaya, completely liberated. So many fell there.
Further on, a glitter: Managua. The site of so many battles.
(The Bunker). Still the bastion of the Guard.
Diriamba: liberated. Jinotepe, still fighting. So much heroism
shines in those lights. Montelimar — the pilot points it out —:
The tyrant's seaside estate. Beside it Puerto Somoza.
The Milky Way above, and the lights of Nicaragua's revolution.
I can almost make out, to the north, Sandino's campfire.
> *("That light is Sandino")*
The stars above us, and the smallness of this earth
but the importance of it as well, of these
tiny little human lights. I think: everything is light.
The planet comes from the sun. It is light made solid.
This plane's electricity is light. The metal is light. Life's
> *warmth comes from the sun.*
> *"Let there be light."*
There is darkness too. ▶

Hay extraños reflejos — no sé de donde vienen — en
                la superficie transparente de la ventanillas.
Una luminosidad roja: las luces de la cola del avión.
Y reflejos en el mar tranquilo: serán las estrellas.
Miro la lucecita de mi cigarrillo — también viene del sol,
                de una estrella.
Y la silueta de un barco grande. ¿El portavión de los EE.UU.
enviado a patrullar la costa del Pacífico?
Una gran luz a la derecha nos sobresalta. ¿Un jet contra nosotros?
No. La luna que sale, media luna, serenísima, iluminada por el sol.
        El peligro de ir volando en una noche tan clara.
Y el radio de pronto. Palabras confusas llenando el pequeño avión.
¿La Guardia? El piloto dice: "son los nuestros."
        Esas ondas son de nosotros.
Ya estamos cerca de León, el territorio liberado.
Una intensa luz rojo-anaranjada, como la brasa de un puro: Corinto:
la potente iluminación de los muelles rielando en el mar.
Y ahora ya la playa de Poneloya, y el avión entrando a tierra,
el cordón de espuma de la costa radiante bajo la luna.
        El avión bajando. Un olor a insecticida.
Y me dice Sergio: "¡El olor de Nicaragua!"
Es el momento de mayor peligro, la aviación enemiga
        puede estar esperándonos sobre este aeropuerto.
Y ya las luces del aeropuerto.
Estamos en tierra. Salen de la oscuridad los compas verde-olivo
a abrazarnos.
Sentimos sus cuerpos calientes, que también vienen del sol,
que también son luz.
        Es contra las tinieblas esta revolución.
Era la madrugada del 18 de julio. Y el comienzo
        de todo lo que estaba por venir.

There are strange reflections — I don't know where they come from —
*   on the clear surface of the window.*
A red luminosity: the plane's tail lights.
And reflections on the calm sea: they must be the stars.
I look at my cigarette's glow — it too comes from the sun,
*   from a star.*
And the silhouette of a big ship. A U.S. aircraft carrier
sent to patrol the Pacific coast?
A big light at the right startles us. A jet against us?
No. The moon coming up, a halfmoon, so serene, lit by the sun.
*   The danger of flying on such a clear night.*
And suddenly the radio. Confused words filling the little plane.
The Guard? The pilot says: "they're ours."
*   Those waves are ours.*
Now we're near León, liberated territory.
An intense reddish-orange light, like the red-hot glow of a cigar: Corinto:
the powerful dock lights shimmering on the sea.
And now the Poneloya beach, and the plane flying over land,
the coast a line of foam radiating light beneath the moon.
*   The plane descending. A smell of insecticide.*
And Sergio says to me: "The smell of Nicaragua."
This is the most dangerous part, the enemy airforce
*   could be waiting for us over this airport*
And finally the airport lights.
We've landed. Comrades clad in olive-green come out of the dark
to embrace us.
We feel their warm bodies, which also come from the sun,
which are also light.
*   It's against the darkness, this revolution.*
It was the early morning of July 18. And the beginning
*   of everything that was to come.*

Bio-Bibliographies of the Principal Poets

Rafael Alberti: Born in 1902 in Puerto de Santa María (Cádiz), Spain. His first book, *Marinero en tierra* (one of his best), won the National Prize of Literature in 1925. From 1930 he cultivated, among other things, political poetry as well as the theatre. He traveled to the Soviet Union and founded, in 1934, the magazine *Octubre*. With the defeat of the Republic in 1939 he went into exile, first in Argentina and later in Italy. After the death of Franco in November 1975, he returned to Spain. In the first elections of the post-Franco period, he ran as a candidate of the Spanish Communist Party and was elected deputy of Cádiz. He visited Nicaragua in 1933 and in November 1979.

Jorge Eduardo Arellano: Born in Granada, Nicaragua, in 1946. He has published a collection of poems entitled *La estrella perdida* (1969), which is a selection from a larger work still unpublished. He is the author of an anthology of young poets, *Poesía joven nicaragüense: 1960-1970,* and also of an anthology of poetry dedicated to the memory of Sandino. He has published a history of Nicaraguan literature, *Panorama de la literatura nicaragüense* (Managua, Ediciones Nacionales, 3rd. edition, 1977). He is presently Director of the National Archives.

Gioconda Belli: Born in Managua, Nicaragua, in 1948. She has published poems in *La Prensa Literaria, El Gallo Ilustrado* and other publications in Latin America. In 1972, she received the Mariano Fiallos Gil prize for her poetry from the National Autonomous University of Nicaragua. In 1974, her book of poems entitled *Sobre la grama* appeared. A year later, she went into exile and lived for several years in Costa Rica. In 1978, she won the Casa de las Américas prize for her latest book, *Línea de fuego* (La Habana, 1978). Belli has returned to Nicaragua in order to participate in the National Reconstruction.

Mario Cajina Vega: Born in Masaya, Nicaragua, in 1929. Mainly a writer of short stories, he also has published books of poems. He has worked in his own publishing house ("Editorial Nicaragüense") in which he has published fine editions of poetry. In 1979, he wrote poetry in the barricades of Masaya. He is in charge of the Nicaraguan edition of *Nicaragua in Revolution.*

Ernesto Cardenal: Born in Granada, Nicaragua, in 1925. At age 31, he entered a Trappist monastery. Later, he studied for the priesthood in Colombia and became a priest in 1965. He then went to Nicaragua, where he founded the contemplative community Solentiname on Lake Nicaragua, where peasants and fishermen went on Sundays to attend mass and participate in dialogues on the Gospels. Some of these dialogues have been preserved in *El evangelio de Solentiname*. Cardenal was decisively impressed by a stay in Cuba, and as a testimonial he wrote a book of reportage entitled *En Cuba*. His poetry has been collected in a series of volumes, including: *Gethsemany Ky* (1960), *Marilyn Monroe y otros poemas* (1965), *El estrecho dudoso* (1966), *Salmos* (1964), *Homenaje a los indios de América* (1969), *La hora cero* and *Canto nacional* (1972), and *Oráculo sobre Managua* (1973). At present he is the Minister of Culture in the Government of National Reconstruction.

Otto René Castillo: Born in Quezaltenango, Guatemala, in 1936. A student leader, he was exiled to El Salvador in 1954. In the following year he won the Central American Poetry Prize. He joined the Communist Party of El Salvador and attended the university in that country. Castillo returned to Guatemala in 1964, was deported, and again returned to join the guerrillas of the Rebel Armed Forces (FAR). In 1967, he was captured, tortured and burned alive, but did not give his torturers any information. In his lifetime, he published two books, *Tecún Umán* (1964), and *Vámonos patria a caminar* (1965). There are also two post-humous editions of his work, *Poemas* (1971), and *Informe de una injusticia* (1975).

Edwin Castro: Born in León, Nicaragua. A central figure in the assassination of Anastasio Somoza, Sr. on September 21, 1956. During Castro's subsequent imprisonment, he wrote a great deal of poetry, which has just been published in book form. On May 18, 1960, Anastasio Somoza, Jr., in the middle of a drunken party, killed both Castro and his comrades, Ausberto Narváez and Cornelio Silva Argüello.

Manolo Cuadra: Born in Malacatoya, Nicaragua, in 1907. In addition to being a poet, he was a telegraph operator, a soldier in the civil war, a radio operator, a healer, a hotelier and a steve-dore on the docks of the United Fruit Co. He also enlisted in the National Guard and fought against Sandino's troops (though he expressed his admiration for the guerrilla leader). He later told of this experience in a prose work entitled *Contra Sandino en la montaña*, which was favorable to Sandino. He opposed the Somoza dictatorship from its beginning and was persecuted, jailed and exiled. He was confined to an island in the Carribbean and recounted this in *Itinerario de Little Corn Island*. Shortly before his death, his friends published a collection of his poetry, *Tres amores* (1955).

Pablo Antonio Cuadra: Born in Managua in 1912. He is the director of *La Prensa Literaria* (the literary supplement of Managua's opposition newspaper, *La Prensa*). At age 22, he published his first work, *Poemas nicaragüenses* (1934), with which he was one of the initiators of a native Nicaraguan poetry. Among his most important books are: *Canto temporal* (1943), *La tierra prometida* (1952), *Libro de horas* (1956), *El jaguar y la luna* (1959), *Poesía: Selección 1929-1962)* (1964), and *Cantos de Cifar* (1971). After the assassination of Pedro Joaquín Chamorro, he became director of *La Prensa*.

Rubén Darío: Born in Metapa (later named Ciudad Darío after him), Nicaragua, in 1867. He died in León in 1916. He is by far the best known of Nicaragua's poets. He is considered the founder of Hispanic modernist poetry and the most important Latin American poet of that school. His international fame dates from his early years as a poet, when the young Spanish modernists of the turn of the century recognized him as the master of Hispanic lyric poetry. In recent years his work has given rise to a series of critical reappraisals which have attempted to study the historical roots of modernist aestheticism.

Francisco de Asís Fernández: Born in Granada, Nicaragua, in 1945. He was a very precocious poet: some of his early poems, written at age sixteen, are among his best works. In 1968 he published in Mexico a book of verse illustrated by Cuevas entitled *A prinicipio de cuentas*. Another collection of poems, *La sangre constante*, was published in 1974. Until recently, he lived in Mexico, where he was active in Mexico's Nicaragua Solidarity Committee, and published an anthology, *Poesía política nicaragüense* (1979). After the victory, he returned to Managua, where he works for the Government of National Reconstruction.

Carlos Fonseca Amador: Secretary General of the Sandinista National Liberation Front, born in the province of Matagalpa in 1936. From 1956 to 1959 he was active in the Nicaraguan Socialist

Party. In 1957, he went to the Soviet Union and the German Democratic Republic as a youth delegate. In 1959 he was wounded at El Chaparral. In 1961 he was active in the foundation of the FSLN. He defined its ideological outlook and oriented it toward the development of a mass movement. In 1961 he was deported to Guatemala; on his return in 1963 he was captured. After six months in prison, he was deported to Mexico. In 1967 he led the guerrillas at Pancasán. In 1970 he was captured once again, this time in Costa Rica. In the same year, a commando unit of the Front seized a Costa Rica Airlines plane and exchanged it for Fonseca Amador, Humberto Ortega, Rufo Marín, and Plutarco Hernández. He returned to Nicaragua in 1976, and died fighting on November 9 of that year. Accoring to Manuel Andara Ubeda, it was Carlos Fonseca who put Riboberto López Pérez's "Will" into verse form.

Raul Javier García: Born in Granada, Nicaragua, in 1938. He has published his poetry in a number of reviews and in *La Prensa Literaria*. He is a carpenter.

Fernando Gordillo: Born in Nicaragua in 1940. At an early age he suffered a grave illness from which he died at age twenty-seven. In spite of having spent much of his life either bed-ridden or in a wheel chair, he was an influential Marxist student leader. Along with Sergio Ramírez, he founded and directed a review, *Ventana,* and a literary group of the same name. He wrote essays, short stories, and poems, and he published in newspapers and reviews, but he never published a book.

Nicolás Guillén: Born in Camagüey, Cuba, in 1902. He is unquestionably one Cuba's most important poets. He is the director of the National Association of Cuban Writers and a member of the Central Committee of the Communist Party of Cuba. His collected poetry is vast and has been translated into many languages. Although he is known principally for his poetry, he is a prose writer of the first rank. In both his prose and his poetry, he has confronted vitally important themes for the modern world such as class consciousness, race relations, and the problems of exploitation and revolution.

Ernesto Gutiérrez: Born in Granada, Nicaragua, in 1929. At present, he is the director of the Department of Publications at the National Autonomous University of Nicaragua at León, where he has done important work in publishing contemporary Nicaraguan poetry. His first book of poems, *Yo conocía algo hace* *tiempo,* was published in 1953. Since then he has published *Años bajo el sol* (1963), *Terrestre y celeste* (1969), and a brief *plaquette* of anti-imperialist and anti-Somoza poems entitled *Poemas políticos* (1971). He has also edited an anthology, *Poesía nicaragüense posdariana,* published by the National University in 1967. Member of the Casa de las Américas jury, Cuba, 1980.

HuGóS: Born in La Otra Banda, Granada, Nicaragua. Lived for some time in Los Angeles, California, where he published poetry in several magazines. He has also published in the Nicaraguan journal, *Taller.* A worker and writer of proletarian poetry. He returned to Nicaragua with the triumph of the Revolution.

Rigoberto López Pérez: Born in León, Nicaragua, in 1929. He openly expressed his repudiation of the Somoza regime and announced his intention to kill the tyrant. Early in 1956, he went to El Salvador, where he was trained in target shooting. He then returned to Nicaragua. On September 21, 1956, Somoza attended the celebration of his re-election to another term as president. This was the opportunity chosen by Rigoberto and his co-conspirators to kill the tyrant. The latter were to shut down the Managua electric plant while Rigoberto killed Somoza, thus enabling Rigoberto to escape. However, Somoza left the celebration much sooner than planned, forcing Rigoberto to kill him immediately. For this action, Rigoberto paid with his life. The poet's "Will" in letter form, has been widely circulated, and is a moving document in the history of Latin American revolutionary struggles.

David Macfield: Born in Ciudad Rama, Nicaragua, in 1936. He has published two books of poetry, *En la calle de en medio* and *Poemas para el año del elefante* (1970). He has taught at the Managua Polytechnic Institute and at the National Autonomous University of Nicaragua.

Carlos Martínez Rivas: Born in Guatemala City in 1924. At eighteen, he wrote his long poem, *El paraíso recobrado,* a work that has been considered one of the most important events in the history of Nicaraguan poetry. His book of poems, *La insurrección solitaria* (1953), strongly influenced many young Nicaraguan poets. He is now at work developing cultural projects for Nicaragua's Agrarian Reform Program (INRA).

Carlos Mejía Godoy: An excellent composer, singer, and

collector of traditional Nicaraguan music, he has placed his songs at the service of the Nicaraguan people and the Sandinista Front. He has made a number of records in Spain and Costa Rica, one of the best known being *La calle de en medio*. In collaboration with Los de Palacagüina he has recorded the *Misa campesina nicaragüense*, which expresses the religious and militant experience of the community of Solentiname.

Luis Mejía Godoy: Nicaraguan composer and singer. Like his brother Carlos, he has dedicated his musical work to the Nicaraguan people and the FSLN. Carlos Mejía Godoy has said of him that "my brother Luis has experimented with Latin American rhythms and his songs are a bridge to new Latin American political music." At present he directs the music section of the Ministry of Culture.

Ernesto Mejía Sánchez: Born in Masaya, Nicaragua, in 1923. His poetry ranges from immediate observations of daily existence to open opposition to the Somoza regime. His prose poems are considered to be his greatest contribution to contemporary Nicaraguan poetry. Some of his most important books are *Ensalmos y conjuros* (1947), *La carne contigua* (1948), *La impureza* (1950), *El retorno* (1952), and *Contemplaciones europeas* (1957). He has recently accepted a position as Nicaraguan Ambassador to Spain.

Pedro Mir: Born in 1913 in the Dominican Republic. He began writing poetry relatively late in life, and until the '60s he was little known outside his own country. Since the publication in Mexico of his *Viaje a la muchedumbre* (1972), he has become recognized as one of Latin America's most profound and authentic political poets. Other important books include *Hay un país en el mundo* (1949), *Contracanto a Walt Whitman: Canto a nosotros mismos* (1953), *Amén de mariposas* (1969), and *El huracán Neruda: elegía con una canción desesperada* (1975).

Beltrán Morales: Born in Nicaragua in 1944. He has published one book of verse, *Algún sol* (1969); another, *Aproximaciones* (1968), has circulated in mimeograph. He has also published a book of criticism, *Sin páginas amarillas* (1975). He is currently under contract to write a book for the Ministry of Culture.

Ricardo Morales Avilés: Born in Diriamba, Nicaragua, in 1939. In 1958, he went to live in Mexico and became a member of the FSLN. In 1967 he returned to his country, called by the FSLN, which incorporated him into its National Directorate. In the middle of 1968, he was arrested and tortured. While he was in prison, he wrote the greater part of his poetry. As a result of pressures from the student movement, he was appointed professor in the National University, a position which he held until his death. He was recaptured and assassinated in September, 1973.

Michele Najlis: Born in Granada, Nicaragua, in 1946. Her first poems were published in *La Prensa Literaria*. She is known for her great revolutionary fervor. She has published a book of poems entitled *El viento armado* (1969). She has taught literature at the National University.

Pablo Neruda: Born in Parral, Chile, in 1904. He published his first book, *Crepusculario,* in 1923, followed the next year by *Veinte poemas de amor y una canción desesperada.* In 1933, he published the first *Residencia en la tierra* which initiated his long and prestigious career as a poet. He resided in Spain from 1934 to 1936 as the Chilean consul. As a result of this visit, and of the impact of the Spanish Civil War, he wrote *España en el corazón.* He published *Tercera residencia* in 1947 and *Canto general* in 1950. From 1945 on, he was a member of the Communist Party of Chile, as a result of which he was forced to go into exile for several years. After the electoral triumph of the Popular Unity Party, Salvador Allende appointed him Ambassador to France. A year later, in 1971, he received the Nobel Prize for Literature. After the overthrow of the Government of Popular Unity by the fascist military coup on September 11, 1973, his house was broken into and his papers and possessions stolen and destroyed by fascists. Neruda died several days later.

Daniel Ortega: For several years, he has been one of the principal Sandinista leaders. He was one of those to sign the unity pact in March of 1979 which made possible the final offensive of the FSLN. In June, he became a member of the Junta of National Reconstruction, and since the victory he has been one of the most important members of the Government of National Reconstruction, and one of its most outstanding critics of imperialism.

Azarías H. Pallais: Born in León, Nicaragua in 1885. He was a priest and a prophet as well as a great poet. He was perhaps the first to speak of socialism in Central America. His disgust for capitalism and imperialism expressed itself in feelings of nostalgia for the great cultures of the past, especially the Middle Ages. He died in 1954. His most important books are *Caminos, Bello tono menor, El libro de las palabras evangelizadas, Epistola católica a Rafael Arevalo Martínez,* and *Piratería.*

Joaquín Pasos: Born in Granada, Nicaragua in 1914. In spite of the fact that he died at the age of 32, he is one of Nicaragua's most important poets. Although he never left Nicaragua, he wrote a great deal of travel poetry entitled, *Poemas de un joven que no ha viajado nunca.* Other important volumes of his poetry are: *Poemas de un joven que no ha amado nunca, Poemas de un joven que no sabe inglés* (includes poems written in English), and *Misterio indio.* He never published any of these books. After his death a short anthology of his poetry entitled *Breve suma* (1947) was published. All of his collected poetry was published under the title, *Poemas de un joven* (1962).

Octavio Robleto: Born in Juigalpa, capital of the province of Chotales, Nicaragua, 1935. He studied law at the National University in León, and has worked in the Department of Culture of the National University in Managua. He has published five books: *Vacaciones del estudiante* (1964), *Enigma y esfinge* (1965), *Epigramas con catarro* (1972), *Noches de Oluma* (1972) and *El día y sus laberintos* (1976).

Luis Rocha: Born in Granada, Nicaragua in 1942. He is the son of poet Octavio Rocha, of the "Vanguard" generation. He has written for many magazines and newspapers and is a frequent contributor to *La Prensa Literaria*. Together with Pablo Antonio Cuadra, he edited the magazine *El Pez y la Serpiente*. His poem "Treinta veces treinta" was published for the first time in this magazine in 1964. His book of poems entitled *Domus aurea* has been published in two editions.

Leonel Rugama: Born in Estelí, Nicaragua, 1950. He entered a Catholic seminary in Managua while very young. There he completed the greater part of his studies. In 1967 he made contact with the FSLN and was assigned to do political work in rural mountain areas. Beginning as a Christian revolutionary, he turned toward Marxism and wrote poems which expressed his conversion. Around the middle of 1969, he joined the underground and participated in several actions against banks in León and Managua. On January 15, 1970, he died fighting in Managua. "In spite of his youth," said Cardenal, "he showed promise of being one of Nicaragua's greatest poets." Rugama's poems have appeared in several anthologies. They were collected for the first time by Jaime Wheelock in *Taller*.

Salomón de la Selva: Born in León, Nicaragua, in 1893. He attended high school and obtained a university degree in the United States. He wrote poems in English, some of which have been collected in the anthology entitled *Tropical Town*, and several anthologies in the United States include his name as a North American writer. His principal books are: *Evocación de Horacio* (1949), *La ilustre familia* (1954), *Canto a la Independencia Nacional de México* (1955), *Evocación de Píndaro* (1957), and *Acolmixtli Nezahuacoyotl* (1958).

Rogelio Sinán: Born in Panama in 1904. Poet, story teller and playwright, he published his first book of poems, *Onda*, in 1929. He has won the National Prize for Literature of Panama twice, first for his novel *Plenilunio* (1943), and later for the book of poems, *Semana Santa en la niebla* (1949). His stories have been published in numerous Latin American collections and have been translated into English, German, and Bulgarian. In 1969, he published a collection of his poems entitled *Paloma sin palomar*.

Iván Uriarte: Born in Nicaragua in 1942, he belongs to the "Betrayed Generation." He is a short-story writer as well as a poet. He has published many stories, poems and articles of literary criticism in magazines and in *La Prensa Literaria*. He has also published two collections of poems: *7 poemas atlánticos* (1968) and *Este que habla* (1969). He holds a law degree and is a student in the Department of Hispanic Studies at Pittsburgh where he works with the local Nicaragua Solidarity Committee.

Roberto Vargas: Chicano poet of Nicaraguan origin, he has lived a good part of his life in San Francisco. He writes bilingual poetry which situates the Chicano struggle within that of the Third World in general. During the decade of the '70s, he has undertaken a tremendous amount of political and poetical work in support of the struggle of the Nicaraguan people. In 1979, he went to Nicaragua and fought in the war of liberation.

Bio-Bibliographies of the Editors

Bridget Aldaraca: Born in Spokane, Washington, U.S.A. She is currently finishing her doctoral dissertation on the novelist Pérez Galdós, and teaches Spanish language and culture at the University of Minnesota. She has published articles in Spanish and North American magazines on feminism and Marxism. As a member of the Committee of Solidarity with Nicaragua, she has given readings of Nicaraguan revolutionary poetry and collaborated on the pamphlet *Canto y lucha.*

Edward Baker: Born in Brooklyn, New York, U.S.A. He is the author of several works on contemporary Spanish literature and a study on the prose of Antonio Machado. He is currently teaching at the University of Minnesota and is a member of the editorial board of *Ideologies and Literature,* the North American magazine of Hispanic Studies. He has given readings of Nicaraguan revolutionary poetry as part of his work for the Committee of Solidarity with Nicaragua, and collaborated on the pamphlet *Canto y lucha.*

Ileana Rodríguez: Born in Chinandega, Nicaragua. Since 1975, she has taught in the Department of Spanish and Portuguese at the University of Minnesota. She has published numerous articles on Caribbean and Central American literature and is a member of the editorial board of *Ideologies and Literature.* She has been active in solidarity work with the FSLN for many years. She has written reviews of works by Sergio Ramírez and Jaime Wheelock and is the author of an analysis of the different periods of the Nicaraguan struggle. She collaborated on the pamphlet *Canto y lucha.* She is currently living in Managua and working in the Literature Section of the Ministry of Culture.

Marc Zimmerman: Born in New Jersey, U.S.A. He has published numerous Marxist articles on literary, cultural and theoretical subjects. He is a member of the editorial board of the journal *Praxis,* and has been a university professor for many years. Since 1975, he has worked for various social service agencies for Chicanos and Latinos in Minnesota. After a stay in Managua in the summer of 1971, he became active in solidarity work with the FSLN. He has coauthored articles on Darío and Rugama, and collaborated on the pamphlet *Canto y lucha.* He is currently living in Managua where he is employed in the Literature Section of the Ministry of Culture.

Bibliography

Anonymous. *Poesía revolucionaria nicaragüense.* Managua: Patria y Libertad, 1968.

Anonymous. *El carácter de la intervención imperialista en Nicaragua.* Mexico: Asociación de Exiliados Nicaragüenses Pro Derechos Humanos, 1977.

Arcano, Iván. *Sandino redivivo. Sangramos a la hiena.* San Francisco: La Latina, 1978.

Arellano, Jorge Eduardo. *Panorama de la literatura nicaragüense.* Managua: Ediciones Nacionales, 1977, 3rd revised edition.

(ed.) *50 poemas sobre el General Sandino.* Managua: 1972.

Belli, Gioconda. *Línea de fuego.* Havana: Casa de las Américas, 1978.

Benedetti, Mario (ed.) *Poesía trunca.* Havana: Casa de las Américas, 1977.

Cardenal, Ernesto. *Antología.* Santiago de Chile: Impresora Horizonte, 1967.

Canto nacional. Mexico: Siglo XXI, 1973.

Epigramas. Buenos Aires: Ediciones Carlos Lohlé, 1972.

Homenaje a los indios americanos. Santiago de Chile: Editorial Universitaria, 1970.

La hora cero y otros poemas. Barcelona: El Bardo, 1971.

Marilyn Monroe and Other Poems. London: Search Press, 1975.

(ed.) *Poesía nueva de Nicaragua.* Buenos Aires: Ediciones Carlos Lohlé, 1972.

Poesía escogida. Barcelona: Barral Editores, 1974.

Castañeda Shular, Antonia, Tomás Ybarra Frausto, Joseph Sommers. *Literatura chicana / Chicano Literature: Texto y contexto / Text and Context.* Englewood: Prentice Hall, 1972.

Cuadra, Pablo Antonio. *Esos rostros que asoman en la multitud.* Managua: El Pez y la Serpiente, 1976.

Cuadra Downing, Orlando. *Nueva poesía nicaragüense.* Madrid: Instituto de Cultura Hispánica, 1949.

Gaceta Sandinista. Caracas: Órgano del Comité Venezolano de Solidaridad con el Pueblo de Nicaragua, I, 3-4, May, 1977. San Francisco: I, 2, October, 1975. Mexico: I, 3, September, 1975.

Guillén, Nicolás. *Tengo.* Montevideo: El Siglo Ilustrado, 1967.

Hernández Segura, Francisco. *Cantares del Cocibolca.* Mexico: Impresora Juan Pablos, 1960.

Lucha Sandinista. Somewhere in Nicaragua: Órgano de la Comisión Exterior del Frente Sandinista de Liberación Nacional, May 2, 1978; June 3, 1978.

Latin America and Empire Report. NACLA, X, 2, February, 1976.

Mir, Pedro. *Viaje a la muchedumbre.* Mexico: Siglo XXI, 1972.

Márquez, Robert (ed.) *Latin American Revolutionary Poetry / Poesía revolucionaria latinoamericana.* New York: Monthly Review, 1974.

Mejía Godoy, Carlos. *Nicaragua, guitarra y fusil.* Panama: Comité Panameño de Solidaridad con Nicaragua, 1978.

Neruda, Pablo. *Obras completas.* Buenos Aires: Losada, 1968, 2 volumes, 3rd edition.

Poesía revolucionaria nicaragüense. Mexico: Confederación de escritores iberoamericanos, 1974.

La Prensa Literaria. Managua: 1960-1979.

Ramírez, Sergio (ed.) *El pensamiento vivo de Sandino.* San José: Educa, 1976.

Selser, Gregorio. *Sandino: General de hombres libres.* Havana: Ciencias Sociales, 1976.

Sandino Vive. Mexico: Órgano de la Asociación de Exiliados Nicaragüenses Pro Derechos Humanos, I, 1, June-August, 1977.

Vanguardia. Somewhere in Nicaragua: Frente Sandinista de Liberación Nacional, February, 1975.

Wheelock Román, Jaime (ed.) *Homenaje a Leonel Rugama. Taller,* 4, February, 1970.
Imperialismo y dictadura: Crisis de un formación social. Mexico: Siglo XXI, 1975.

STUDIES IN MARXISM

STUDIES IN MARXISM is a series of books providing discussions of important issues in all fields of knowledge from the dialectical-materialist perspective.

Conference proceedings volumes:

Vol. 1: MARXISM AND NEW LEFT IDEOLOGY. Proceedings of the First Midwest Marxist Scholars Conference, 1976. *Ed. by Ileana Rodríguez and William L. Rowe.* 1977.

Vol. 2: SOCIAL CLASS IN THE CONTEMPORARY UNITED STATES. Papers from the Second Midwest Marxist Scholars Conference, May 1977. *Ed. by Gerald M. Erickson and Harold L. Schwartz.* 1977.

Vol. 4: THE UNITED STATES IN CRISIS: MARXIST ANALYSES. Papers from the Third Midwest Marxist Scholars Conference, March 1978. *Ed. by Lajos Biro and Marc J. Cohen.* 1979.

Vol. 6: THE UNITED STATES EDUCATIONAL SYSTEM. MARXIST APPROACHES. Papers from the Fourth Midwest Marxist Scholars Conference, March, 1979.*Ed. by Marvin J. Berlowitz and Frank E. Chapman, Jr.* 1980.

Volumes on special topics:

Vol. 3: THE SOCIALIST COUNTRIES: GENERAL FEATURES OF POLITICAL, ECONOMIC AND CULTURAL LIFE. *By Erwin Marquit.* 1978.

Vol. 5: NICARAGUA IN REVOLUTION: THE POETS SPEAK. *Ed. by Bridget Aldaraca, Edward Baker, Ileana Rodríguez, Marc Zimmerman*

Vol. 7: PHILOSOPHICAL PROBLEMS IN PHYSICAL SCIENCE. *By Herbert Hörz, Hans-Dieter Pöltz, Heinrich Parthey, Ulrich Röseberg, and Karl-Friedrich Wessel.* First publication in English of outstanding text from the German Democratic Republic. 1980.

Forthcoming books:

THE SCHOLAR AS ALLY OF LABOR. Papers from the Fifth Midwest Marxist Scholars Conference, May 1980.

DEATH RATTLES: PHILOSOPHICAL CRITIQUE OF CRISIS-CONSCIOUSNESS IN BOURGEOIS SOCIETY. *By András Gedő.* Penetrating analysis by outstanding young Hungarian philosopher.

MYTHS, ILLUSIONS, REALITIES: MARXIST CRITIQUES OF CAPITALIST CULTURE IN THE UNITED STATES. Papers from the First Eastern Marxist Scholars Conference, October 1980.

A MARXIST INTERPRETATION OF PROGRESSIVE EDUCATION. *By Gilbert Gonzalez.* Includes special section on harmful consequences of application of Dewey's theories to Chicano community in Los Angeles.

Order from: MARXIST EDUCATIONAL PRESS, c/o Anthropology Department, 215 Ford Hall, University of Minnesota, 224 Church Street. S.E., Minneapolis, Minnesota 55455.